The
Cross
&
The
Crescent

An Interfaith Dialogue between
Christianity and Islam

The Cross & The Crescent

An Interfaith Dialogue between
Christianity and Islam

Jerald Dirks

M.Div., Psy.D.

amana publications

First Edition
(1422AH/2001AC)
© Copyright 1422AH/2001AC
amana publications
10710 Tucker Street
Beltsville, Maryland 20705-2223 USA
Tel: (301) 595-5777 / Fax: (301) 595-5888
E-mail: amana@igprinting.com
Website: www.amana-publications.com

Library of Congress Cataloging-in-Publications Data

Dirks, Jerald.
   The cross & the crescent / Jerald Dirks.
      p. cm.
   Includes bibliographical references and index.
   ISBN 1-59008-002-5
      1. Islam--Relations--Christianity. 2. Christianity and other religions--Islam I. Title:
   Cross and the crescent. II. Title.

BP172.D584 2001
261.2'7--dc21

                                                                2001046093

Printed in the United States of America by
International Graphics
10710 Tucker Street
Beltsville, Maryland 20705-2223   USA
Tel: (301) 595-5999 Fax: (301) 595-5888
Website: igprinting.com
E-mail: ig@igprinting.com

Contents

All quotations of the English translation of the meaning of the *Qur'an* are taken from   *The Meaning of the Holy Qur'an, translated by 'Abdallah Yusuf 'Ali,* copyright 1989, Amana Publications, Beltsville, Maryland 20705, U.S.A.

All Biblical quotations appearing in the text, unless specifically identified as being from another source, the following statement is noted in conformity with the request of the copyright holder.

Preface

In the name of God

As recently as last century, it was not uncommon to find Christian men and women prefacing a book by invoking the name of God. Today, that is a rare occurrence, and often the cause of a raised eyebrow in what is becoming an increasingly secular world. Within Christianity, such a formal invocation of the name of God has become anachronistic and out of fashion. In contrast, most publications by Muslim writers commence with the invocation "*Bismillah al-Rahman al-Rahim*", which reads "in the name of God, most Gracious, most Merciful". As such, one still finds within the Muslim world the continuation of a practice that was formerly quite common within the Christian world.

Similarly, in days gone by, Christians frequently interspersed a statement of their intentions or of their predictions by saying "God willing". This served as an acknowledgment by Christian men and women that, in the final analysis, their intentions and predictions would be fulfilled only with the grace of God. Such Christian verbiage is now considered a relic of the past. However, Muslim men and women still constantly pepper their statements with the phrase "*insha 'Allah*", meaning "God willing".

This manner of invoking the name of God, and of acknowledging the sovereignty of the Almighty God in all that we do and plan, serves to highlight the central tenet of this collection of essays, which draws close parallels between Islam and Christianity. Further, as one investigates historical Christianity, and gets closer to the roots of Christianity, that shared commonality and the interrelationship between Islam and Christianity becomes ever stronger and more pronounced. Unfortunately, this close interrelationship between these two religions is often overlooked. For many Occidental Christians, Islam is seen as being decidedly foreign, as being the religion of another place and of a foreign people, i.e., Arabia and the Arabs. In reality, this perception is far from being accurate. Islam, no less than Christianity, claims to be a universal religion, which cannot be appropriated by any national or ethnic group nor by any geographic area. Arabs represent only a minority of the world's Muslims, and Islam has spread far beyond the borders of the Middle East. Moreover, at present, Islam is the fastest growing religion in the United States, having approximately seven million adherents. Clearly, the need for mutual understanding and appreciation between Christians and Muslims becomes ever more imperative.

Unfortunately, for most Western Christians, differences in language and in certain literary conventions add to the perceived foreign nature of Islam. As one example, Western Christians are used to the word "God", and typically find the word "Allah" somewhat mysterious and troubling. They do not understand that "Allah" is nothing more than the contraction of two Arabic words, which mean "the God", or by implication "the One God". As such, it is not surprising that Arab Christians commonly use the word "Allah" when speaking of the deity. As a second example, Western Christians are often uneasy about the Islamic convention of conferring the phrase "peace be upon him" to the names of the prophets of Allah. Yet, a third example finds Muslims typically objecting to the use of such dating conventions as BC (before Christ) and AD (*annos domini,* i.e., in the year of our Lord), since they maintain that none other than Allah is Lord.

Obviously, such linguistic sensitivities need to be overcome, in order for Christians and Muslims to develop a proper appreciation of the commonality between their religions. Given the nature and central theme of this book, such linguistic sensitivities raise special challenges for one who is writing for both Christian and Muslim readers. With regard to the use of "God" rather than "Allah", one is tempted to use the word "God", this being the common English vernacular. However, it is felt that Occidental Christian readers need to begin to feel as comfortable with the word "Allah" as are their Arab Christians brothers, in order for them to begin to overcome their misperception that Islam is somehow completely foreign to their own religious beliefs. However, one does not become comfortable with a word by avoiding it, but only by repeatedly using it. As such, beginning now, unless there is some specific, doctrinal reason for not using the word "Allah", the general linguistic rule employed in this book is to refer to the deity as Allah. As far as the phrase "peace be upon him" is concerned, a compromise has been adopted between Christian and Muslim sensitivities and so within each chapter of this book, the phrase "peace be upon him" is used following the first mention of the name of a prophet of Allah and this usage is discontinued thereafter. Readers may kindly note that the in regard to dating conventions, this book uses the more neutral conventions of BCE (before the common era) and CE (common era).

Having said the above, I find it useful to introduce myself to the reader, so that he may have some understanding of my qualifications to discuss the issues at hand. I hold a Master of Divinity degree from Harvard Divinity School, and was formerly an ordained minister (deacon) in the United Methodist Church. My personal experience of the interrelationships between Christianity and Islam and their common roots covers a journey of many years, that has evolved in depth and breadth with time. It began almost thirty years ago in a course at Harvard on comparative religion. It developed further during the last two decades as I studied the history of the Arabian horse, and grew to fruition as I started moving within the Muslim communities in America and in the Middle East.

In writing this book, I would like to touch the lives of those Christians who have not been given the knowledge that I have gained, both about Islam from my direct contact with Muslims and about Christianity from my seminary education. I want to share with those Christians who are willing to listen what is so often known by their clergy and church leaders, but seldom finds its way into their knowledge of their own religion. Likewise, I would like to reach out to the Muslims, in order to help them understand the religious commonality that they share with Christians. While a good deal of the information presented within these essays is somewhat obscure, such information highlights much of what was once common between Christianity and Islam, but which has subsequently been altered and misrepresented to affect a gulf between these two religions.

Given these somewhat challenging goals, the readers may at times, feel that the author is addressing in a particular essays, two different audiences, each with its own language and with its own conceptual frame of reference. To a certain extent, this has been intentional on my part, for I find it the optimal way of reaching the goals set in this book.

The first essay in the book is a simple recounting of my own personal experience of the commonality to be found between Christianity and Islam, and is entitled "Parallels between Christianity and Islam". Its targeted readership includes both Muslims and Christians, but for each group a separate message has been intended. The second essay, "Judaism, Christianity, and Islam: Origins and Relationships", seeks to resolve certain barriers to communication existing among members of these three religious groups. In that regard, Muslims may better understand the conceptual and communication barriers which separate Christians and Jews from them, while Christians and Jews may appreciate those conceptual and communication barriers separating Muslims from them. The third essay presents a comparison and analysis of the structure and provenance of the *Qur'an*, the received *Torah*, the *Psalms*, and the canonical gospels of the *New Testament*. This essay presents some fairly technical information, which sheds significant light on the formation of these sets of scripture, and thus illuminates some aspects of the origins of Judaism, Christianity, and Islam not covered in the prior essay.

The next five essays focus on specific topics in the Judeo-Christian tradition. These essays contain a great deal of information regarding the basic foundations of Christianity, and how they relate to Islam. To a great extent, this consists of information not known to the Christian laity, but information that is known to the better educated of their clergy. The primary reason behind writing these essays is to educate Christians about the origins and foundations of their own religion, in the hope that this may lead them to appreciate the heritage, which they so closely share with Islam. Additionally, Muslims may gain a much better appreciation of just how similar certain branches of early Christianity were to the teachings of Islam.

The last essay, "A Concise Introduction to Islam: Articles of Faith and Pillars of Practice", is an introduction to Islam for the Christian reader. In that respect, I have attempted to bridge the Judeo-Christian tradition and Islam wherever possible, in order to help the Christian reader gain a better understanding of Islam and of its similarity to his or her own religious tradition. As such, this introduction to Islam approaches certain issues from a slightly different perspective than most such presentations on Islam do. In conclusion, while this final essay was written primarily for the Christian reader, its my sincere desire that the Muslim reader may also find it a worthwhile reading.

Having stated my intentions and goals in writing these essays, I wish to express my appreciation to my wife of thirty years, Debra, who proofread the entire manuscript, offering valuable suggestions. However, the success or failure of any action is not solely controlled by the human actor who perpetrates it. In the final analysis, the results of any human endeavor rests in the hands of God. Despite my own shortcomings and failures, I pray that Allah, i.e., the God of us all, will accept this modest endeavor, and that He will utilize it as He wills for His purpose.

June 22, 2001
Jerald F. Dirks,
M.Div., Psy.D.

Chapter 1

Parellels between Christianity and Islam

Thanks and praise to Allah[1] that I was fortunate enough to be born into and raised in a small, agricultural community in rural Kansas. Within that community, and especially within my family, there was an emphasis on certain "old fashioned" values and conceptions of morality and self-responsibility, which were still prevalent during my childhood days of 1950s. Within the context of that security, my upbringing may appear strange to many contemporary Americans, but may nostalgically remind them of a bygone American era. At that time and place, doors to the house were seldom locked, a man's word was his bond, and a handshake was worth more than any legally binding contract. A child's mother was usually in the home for him 24 hours a day, grandparents were near at hand, and one's neighbors when one was two were one's neighbors when one was sixteen, resulting in a familial and social stability that is almost non-existent today. Teachers were citizens of respect within the community, and violence was unheard of, whether in the school or elsewhere. Divorce would have been cause for a social scandal, and I cannot remember even one nuclear family that was not intact. The church was the center of community life, prayers were still said at the beginning of every school day, and weekly Sunday School inoculated each child with a simple, but worthy, moral code of conduct, based squarely upon the Ten Commandments,[2] as well as on the reported words of Jesus, peace be upon him.[3]

He said to him, 'You shall love the Lord your God with all your heart, and with all your soul, and with all your mind.' This is the greatest and first commandment. And a second is like it: 'You shall love your neighbor as yourself.'[4]

If this all seems to be a re-run from *Leave It to Beaver, Ozzie and Harriet*, or *Father Knows Bes*t, perhaps it was. However, it was no celluloid illusion created by the mythmakers of Hollywood. Rather, it was our daily life.

While some older and middle-aged Americans can perhaps relate to the setting I am writing about, there was one aspect of that community that would probably seem foreign even to them. The community in which I was raised was primarily *Mennonite*[5] in its religious affiliation, and the paternal side of my family traced to Mennonite roots, although my own nuclear family was Methodist in denominational affiliation. Given that influence, there were certain aspects of my early life, which helped me prepare to appreciate many aspects of Islam. During my early childhood, the Old Mennonite women of my home town most of the time wore "prayer bonnets" that provided a semi-transparent covering for at least part of the hair; dress was conservative and modest, for both men and women, with hem lines never moving higher than the bottom of the knee, and with shorts being a foreign concept. While men and women typically ate at a common table, when company was over the two genders tended to congregate in separate rooms of the house both before and after the meal. Whenever married couples went out together, the men always sat in the front seat of the car, while the women sat in the back seat. Though dating was allowed among teenagers, it was closely supervised during the early teen years, and social dancing was altogether forbidden. While most individuals kept away from alcohol, a few imbibed on a minimal basis. Later on in life, I could draw many more parallels between the social customs of my childhood community and the Islamic *Ummah* ("community" or "nation").

At the age of four I became a victim of the great polio epidemic that swept across America in 1954. I woke up one morning, crying from pain in my neck. The pain that morning, a vague memory of undergoing a spinal tap at the hospital, and an even vaguer memory of another boy in a wheelchair constitute most of the true memories I have of that traumatic time.

The attack left me paralyzed. I was rushed to the hospital and on examining me, the doctors told my parents that I may perhaps not survive the night My mother responded with a round-the-clock bedside vigil, in which she constantly prayed for me, and, in her own way, dedicated my life to Allah. The next morning, my condition had improved, and the physicians decided that the chance of my survival had increased to the point where they could allocate one of their few "iron lungs" in an effort to try and save me. Before I could be transferred to the "iron lung", my condition had inexplicably improved to the point that the "iron lung" was no longer necessary. Three days later, I was discharged from the hospital. I could walk with a rather pronounced limp, but I could not run without getting my legs tangled together, and without falling down within a few strides.

Apparently, my mother's prayers had been heard. Certainly, there was no medical explanation for the strange and baffling course of my bout with polio. While my mother's prayerful dedication was never forced upon me, nor even directly mentioned to me, my later childhood became more and more focused on the church. By the time I was in high school, I was a regular "preacher" during Youth Sundays, and would occasionally make rounds to "preach" at various churches in my own and in neighboring communities. By the time I graduated from high school, I had "filled the pulpit" at about a half dozen different churches, and held an elective conference office in my denomination's youth organization. I had also decided to enter the ministry.

Academic Encounters with Islam: Familiar Names

In pursuing my decision to enter the ministry, I attempted to receive the best education that I could. Thanks to Allah once again, I was lucky to be admitted to Harvard College (Harvard University) on scholarship. During my freshman year, I enrolled in a two-semester course in comparative religion, which was taught by Wilfred Cantwell Smith, whose specific area of expertise was Islam.[6] As I began my study of Islam, I was surprised more than ever before to learn how similar Islam was in so may aspects to my own Christianity. Certainly, the religious history and heritage of the two religions seemed almost similar, if not nearly identical. After all, my initial reading of the Qur'an revealed numerous references to Adam, Noah, Abraham, Isma'il, Isaac, Jacob, Joseph, Moses, David, Solomon, John the Baptist, and Jesus, peace be upon them. In fact, those of the Judeo-Christian tradition may be surprised to learn than the *Qur'an* specifically names many Biblical figures far more often than it refers to Muhammad, by name. In that regard, using 'Abdullah Yusef 'Ali's English translation of *The Meaning of The Holy Qur'an,*[7] and counting the number of times a name is cited in the text, one finds that Adam, Noah, Abraham, Isaac, Jacob, Joseph, Moses, David, Solomon, and Jesus are all mentioned far more frequently than are Isma'il and Muhammad. This information is summarized in Table 1 below.

Table 1: Frequency of Citation of Various Prophets in the *Qur'an*

Name of Prophet	Frequency of Citation [8]
Moses	177
Abraham	74
Noah	47
Jesus[9]	37
Joseph	34
Adam	25
Solomon	19
Jacob	18
Isaac	16
David	16
Isma'il	6
John the Baptist	5
Muhammad	4

The above list does not include every prophet mentioned by name in the *Qur'an*. Further, it needs to be noted that not every prophet mentioned in the *Qur'an* is mentioned in the *Bible* either. However, the above list is illustrative of the marked similarity in orientation between Islam and the Judeo-Christian tradition. As shown in the above list, Moses is by far the most frequently mentioned prophet in the *Qur'an*, with his name being mentioned more than twice as often as that of Abraham, the second most frequently cited prophet in the *Qur'an*. Following the name of Abraham in frequency of citation are those of Noah, Jesus, and Joseph.

Parallel Stories in the *Qur'an* and the *Bible*

In reading the *Qur'an*, I quickly discovered that the similarities between the *Qur'an* and the *Bible* (Islam and the Judeo-Christian tradition) are not limited to the use of names of prominent Biblical characters alone. Within the pages of the *Qur'an*, one finds many stories that are an impressive parallel to those recorded in the *Bible*. Occasionally, the stories in the *Qur'an* offer a slightly different perspective and detail from the parallel ones in the *Bible*. The overall similarity is impressive, as is shown in the following few examples.

The Creation and Fall of Adam

Both the *Bible* and the *Qur'an* address the issue of the creation of the first man, Adam, and of his subsequent expulsion from the Garden of Eden. The Biblical narration is recorded in *Genesis* 2:4-3:24, and details that Adam was created "from the dust of the ground; and Allah "breathed into his nostrils the breath of life", and Adam became a living being and was asked to give names to every animal. Eve, Adam's wife, was formed by Allah from one of Adam's ribs. Allah then declared that the two were free to eat from the fruit of the trees in the garden, barring one particular tree. The Satan, in the guise of a serpent, persuaded Eve, who in turn persuaded Adam, to eat the fruit of the forbidden tree, disobeying the command of their Creator. Thereupon, their nakedness became manifest to them and they were ashamed of it. In punishment of their disobedience, they were expelled from the Garden of Eden. In a distinct similarity of description, the *Qur'an* draws a close parallel to this instance:

> Behold! Thy Lord said to the angels: "I am about to create man, from sounding clay from mud moulded into shape; when I have fashioned him (in due proportion) and breathed into him of My spirit, fall ye down in obeisance unto Him."[10]

> And He taught Adam the names of all things...[11]
> "O Adam! Dwell thou and thy wife in the garden, and enjoy (its good things) as ye wish: but approach not this tree, or ye run into harm and transgression." Then began Satan to whisper suggestions to them, in order to reveal to them their shame that was hidden from them (before): he said: "Your Lord only forbade you this tree, lest ye should become angels or such beings as live forever". And he swore to them both, that he was their sincere adviser. So by deceit he brought about their fall: when they tasted of the tree, their shame became manifest to them, and they began to

sew together the leaves of the garden over their bodies. And their Lord called unto them: "Did I not forbid you that tree, and tell you that Satan was an avowed enemy unto you?" They said: "Our Lord! We have wronged our own souls: if Thou forgive us not and bestow not upon us Thy mercy, we shall certainly be lost". (Allah) said: "Get ye down, with enmity between yourselves, on earth will be your dwelling-place and your means of livelihood—for a time". He said: "Therein shall ye live, and therein shall ye die; but from it shall ye be taken out (at last)."[12]

Cain Murders Abel

Genesis 4:1-16 states that Adam and Eve had two sons, i.e. Cain, the elder, and Abel, the younger. Upon reaching maturity, both Cain and Abel offered sacrifices to Allah, but only Abel's sacrifice was acceptable to Allah. Realizing this, Cain was furious and in a rage of anger and frustration murdered Abel. Allah cursed and punished Cain for his homicidal behavior. The *Qur'an* offers an almost identical narration, but with some additional details about Abel's refusal to fight his brother, Cain:

> Recite to them the truth of the story of the two sons of Adam. Behold! They each presented a sacrifice (to Allah): it was accepted from one, but not from the other. Said the latter: "Be sure I will slay thee." "Surely," said the former, "Allah doth accept of the sacrifice of those who are righteous. If thou doest stretch thy hand against me, to slay me, it is not for me to stretch my hand against thee to slay thee: for I do fear Allah, the cherisher of the worlds. For me, I intend to let thee draw on thyself my sin as well as thine, for thou wilt be among the companions of the fire, and that is the reward of those who do wrong." The (selfish) soul of the other led him to the murder of his brother: he murdered him, and became (himself) one of the lost ones.[13]

Moses and the Promised Land

According to the *Bible* (Numbers 13:1-14:38 and Deuteronomy 1:19-40) Moses and the Israelites, having escaped from Egypt, were directed by Allah to invade and take the land of Palestine. Before beginning their invasion, the Israelites sent out spies into Palestine. Except for Joshua and Caleb, all the other spies reported that a successful invasion was not feasible, since the inhabitants of Palestine were far taller and stronger than the Israelites. Even though Joshua and Caleb urged invasion and reliance upon Allah, the people refused to obey them. At this point, according to Numbers 13:11-12, Allah reportedly threatened to disinherit the Israelites, a punishment that Numbers 13:13-14:38 states was only averted by the pleading of Moses to Allah. However, as punishment, the Israelites were forced to continue wandering in the wilderness for 40 years, before they were allowed to enter Palestine. A similar description appears in the *Qur'an*, too, but with some greater detail.

Remember Moses said to his people: "O my people! Call in remembrance the favor of Allah unto you, when He produced prophets among you, made you kings, and gave you what He had not given to any other among the peoples. O my people! Enter the holy land which Allah hath assigned unto you, and turn not back ignominiously, for then will ye be overthrown, to your own ruin." They said: "O Moses! In this land are a people of exceeding strength: never shall we enter it until they leave it: if (once) they leave, then shall we enter." But among (their) God-fearing men were two on whom Allah had bestowed His grace: they said: "Assault them at the (proper) gate: when once ye are in, victory will be yours; but on Allah put your trust if ye have faith." They said: "O Moses! While they remain there, never shall we be able to enter, to the end of time. Go thou, and thy Lord, and fight ye two, while we sit here (and watch)." He said: "O my Lord! I have power only over myself and my brother: so separate us from this rebellious people!" Allah said: "Therefore will the land be out of their reach for forty years: in distraction will they wander through the land: but sorrow thou not over these rebellious people."[14]

However, there is one marked difference between the narration of this incident in the two Holy Books. While the *Qur'an* reports that it was Moses who asked Allah to separate him from the Israelites, the *Bible* maintains that Moses pled for Allah's forgiveness of the "rebellious people" – the Israelites – after Allah threatened to disinherit them from His favors. Nonetheless, the Biblical and Qur'anic accounts, in spite of this slight variation, are amazingly similar.

The Story of Jonah

The Biblical book of *Jonah* tells the story of Jonah, the son of Amittai, a prophet to the Assyrian city of Nineveh. Reportedly, because he did not want the inhabitants of Nineveh to be saved, Jonah disobeyed Allah's command for him to go to Nineveh, and preach to its inhabitants. Instead, Jonah fled to Joppa, where he boarded a ship sailing for Tarshish. Once the ship had set sail, Allah created a great storm, which threatened to sink the ship. In response, the crew cast lots to see on whose account the storm had been created, and "the lot fell on Jonah". After hearing Jonah's story, the crew continued to try to row to safety, but the storm continued unabated. Finally, the crew threw Jonah overboard as a sacrifice, in hopes that this sacrifice would result in a calming of the storm. Jonah was swallowed by a large fish, and he remained in its belly for three days and three nights. Therein, Jonah prayed to Allah for forgiveness, and the fish then spat Jonah out on dry land. Having been freed from the belly of the fish, Jonah went to Nineveh, and preached to the inhabitants of the city. Over 120,000 people responded to Jonah's preaching and prayed to Allah seeking His forgiveness. Thereafter, Jonah retired outside the city angry that Nineveh had been saved. As he sat there lamenting, Allah caused a "bush" to grow up over Jonah, and to offer a comforting shade to Jonah. The next day, Allah reportedly caused the bush to wither.

The above story is very eloquently related in the following passage from the *Qur'an*, wherein one has most of the details from the Biblical book of *Jonah* (Yunus). The similarities between the two descriptions are truly impressive.

"So also was Jonah among those sent (by Us). When he ran away to the ship (fully) laden, he (agreed to) cast lots, and he was condemned: then the big fish did swallow him, and he had done acts worthy of blame. Had it not been that he (repented and) glorified Allah, he would certainly have remained inside the fish till the Day of Resurrection. But We cast him forth on the naked shore in a state of sickness, and We caused to grow, over him, a spreading plant of the gourd kind, and We sent him (on a mission) to a hundred thousand (men) or more. And they believed so We permitted them to enjoy (their life) for a while." [15]

The Birth of John The Baptist

It is not only in the *Old Testament*, but the similarities between the *Bible* and the *Qur'an* also exist in the *New Testament* as well. In that regard, one can turn to the events leading up to the birth of John ("Yahya" in

Arabic) the Baptist, as reported in Luke 1:2-24, 57-66. According to the story (as reported in Luke), Zechariah and his wife, Elizabeth, were an aged couple, who had never had children – Elizabeth being barren. Once, when Zechariah was praying in the sanctuary, the angel Gabriel appeared, and announced to Zechariah that his prayer had been heard and accepted by Allah. Zechariah and Elizabeth were soon to have a son who would be named John, and who would be a prophet to his people. Zechariah asked for a sign to confirm this message regarding the birth of a son. According to the account of *Luke*, the sign was that Zechariah was made mute, and allegedly remained mute throughout the conception, gestation, birth, and first eight days of John the Baptist. Only upon confirming his wife's choice of the name John for their son, did Zechariah regain his speech. The above account parralels the *Qur'an*, which, too, speaks of this event.

> "There did Zakariya pray to his Lord, saying: "O my Lord! Grant unto me from Thee a progeny that is pure: for Thou art He that heareth prayer!" While he was standing in prayer in the chamber, the angels called unto him: "Allah doth give thee glad tidings of Yahya, witnessing the truth of a word from Allah, and (be besides) noble, chaste, and a Prophet—of the (goodly) company of the righteous. "He said: "O my Lord! How shall I have a son, seeing I am very old, and my wife is barren?" "Thus," was the answer, "Doth Allah accomplish what He willeth." He said: "O my Lord! Give me a Sign!" "Thy Sign," was the answer, "Shall be that thou shalt speak to no man for three days but with signals, then celebrate the praises of thy Lord again and again. And glorify Him in the evening and in the morning." [16]

Bearing in mind that "Yahya" is merely the Arabic name for "John", the above passage from the *Qur'an* offers impressive similarity to the account reported in Luke. The only significant discrepancy is in regard to the length of time that Zechariah remained mute, which the *Qur'an* limits to only three days.

The Birth of Jesus

The Biblical account of the angelic announcement to Mary of the coming birth of Jesus is related in *Luke* 1:26-38. Skipping over the later theologizing to be found in this passage from *Luke*, the basic outline is that the angel Gabriel informs virgin Mary that she has found favor in the sight of Allah, and that she will soon give birth to a son, who will be named Jesus; Mary in a puzzled state asks as to how she could possibly give birth, when she is still a virgin, to which Gabriel reportedly answers that: "The Holy Spirit will come upon you, and the power of the Most High will overshadow you; therefore the child to be born will be holy; he will be called Son of God." The words attributed to Gabriel in the above quoted passage call to mind the polytheistic Greek myths of the gods descending from Mount Olympus to rape and impregnate mortal women. In contrast to this polytheistic residual as found in Luke, the *Qur'an*, while paralleling the account from Luke in most other respects, presents the virgin birth of Jesus as an act of miraculous creation, not as an act of impregnation.

> "Behold! The angels said: O Mary! Allah hath chosen thee and purified thee—chosen thee above the women of all nations. O Mary! Worship thy Lord devoutly: prostrate thyself, and bow down (in prayer) with those who bow down." This is part of the tidings of the things unseen, which We reveal unto thee (O Prophet!) by inspiration: thou wast not with them when they cast lots with arrows, as to which of them should be charged with the care of Mary: nor wast thou with them when they disputed (the point). Behold! The angels said: "O Mary! Allah giveth thee glad tidings of a word from Him: his name will be Christ Jesus. The son of Mary, held in honor in this world and the hereafter and of (the company of) those nearest to Allah; he shall speak to the people in childhood and in maturity. And he shall be (of the company) of the righteous." She said: "O my Lord! How shall I have a son when no man hath touched me?" He said: "Even so: Allah createth what He willeth: when He hath decreed a plan, He but saith to it, 'Be,' and it is! And Allah will teach him the book and wisdom, the law and the gospel,..." [17]

Summary and Conclusions

There are many more parallels that can be illustrated between the *Qur'an* and the *Bible*. In both books, one finds the story of Noah's ark and the flood. In both books, one finds similar and additional stories regarding Moses, e.g., the conflict between Moses and the pharaoh of

Egypt, the story of Moses receiving the covenant at Mt. Sinai, etc. Likewise, one finds the story of Joseph, the Israelite vizier of Egypt, which unfolds remarkably and in great detail, in the *Qur'an*. Furthermore, the *Qur'an* tells the story of David's killing of Goliath, the story of King Saul, the story of Abraham's trials, etc. Unfortunately, time and space do not permit that all of these parallel stories between the *Qur'an* and the *Bible* can be individually addressed.

Biblical characters in the *Qur'an*

However, it is also the case that the *Qur'an* reports numerous stories, regarding well-known Biblical characters that cannot be found in the *Bible*. One example of the *Qur'an* reporting a story not found in the *Bible* would be the allusion in the immediately quoted passage from the *Qur'an* of various individuals casting arrows to see who would be charged with the care of Mary during her pregnancy.[18] Quite simply, this story is not to be found in the contemporary *Bible*. Another example would be the passage in the *Qur'an* that refers to Jesus fashioning a bird out of clay, and then, by Allah's leave, causing that clay bird to come to life.[19] Once again, this story cannot be found anywhere in the modern *Bible*. Nonetheless, one can see that such stories do find expression in the early Christian literature, most especially in the so-called apocryphal books of the *New Testament*. As such, these stories illustrate that the *Qur'an* is often more consistent with the early roots of Christianity, than is modern Christianity, itself.

Encounters with Early Christianity Graduating from Harvard College in 1971, I was accepted on scholarship to the Master of Divinity program at the Harvard Divinity School (Harvard University), having previously obtained my License to Preach from the United Methodist Church in 1969. After completion of the first year of a three-year study program at Harvard Divinity School, I was ordained into the deaconate of the United Methodist Church in 1972, and was from that point an ordained minister.

There is some irony in the fact that the supposedly best, brightest, and most idealistic of ministers-to-be are selected for the very best of seminary education (e.g., that offered at that time at the Harvard Divinity School). The irony is that, with such an education, the seminarian is exposed to a vast knowledge of historical truth – such as the formation of the early, "mainstream" church, and how it was shaped by geopolitical considerations; the "original" reading of various Biblical texts, many of which are in sharp contrast to what most Christians read when they pick up their *Bible*, although gradually some of this information is being incorporated into newer and better translations of the *Bible*; the evolution of such concepts as a triune godhead and the "sonship" of Jesus; the non-religious considerations that underlie many Christian creeds and doctrines; the existence of those early churches and Christian movements which never accepted the concept of a triune godhead, and which also never accepted the concept of the divinity of Jesus; and those early Christian writings, once regarded as scripture by many early Christian churches (known as the *New Testament* apocrypha). Moreover the information contained therein differed from the information in the canonical New TestamentNew Testament that emerged some centuries later.

Dwelling briefly on the subject, one must consider the issue of those early Christian writings — not incorporated into the later formation of the *New Teatment*.

During my seminary encounters in tracing the roots of early Christianity, I amazingly discovered that certain specific stories in the *Qur'an*, (not found in the contemporary *Bible*, and occasionally even at odds with those contained in the *Bible*), were preserved and recorded identically in the *New Testament* apocrypha. Some examples of such occurrences are enumerated below.

The Birth and Lineage of the Virgin Mary

The books of the contemporary *New Testament* offer nothing or very little substance with regard to the background of Mary, the mother of Jesus. The only readily available information can be seen in Luke, where Mary is said to have been a relative of Elizabeth, the mother of John the Baptist, and where it is stated that Mary spent three months of her pregnancy in the house of Zechariah and Elizabeth, the parents of John the Baptist.[20] In contrast, the *Qur'an* offers a great deal of information regarding Mary.

> Behold! a woman of 'Imran said: "Oh my Lord! I do dedicate unto Thee what is in my womb for Thy special service: so accept this of me: for Thou hearest and knowest all things." When she was delivered, she said: "O my Lord! Behold! I am delivered of a female child!"—And Allah knew best what she brought forth—

"And no wise is the male like the female. I have named her Mary, and I commend her and her offspring to Thy protection from the evil one, the rejected." Right graciously did her Lord accept her: He made her grow in purity   and beauty; to the care of Zakariya was she assigned. Every time that he entered (her) chamber to see her, he found her supplied with sustenance. He said: "O Mary! Whence (comes) this to you?" She said: "From Allah: for Allah provides sustenance to whom He pleases, without measure." [21]

Three points emerge from the foregoing Qur'anic quote. First, the reference to "a woman of 'Imran' appears to be a statement that the lineage of Mary's mother traced back to the Biblical Amram, the son of Kohath, a member of the Levite tribe of Israel, and the father of Moses.[22] As there was a pronounced tendency among the Israelites to marry within their own clan / tribe, in all probabilities, Mary was of the Levite tribe. Second, the quotation specifically states that Mary was miraculously "supplied with sustenance" from Allah. Third, the same passage from the *Qur'an* distinctly says that Mary was placed in the care of Zechariah, while Luke merely says that Mary visited Zechariah and Elizabeth for three months during her pregnancy. As an additional fourth point, and referring back to a previously quoted passage from the *Qur'an*, it is noted that several individuals cast lots with arrows to see who would be entrusted with the care of Mary.[23]

The above four points find specific support in the so-called *New Testament* apocrypha. The Gospel of the Birth of Mary, preserved in a reference given by Faustus, the Bishop of Riez in Provence, directly states that Mary was a Levite.[24] Further, a passage from the *New Testament* apocrypha says that angels fed Mary during her stay at the Temple in Jerusalem.[25] Third, regarding Mary being entrusted into Zechariah's care, the *New Testament* apocrypha provides support, by noting that Zechariah petitioned the High Priest about Mary.[26] Further, two passages in the *New Testament* apocrypha provide evidence for such an event, with Joseph being the one who was chosen to succeed Zechariah in taking care of Mary.[27]

Jesus Speaks in Infancy

In a moving passage, the *Qur'an* describes the reaction of people to Mary having given birth to Jesus. Apparently, they were all too ready to think the worst about this righteous young woman, her pregnancy, and her subsequent child. To all of them, Mary said nothing in defense, but pointed to her infant child. Thereupon, the infant Jesus spoke, defending his mother's honor and preaching to the onlookers.

When she brought the infant Jesus to her people, They reacted sharply: "O Mary! Truly an amazing thing hast thou brought! O sister of Aaron! Thy father was not a man of evil, nor was thy mother a woman unchaste!" But she pointed to the babe. They said: "How can we talk to one who is a child in the cradle?" He said: "I am indeed a servant of Allah: He hath given me revelations and made me a prophet; and He hath made me blessed wheresoever I be, and hath enjoined on me prayer and charity as long as I live: (He) hath made me kind to my mother, and not overbearing or miserable;..." [28]

The foregoing account of the birth of Jesus does not appear in the current *New Testament*. However, the story of Jesus speaking while still an infant in the cradle is preserved in the *New Testament* apocrypha.[29]

Jesus and the clay pigeons

Two different passages in the *Qur'an* refer to Jesus fashioning a clay bird, and then, by Allah's will, making it come alive.

She said: "O my Lord! How shall I have a son when no man hath touched me?" He said: "Even so: Allah createth what He willeth: when He hath decreed a plan, He but saith to it, 'Be', and it is! And Allah will teach him the book and wisdom, the law and the gospel, and (appoint him) a messenger to the children of Israel, (with this message): 'I have come to you, with a sign from your Lord, in that I make for you out of clay, as it were, the figure of a bird, and breathe into it, and it becomes a bird by Allah's leave: and I heal those born blind, and the lepers, and I quicken the dead, by Allah's leave; and I declare to you what ye eat, and what ye store in your houses. Surely, therein is a sign for you if ye did believe;...'" [30]

Then will Allah say: "O Jesus the son of Mary! Recount My favor to thee and to thy mother. Behold! I strengthened thee with the holy spirit, so that thou didst speak to the people in childhood and in maturity. Behold! I taught thee the book and wisdom, the law and the gospel. And behold! Thou makest out of clay, as it were, the figure of a bird, by My leave, and thou breathest into it, and it becometh a bird by My leave, and thou healest those born blind, and the lepers, by My leave. And behold! Thou bringest forth the dead by My leave. And behold!

I did restrain the children of Israel from (violence to) thee when thou didst show them the clear signs, and the unbelievers among them said: 'This is nothing but evident magic'." [31]

The story of Jesus causing, by the will of Allah, a clay bird to come to life is not found in the contemporary *New Teatment*. But, this story in the *Qur'an* can be found in the *New Testament* apocrypha.[32]

Summary and Conclusions

Taken together the *Bible* and the *New Testament* apocrypha offer dramatic parallels to many passages in the *Qur'an*. Such parallels suggest that Christians are well advised to explore the substantial interface between Islam and Christianity. With this very view, the chapters in this book are presented.

Chapter 2

Judaism, Christianity, and Islam
– Origins and Relationships

One of the chief barriers to effective communication between people is when one assumes he is speaking the same language, being unaware of the fact that some key words and concepts of his conversation mean radically different things to others. One party to the conversation quickly concludes that the other does not understand what is being discussed, yet neither realizes that the common words they are using do not have a shared, common meaning for the two of them. This specific type of lack of communication is frequently encountered when people of different religious backgrounds are discussing the interrelationship of Judaism, Christianity, and Islam. Each discussant is operating from a different definition of Judaism, of Christianity, and of Islam, depending upon his or her prior religious education and training, which has inoculated each speaker with a different understanding of the origin of the religion in question.

In some ways, it may seem strange that adherents of these three religions, which share so much common heritage, would have so much trouble communicating with each other. It is perhaps because of this common heritage that confusion is probable. When one is confronted by a radically different concept, which has no relationship to one's typical mindset and mental representation of the world, one is forced to accommodate to that new concept, and to build a new mental framework for understanding the concept in question. However, when an apparently familiar concept, but one that is being used in a slightly different way confronts one, the temptation arises either to ignore the differences or to assimilate the concept to the individual's pre-existing mental framework. In either case, the use of the concept is distorted. As such, it may be much easier, for example, for the Christian to develop a reasonably accurate understanding of advaitistic Hinduism, than of Islam.

Advaitistic Hinduism is so foreign to the Christian's everyday understanding of religious concepts, that he is forced to develop new and unbiased mental representations. However, Islam is so close to Christianity in so many ways that the Christian simply assumes he understands what the Muslim means, when the latter mentions terms such as "revelation", "Torah", and "gospel". Likewise, the Christian is likely to assume that he understands who the Muslim means, when the Muslim names various prophets of Islam, such as Adam, Abraham, Jesus, and Muhammad, peace be upon them all.[1] Not to be outdone, the Muslim is likely to be just as misled by a false assurance that he understands those same terms and names when used by the Christian.

In the author's experience, one of the easiest and simplest ways of clearing up these difficulties in communication is to examine the origins of the three religions in question. As soon as one begins to do that, it becomes obvious that there is a major gulf separating the Judeo-Christian perspective of the origins of Judaism, Christianity, and Islam, from the Islamic perspective of the origins of these same three religions. Even a modest study of the conceptualization of religious origins highlights some of the common causes of miscommunication between the adherents of the Judeo-Christian tradition and the adherents of the Islamic tradition. As such, in the hope of bridging that gap in communication, the present essay examines the origin and evolution of Judaism, Christianity, and Islam from two markedly different perspectives, i.e., the Judeo-Christian perspective and the Islamic perspective.[2] In doing so, the present essay is necessarily somewhat simplistic and is definitely incomplete. A complete, thorough, and penetrating analysis of the topic in question would require its own multi-volume book, not a mere essay.

The Judeo-Christian Perspective

The Judeo-Christian perspective is one that is systematically taught throughout Western academic institutions, beginning in junior high school history classes and continuing throughout college level courses. It can be seen in such junior high school textbook statements as, "Judaism was the first monotheistic religion", a statement which is vehemently rejected by the Islamic perspective, which will be presented later. As a brief digression, it is noted that most Muslim parents in the United States probably fail to grasp that their children are being systematically proselytized with this Judeo-Christian perspective as part of their children's public school education. Complicating the problem, because of their lack of familiarity with the Islamic perspective, the public school teachers of these Muslim children probably fail to realize that they are even engaged in an act of proselytizing.

While the major points of the Judeo-Christian perspective are typically well known to most Christians and Jews, some of the specificity presented below may represent a level of knowledge not readily available to them. This is especially likely to be the case about the nature and causes of various sects within Judaism and Christianity, and concerning specific dates and events reported below.

Ur-Judaism and the Covenant with Noah

The Judeo-Christian perspective begins with Adam, peace be upon him, and traces the descent of man down through the various *Old Testament* patriarchs, until arriving at Noah, peace be upon him. The actual lineage proposed by *Genesis* is Adam to Seth to Enos to Cainan to Mahalaleel to Jared to Enoch to Methuselah to Lamech to Noah.[3] It is with the arrival of Noah that something new enters the framework of the Judeo-Christian perspective. Reportedly, Noah was the first person with whom Allah[4] entered into a covenant.[5] Now, this covenant was reportedly quite primitive and limited, and very few details regarding the covenant are reported in *Genesis*. In fact, the only details listed in Genesis regarding this covenant are that Noah was to build the ark, and stock it with the animals of the earth[6]; that Allah would never again destroy all mankind through a flood, and His promise of that was symbolized in the rainbow.[7] It is of note that there is next to nothing in this report of *Genesis* about a monotheistic commitment of worship, etc. Nonetheless, this covenant of Noah can serve as the first possible point of origin for Judaism, or what might be better-termed proto-Judaism or ur-Judaism.

Judaism and the Covenant with Abraham

More often, the Judeo-Christian tradition traces the origin of Judaism to Abraham, who lived approximately eleven generations after Noah.[8] Here, one encounters the second covenant between Allah and man, as

Allah reportedly established a new covenant with Abraham. Once again, *Genesis* only sparsely reports the details of this covenant. In short, this covenant can is summarized to mean that: Abraham and his descendants were to keep the covenant, and were to practice circumcision[9]; Allah promised He would be the god of Abraham and his descendants through Isaac, peace be upon him; and that Abraham and his descendants would be multitudinous. Further, Abraham and his descendants through Isaac would inherit the land of Palestine, and the covenant.[10] The whole of history then pivoted on this covenant, the relationship between Allah and man was forever changed, and a special relationship had been established between Allah and the descendants of Isaac.

It is important to note that the Judeo-Christian tradition sees this covenant between Allah and Abraham as being one of exclusive inheritance. Only Isaac and his descendants, of all of Abraham's many children, could inherit the covenant with Allah.[11] The exclusivity of inheritance was further refined, when it was maintained that the inheritance of the covenant passed over Isaac's elder son, Esau, in favor of Isaac's younger son, Jacob, peace be upon him.[12] As Jacob's name was later changed to Israel[13], making him the eponymous ancestor of the 12 tribes of Israel, the exclusivity of the covenant was seen to reside thereafter with Israel, and with Israel alone.

Judaism Refined and the Mosaic Covenant

Several centuries after Jacob, Allah reportedly refined his covenant with the 12 tribes of Israel. This refinement, which for the first time left a recording of specified and explicit details regarding the worship of Allah and the laws of Judaism, was given to Moses, peace be upon him. The various stipulations of the Mosaic covenant are much too detailed and voluminous to go into at this point. However, it does need to be noted that, according to the Judeo-Christian perspective, this is the second point in time, in which history pivoted, and in which the relationship between man and Allah is seen as having been irrevocably changed. For those in the Judeo-Christian tradition, who resist seeing the covenant with Abraham as being the origin of Judaism, this Mosaic covenant is seen as constituting the beginning of Judaism as an organized religion.

The Role of the Prophets

A fully evolved religious structure having been decreed by the Mosaic covenant, it was inevitable that the Israelites, or at least some significant portion of them, would stray from fulfilling the obligations of the covenant. As such, Allah periodically sent prophets, i.e., those authorized to speak for Allah, to call the wayward and backsliding Israelites back to the true fulfillment of the Mosaic covenant. From the contemporary Judeo-Christian perspective, these prophets are seen as admonishing the Israelites to return to Judaism

Despite the clarion call of these prophets, a sizable portion of the Israelites failed to listen, especially among those in the ruling class. As such, the Davidic and Solomonic Kingdom of Israel was fragmented into a northern Kingdom of Israel and a southern Kingdom of Judah around 930 BCE. From this point on, prophets were variously sent to both king-doms. However, again, many failed to heed the message of warning, which was delivered by these prophets. As further punishment, Allah ordained the destruction of the northern Kingdom of Israel by the Assyrian Empire around 722 BCE. The Israelites of the northern Kingdom of Israel, comprising 10 of the 12 tribes of Israel, were carried away into captivity, and failed ever to re-emerge on the pages of history as an identifiable people, thus giving rise to the 10 lost tribes of Israel.

The southern Kingdom of Judah, being primarily comprised of the tribes of Benjamin and Judah, continued in a rocky existence for about 150 years more. Prophets continued to be sent to these people, but true adherence to Judaism, as specified in the Mosaic covenant, was lacking. Thus, Allah allowed the fall of the southern Kingdom of Judah to the Babylonian Empire around 586 BCE. The Solomonic Temple (see below under "The Temple Cult") was destroyed, many of the Jews were carted off into exile in Babylon, and the period of exile had begun.[14]

In understanding the role of the prophets from the Judeo-Christian perspective, it cannot be emphasized enough that these prophets were perceived as simply calling the people back to Judaism. They did not bring any real revision to the Mosaic covenant, although they may have offered some interpretation of it. However, even this "new" interpretation should be seen as simply correcting a prior, erroneous interpretation, which had arisen among the people. As such, although these prophets were seen as speaking for Allah, they did not bring any new revelation or any real modification of the Mosaic covenant. In that regard, revelation can be seen within the Judeo-Christian perspective as having been static since the time of Moses. Further, it must be emphasized that the Judeo-Christian perspective frequently portrays these prophets as having spiritual feet of clay, i.e. of being as prone to sin, temptation, and degradation as those to whom they preached.

The Temple Cult

In the fourth year of the reign of King Solomon, peace be upon him, construction began on a magnificent temple in Jerusalem[15], which measured about 90 feet in length, 30 feet in breadth, and 45 feet in height[16], and was surrounded by various courtyards and interconnected rooms.[17] With the construction of this Temple of Solomon in the 10th century BCE, the religion of Judaism became centered on the concept and ritual of temple sacrifice.[18] During three separate religious holidays or pilgrim feasts, Jews were enjoined to journey to Jerusalem to give a sacrifice from the first fruits of the harvest at the Solomonic Temple. These religious festivals included Passover (at the time of the harvest of barley), The Feast of Weeks (at the time of the harvest of wheat; conforming to the Christian holiday of Pentecost), and Tabernacles or the Feast of Booths (at the time of the harvest of fruits)[19]. In turn, this focus on temple sacrifice elevated the importance of the role of the priests and Levites in the religious life of Judaism.[20]

However, not all of those who claimed to be Jews acknowledged the temple cult in Jerusalem. Among them were the Samaritans, a people of mixed Assyrian and Israelite descent, who had relocated in the area, which had been the northern Kingdom of Israel, after the Assyrian conquest of the Kingdom of Israel in 722 BC. The Samaritans did not finally break away from Judaism until after the return of the Jews from the Babylonian exile (see below). However, they avoided the temple cult in Jerusalem, worshipped at their own site at Mt. Gerisim at Shechem (modern Nablus), which they claimed to be the real and actual holy site selected by Allah (as opposed to Jerusalem). These people had their own version of the *Torah*, which differed in many parts from the *Torah* of the postexilic Jews in Judea.[21]

As noted above, the Babylonian army of Nebuchadnezzar destroyed the Solomonic Temple in 586 BC. Of marked significance to the maintenance of Judaism as a distinct religion, was the building of a new temple in Jerusalem at the start of the second year of the reign (522-486 BCE) of Darius I of Persia.[22] While helping to maintain Judaism as a distinct entity, this second temple had considerably less grandeur than the original Solomonic Temple[23], although it reportedly was larger, having a width and a height of about 90 feet.[24] About five centuries later, around 19 BCE, Herod the Great, the Roman appointed King of the Jews, began building a third and much more elaborate temple, which involved a massive reconstruction and expansion of the temple built in 520 BCE. This Temple of Herod stood until its destruction in August of 70 CE by a Roman army.[25]

Post Exilic Judaism

The Persian Empire conquered the Babylonian Empire around 539 BCE. The following year, Sheshbazzar led the first group of returning Jews back to Palestine. This migration of returning Jews continued sporadically for the next 140 years, and was almost complete with the return of Ezra to Palestine around 397 BCE.

Post exilic Judaism was characterized by the rise of numerous Jewish sects, most of which failed to survive to modern times, but which are known to have existed in the Hellenistic period, beginning with the conquest of Alexander the Great between the years 334 and 323 BCE. Religious and secular-nationalistic-political considerations differentiated these sects, which can be roughly categorized into three main groups: the Sadducees, meaning the "righteous ones"; the Hassidim (Chassidim); and the Zealots.

The Sadducees, also known as the Zadokites, were political opportunists, who were willing to accommodate to other cultures and governments, including the Roman Empire. They were comprised mainly of members of the upper class and hierarchy, and their domain of influence was confined to the city of Jerusalem. Their philosophical rationale centered on a belief in a theocratic government, which was to be vested in the descendants of Zadok, the high priest during the reign of King Solomon. Their religious practice centered on the written law, ignoring the oral law and any written scripture outside the five books of the received *Torah*. For them, religious practice was focused on the rites and sacrifices of the temple. They apparently did not believe in the coming of a Messiah, in the concept of resurrection after death, or in the existence of the angels of Allah. With the destruction of Herod's Temple in August 70 CE, their reason for existence vanished, and they ceased to exist as a viable sect.[26]

The Hassidim, whose name can be translated as "the pious", arose about the beginning of the second century BCE, and shortly thereafter split into two main groups: the Pharisees; and the Essenes.[27] The prominence of these two main subgroups of the Hassidim calls for a separate discussion of each.

The Pharisees were probably the dominant Jewish sect at the time of Jesus, and likely numbered about 6,000. They resisted assimilation of Hellenistic influences, and were more nationalistically oriented than the Sadducees. Likewise, they were more of a "people's" movement, than were the more aristocratic Sadducees, but their influence was primarily felt on the outskirts of Jerusalem. The Pharisees gave rise to the various rabbinical schools and to rabbinical Judaism; and they were great proponents of the oral law, which attempted to interpret the *Torah*. They readily accepted as authoritative scripture the various books of the *Nevi'im* and of the *Ketuvim*, which today find their place alongside the *Torah* in the *Old Testament*. They awaited the coming of a Messiah, and believed in resurrection after death, in a final Day of Judgment, and in the existence of the angels of Allah.[28]

The Essenes, on the other hand, numbering about 4,000, tended to withdraw from society, and established "monasteries" such as that at Qumran, on the shore of the Dead Sea, or closed communities in and around Jerusalem and probably Damascus. Like the Pharisees, they resisted Hellenistic influences, accepted the *Nevi'im* and the *Ketuvim* as scriptural, although apparently not at the same level as the *Torah*, and awaited the coming of a Messiah (if not two Messiahs, one being priestly and one being kingly). They believed in resurrection after death, in a final Day of Judgment, and in the existence of the angels of Allah, as well as in the final, cosmic battle between good and evil, giving a dualistic color to their theology. The Essenes also utilized a number of books, which were not acceptable to the Pharisees, and which never were accepted as part of the *Old Testament* canon. By and large, these books are found in various collections of the pseudepigraphical writings, appear to have had a great influence on the early Christian churches, and are frequently quoted without reference in the *New Testament*. In terms of religious practice, the Essenes were characterized by their great emphasis on ritual ablution, on the repetitious use of immersion in water, by their wearing of white, by a frequently communal and ascetic lifestyle, by extremely strict marital limitations, and by a refusal to even defecate on the Sabbath. After the destruction of Herod's Temple in 70 CE, various Essenic communities either ceased to exist, or were absorbed by the nascent Christian churches and possibly by the early Mandaean movement, which alleged its origin from John the Baptist, peace be upon him.[29]

The Zealots were primarily a political group with extreme nationalistic ambitions, which was fragmented into a variety of sub-sects, including the Galileans and the Sicarii ("dagger men" or "assassins"). They claimed their origin with the aborted uprising of Judas of Gamala (a.k.a. Judas the Galilean) in six CE. Thereafter, they engaged in isolated acts of guerrilla warfare against Rome, which were punctuated by armed uprisings, e.g. in 66 CE and in 132 CE. While Josephus claimed that their religious orientation was like that of the Pharisees, it is more likely that their nationalistic platform masked a variety of different religious practices and sects. To the extent they looked for the coming of a Messiah, they envisioned the Messiah as a warrior king, who would deliver them from foreign control. The Zealots ceased to exist after their final uprising under Simon bar Kochba in 132 CE.[30]

Modern Judaism

With the destruction of Herod's Temple in 70 CE, the Pharisees were able to re-interpret the rites and rituals of the temple into life and worship within the synagogue and within the family.[31] As such, not counting the small Samaritan sect of today, the Pharisees were able to survive into modern times as the only living sect of Judaism[32] even though in the process further sectarian groups emerged. In modern times, these sects are grouped into three main groups, which can be ranked on a conservative to liberal scale to include Orthodox Judaism, Conservative Judaism, and Reform Judaism.

Christianity

So far, the discussion of the Judeo-Christian perspective has focused solely on Judaism. However, with the advent of Jesus Christ, the Judeo-Christian perspective now divides into a Jewish and a Christian perspective. In what follows, the "Christian perspective" is traced. "Christian perspective" refers here to that traditional corpus of beliefs, which today is held by the majority of Christian churches. In defining the "Christian perspective" in this manner, it ought to be pointed out that there was no single, monolithic Christian church, which evolved immediately following the time of Jesus. Rather, there were a multitude of independent churches, each having its own set of recognized scriptures, each under its own independent bishop or leader, and each having its own viewpoint on such issues as: whether or not it was Jesus Christ, who was crucified[33]; the nature of Jesus Christ[34], i.e., whether he was God[35], man, or some combination thereof; and the nature of God, i.e., trinitarian of one formulation or another or one and indivisible. It was not until several centuries later that these issues began to be sorted out, and the traditional consensus of Christian belief began to emerge.

With the above in mind, it can be stated that, from the Christian perspective, the birth of Jesus ushered in yet a third time in which history pivoted, and in which the fundamental relationship between Allah and mankind was forever altered. Although allegedly pre-existing his physical birth[36], Jesus was seen as the begotten son of God via a virgin birth, who opened up the covenant of Allah to all mankind, whose ministry was to both Jew and gentile, and who allegedly was crucified in atonement for the sins of mankind, before allegedly being resurrected. Although precise formulations of the concept of the trinity differ, Jesus was seen as one person among three (the Father, the Son, and the Holy Spirit), who shared the same divine substance.

The Christian perspective typically sees the ministry of Jesus as having evolved out of Judaism, primarily the Judaism of the Pharisaic and Essenic movements, and as having ushered in a new covenant of faith, repentance, and atonement in the "blood of Christ", which totally replaced the prior Mosaic covenant. In short, Christianity replaced Judaism, which was no longer relevant or spiritually operative after the new covenant of Christ. The age of the *Old Testament* prophets was now over, and the age of the Holy Spirit had begun.

As noted previously, it took some several centuries for the above consensus to emerge within Christianity. However, even then, the consensus was shaky. Disagreements as to the independence of and/or hierarchical ranking of the various bishops, and over the exact wording of the definition of the trinity, finally led to the great schism between the Roman Catholic and Orthodox Catholic Churches. The latter quickly fragmented, largely along nationalistic or ethnic lines. Some centuries later, the Roman Catholic Church underwent its own schism during the Protestant Reformation, giving rise to myriad and differing Protestant denominations.

Islam

According to the Judeo-Christian perspective, Islam did not exist until the ministry and preaching of Muhammad in the seventh century CE. Originally portrayed as the anti-Christ by many Christians, the image of Muhammad later began to be portrayed somewhat more favorably among certain elements of the Christian clergy and scholars. However, the Judeo-Christian perspective still perceives that Islam originated with Muhammad, and that Muhammad created Islam by borrowing heavily from both rabbinical Judaism and from Christianity. Concerning the alleged borrowing from Christianity, it is traditionally held that Muhammad most frequently took from the teachings of the Eastern churches and from a variety of apocryphal Christian writings. Thus, from the Judeo-Christian perspective, Islam originated in the seventh century CE as an amalgamation of Judaism and Christianity.

Summary

To summarize, the Judeo-Christian perspective posits the following step-wise evolution of Judaism, Christianity, and Islam. Primitive or proto-Judaism can be traced to the primitive covenant between Allah and Noah. However, Judaism really has its origin with the covenant between Allah and Abraham, a covenant, which was exclusively inherited by Isaac, then by Jacob, and then by the Israelites. The covenant was then reformulated with Moses, and Judaism as a full-blown religion began. Central to the maintenance of Judaism as a distinct religious practice was the temple cult, with its focus on the act of sacrifice at the Solomonic Temple in Jerusalem. Thereafter, various Israelites strayed from observance of the covenant, resulting in Allah sending prophets, who reaffirmed the Mosaic covenant, but neither added to nor modified it. This state of affairs continued until the new covenant of Christ, from which Christianity emerged. Almost 600 years later, Muhammad, borrowing heavily from both rabbinical Judaism and from Christianity, created the religion of Islam. This brief summary is graphically illustrated in somewhat more detail in Table 1 below.

The Islamic Perspective

Most Western non-Muslims do not even realize that there is an Islamic perspective, which is substantially different from that of the Judeo-Christian perspective, particularly with regard to the understanding of the

origins of Judaism, Christianity, and Islam. As a matter of course, it is
the Judeo-Christian perspective, which is systematically taught throughout Western school systems. As such, Muslim children in Western school
systems are routinely indoctrinated with the Judeo-Christian perspective,
often without their parents realizing it, and in direct violation, albeit
unknowingly, of the American principle of separation of church and state.
Ironically, even in Islamic schools in North America, classes in world
history, etc. are often forced to use Western textbooks, which propagate
the Judeo-Christian perspective.

Table 1
The Traditional Judeo-Christian Perspective
– The origins of Judaism, Christianity and Islam

Adam
|
Noah
(The Noahic covenant and ur-Judaism)
|
Abraham
(The Abrahamic covenant and the origin of Judaism)
|
Moses
(The Mosaic covenant and the defining of Judaism)
|
The Prophets
(Called the people back to Judaism)
(Confirmed the Mosaic covenant, but provided no new revelation or modification
of the covenant)
|
The Exile
|
Postexilic Judaism

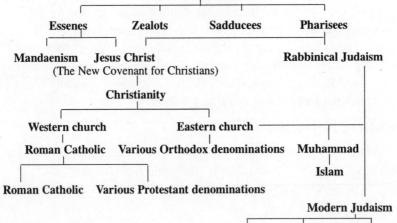

| **Essenes** | **Zealots** | **Sadducees** | **Pharisees** |

Mandaenism   **Jesus Christ**   **Rabbinical Judaism**
(The New Covenant for Christians)

Christianity

Western church   **Eastern church**

Roman Catholic   **Various Orthodox denominations**   **Muhammad**

Roman Catholic   **Various Protestant denominations**   **Islam**

Modern Judaism

Orthodox   Conservative   Reform

If the teacher of such a class were not a Muslim, then the state-certified, non-Muslim teacher would probably blithely teach the Judeo-Christian perspective without even realizing that he or she is subtly proselytizing. Just as alarming, some Muslims, especially those who were educated in a Western-oriented institution of learning, or who were educated in Israeli controlled Palestine, have come to accept the Judeo-Christian perspective, without being fully aware of the Islamic perspective.

Given the above background, the Islamic perspective is presented below. As will be seen, it sometimes parallels and at times deviates from the Judeo-Christian perspective. This is most apparent when considering terms such as Judaism, Christianity, Islam, covenant, and revelation.

Like the Judeo-Christian tradition, Islam traces the origin of mankind to Adam. However, unlike any conceptualization within the Judeo-Christian tradition, Islam posits its beginning with Adam. Islam means "submission", i.e. submission to Allah, and a Muslim is "one who submits" to Allah. Thus, the religion of Adam was Islam, as was the religion of Noah, Abraham, Moses, Jesus, etc.

> The same religion has He established for you as that which He enjoined on Noah—that which We have sent by inspiration to thee—and that which We enjoined on Abraham, Moses, and Jesus: namely, that ye should remain steadfast in religion, and make no divisions therein: to those who worship other things than Allah, hard is the (way) to which thou callest them. Allah chooses to Himself those whom He pleases, and guides to Himself those who turn (to Him).[37]

This is not, however, to say that the Islamic religion of Adam was the same in every detail as that of Noah, or of Abraham, or of Moses, or of Jesus, or of Muhammad. In fact, it was not. However, to understand that difference, one has to understand the Islamic concepts of covenant and of progressive revelation.

Covenanat and Revelation

As noted above, the Judeo-Christian tradition perceives the concept of covenant to represent a fundamental re-ordering of the cosmos, in which the relationship between mankind and Allah is completely redefined, and in which an entirely new concept of religion is introduced. Covenants are thus seen as being few and far between, represented only by: 1) the primitive or proto-covenant with Noah; 2) the defining covenant with Abraham, which was exclusively inherited by Isaac, by Jacob, and then by the Israelites; 3) the revision and elaboration of the Abrahamic covenant with Moses, with inheritance of the covenant limited to Israelites and Jews; and 4) the new covenant with Jesus, which for the first time was open to participation by non-Jews.

In marked contrast, Islam affirms a multiplicity of covenants between Allah and mankind. Every prophet of Allah, most of whose names are not even known to contemporary man[38], has had his own covenant, which was inherited by that prophet's people[39]. The following quotations from the *Qur'an* serve to illustrate this latter point.

> Remember We made the House a place of assembly for men and a place of safety; and take ye the station of Abraham as a place of prayer; and We covenanted with Abraham and Isma'il, that they should sanctify My House for those who compass it round, or use it as a retreat, or bow, or prostrate themselves (therein in prayer.[40]

> Behold! Allah took the covenant of the prophets, saying: "I give you a book and wisdom; then comes to you a messenger, confirming what is with you; do you believe in him and render him help." Allah said: "Do ye agree, and take this my covenant as binding on you?" They said: "We agree." He said: "Then bear witness, and I am with you among the witnesses."[41]

> And remember We took from the prophets their covenant: as (We did) from thee: From Noah, Abraham, Moses, and Jesus the son of Mary: We took from them a solemn covenant.[42]

Further, a prophet of Allah was sent to every people, not just to the Israelites. There are many passages in the *Qur'an* referring to the fact that a prophet was sent to every people.[43] The following represents a brief sample of those passages.

> Before thee We sent (messengers) to many nations, and We afflicted the nations with suffering and adversity, that they might learn humility.[44]

To every people (was sent) a messenger: when their messenger comes (before them), the matter will be judged between them with justice, and they will not be wronged.[45]

For We assuredly sent amongst every people a messenger, (with the command), "Serve Allah, and eschew evil": of the people were some whom Allah guided, and some on whom error became inevitably (established). So travel through the earth, and see what was the end of those who denied (the truth)[46]

Verily We have sent thee in truth, as a bearer of glad tidings, and as a warner:and there never was a people, without a warner having lived among them (in the past).[47]

Thus, between the time of Adam and Muhammad, covenants were plentiful, and were non-exclusive. Every person, regardless of ethnic, national, or racial descent, had the potential opportunity to inherit a covenant with Allah, and to enter into a proper, worshipful relationship with Allah.

This concept of a multiplicity of covenants is linked with the Islamic concept of progressive revelation.[48] Since each prophet received his own covenant with Allah, the revelation of Allah as to how best to worship Him was progressively revealed over an evolutionary period. Unlike the cosmic re-orderings followed by long periods of revelatory stagnation posited by the Judeo-Christian tradition, Islam affirms a gradual evolution in the relationship between man and Allah and in man's worship of Allah. Prior revelations could and were modified, elaborated, and abrogated.[49] In fact, such evolution and progressive revelation occurred not only between prophets, but also within a given prophet's own message and revelation.[50] With regard to this, one needs only look to the progressive revelation within the lifetime of Muhammad, which led from no prohibition against alcohol, to prohibition against alcoholic consumption interfering with the performance of mandatory prayers[51], to total prohibition of alcohol.[52] This concept of progressive revelation is summarized in the following passages from the *Qur'an*.

None of Our revelations do We abrogate or cause to be forgotten, but We substitute something better or similar: knowest thou not that Allah hath power over all things?[53]

We did send messengers before thee, and appointed for
them wives and children: and it was never the part of a
messenger to bring a sign except as Allah permitted (or
commanded). For each period is a book (revealed). Allah
doth blot out or confirm what He pleaseth: with Him is the
mother of the book.[54]

This *Qur'an* is not such as can be produced by other than
Allah; on the contrary it is a confirmation of (revelations)
that went before it, and a fuller explanation of the book—
wherein there is no doubt—from the Lord of the worlds.[55]

When We substitute one revelation for another—and Allah
knows best what He reveals (in stages)—they say, "Thou art
but a forger": but most of them understand not.[56]

Given the above, it can be seen that Islam began with Adam,
gradually evolved through the different covenants and progressive
revelations given to the various prophets, and finally culminated in the
final revelation given to Prophet Muhammad. In this regard, the contrasts
between the Judeo-Christian and Islamic perspectives are dramatic. The
Judeo-Christian perspective posits a few stages of religious evolution,
each of which is markedly different than the one before it.
Metaphorically, one can compare the Judeo-Christian perspective to
the drastic revolutions involved in the developmental stages of the
caterpillar, cocoon, and butterfly. Each stage is fundamentally different
in appearance than the stage before it. In contrast, the metaphor for the
Islamic perspective would be that of the budding and opening of a flower,
in which the message of Adam represents the first budding[57], and in
which the final message of Muhammad represents the flower in full
bloom.[58] However, even within that first bud of Adam's message, there
were two fundamental truths, which have never been abrogated or
modified, and which continued to be the centerpiece of the message of
every later prophet: 1) there is no god but Allah, Who has no partners, and
Allah is to be worshipped and served[59]; and 2) avoid evil and wickedness,
for there will be a day of final judgment.[60]

The Role of the Prophets

In order to affect a proper comparison between the Judeo-Christian and Islamic perspectives, this discussion of the role of the prophets is limited to those prophets, who are recognized in some capacity by both the Judeo-Christian tradition and by Islam. As noted previously, the Judeo-Christian tradition posits that these prophets were sent by Allah to call the backsliding Israelites and Jews back to Judaism. In contrast, the Islamic perspective affirms that these prophets represented the progressive revelation of Islam, and were sent by Allah to bring the people back to Islam. However, many did not listen to the prophets, did not repent of their ways, and did not return to proper submission to Allah. Apostasy and deviation existed, and eventually certain of these deviations came to be codified and ritualized. Such codification and ritualizing of deviation from Islam were the origin of Judaism[61], i.e. of one of the two branches of the People of the Book.[62] This is illustrated by the Qur'anic emphasis on the Jews having distorted and perverted their revealed scriptures.[63] In short, Judaism arose much after Islam, and was the codified remains of deviation from Islam. As such, the prophets were not sent to call the people back to Judaism, but were sent to call the people back to Islam from Judaism, from other forms of deviation, and from frank unbelief.

> The religion before Allah is Islam (submission to His will): nor did the People of the Book dissent therefrom except through envy of each other, after knowledge had come to them. But if any deny the signs of Allah, Allah is swift in calling to account.[64]

> The same religion has He established for you as that which He enjoined on Noah—that which We have sent by inspiration to thee—and that which We enjoined on Abraham, Moses, and Jesus: namely, that ye should remain steadfast in religion, and make no divisions therein: to those who worship other things than Allah, hard is the (way) to which thou callest them. Allah chooses to Himself those whom He pleases, and guides to Himself those who turn (to Him). And they became divided only after knowledge reached them—through selfish envy as between themselves. Had it

not been for a word that went forth before from thy Lord,
(tending) to a term appointed, the matter would have been
settled between them: but truly those who have inherited
the book after them are in suspicious (disquieting) doubt
concerning it.[65]

One other point of difference between the Judeo-Christian and
Islamic perspectives on the role of the prophets needs to be stated. As
noted previously, the Judeo-Christian perspective frequently portrays
the prophets of Allah as being backsliding sinners, who engaged in
all manner of reprehensible behavior. In marked contrast, the Islamic
perspective is that these prophets were men of virtue, piety, and high
moral character.

No prophet could (ever) be false to his trust.[66]

Jesus and the origin of Christianity

Islam affirms the virgin birth of Jesus, but sees this not as an act of
begetting, but as an act of miraculous creation, caused by Allah's verbal
command.[67] The following represents but one of several passages from
the *Qur'an* that testifies to the virgin birth of Jesus.

Behold! The angels said: "O Mary! Allah giveth thee glad
tidings of a word from Him: his name will be Christ Jesus.
The son of Mary, held in honor in this world and the
hereafter and of (the company of) those nearest to Allah; He
shall speak to the people in childhood and in maturity. And
he shall be (of the company) of the righteous." She said: "O
my Lord! How shall I have a son when no man hath touched
me?" He said: "Even so: Allah createth what He willeth:
when He hath decreed a plan, He but saith to it, 'Be,' and it
is!"[68]

However, in regard to the virgin birth, the miraculous origin of Jesus
is seen as being akin to the creation of Adam. Just as Jesus was without
a father, so Adam, having been created from the earth[69], was without a
father and a mother.

> The similitude of Jesus before Allah is as that of Adam;
> He created him from dust, then said to him: "Be": and he
> was.[70]

Islam affirms that Jesus was a prophet of Allah[71], and that Jesus was the Messiah or Christ.[72] However, Islam denies the crucifixion of Jesus[73], and denies the divinity of Jesus.[74] Like those prophets of Israel before him, Jesus' message and ministry were confined to the remnants of Israel and to the Jews[75], and were a call to return to Islam and to proper submission to and worship of the Oneness of Allah.[76] It's worth noting that one part of the message of Jesus was the prophecy of an additional prophet yet to come, who would be called Ahmad, which is a variation of the name Muhammad.

> And remember, Jesus, the son of Mary, said: "O children of
> Israel! I am the messenger of Allah (sent) to you, confirm-
> ing the law (which came) before me, and giving glad tidings
> of a messenger to come after me, whose name shall be
> Ahmad." But when he came to them with clear signs, they
> said, "This is evident sorcery!"[77]

Jesus was not the founder or originator of a new religion, or even of a new religious movement within the Judaism of his times, but was one in a succession of prophets of Allah to the people of Israel. Likewise, attempts to link Jesus with this or that particular school of Judaic thought, whether Pharisaic, Essenic, or other, are rejected, as they distort the fundamental truth that Jesus was a prophet of Allah, who was bringing a portion of the progressive revelation of Islam. All of which is not to say that there was no new component to the message that Jesus brought. The Islamic concept of progressive revelation allows for the possibility that the revelation to Jesus may have partially altered, added to, or abrogated some parts of the revelations of earlier prophets.

So, then how does one account for the origin of Christianity? The Islamic answer is that others, e.g., Paul of Tarsus, quickly distorted the message, ministry, and gospel of Jesus. Probably, none of those who distorted Jesus' message had been an eyewitness to Jesus' life and ministry, and none were actual disciples of Jesus. The actual and complete gospel of Jesus is nowhere to be found in the contemporary *New*

Testament. However, bits and pieces of that gospel probably have been preserved by subsequent "Christian" authors of the various books of the *New Testament*, all of which were written two decades to one century after the completion of Jesus' ministry, and none of which were likely authored by anyone who had first hand contact with Jesus' actual ministry. Additional fragments about the ministry of Jesus were probably preserved in parts of the so-called apocrypha of the Christian era.

In short, just as distortions of earlier revelations from Allah to the prophets had resulted in the formation of Judaism, so distortions of the message of Jesus resulted in the formation of Christianity.

> When Jesus came with clear signs, he said: "Now have I come to you with wisdom, and in order to make clear to you some of the (points) on which ye dispute: therefore fear Allah and obey me. For Allah, He is my Lord and your Lord: so worship ye Him: this is a straight way." But sects from among themselves fell into disagreement: then woe to the wrongdoers, from the penalty of a grievous day![78]

> From those, too, who call themselves Christians, We did take a covenant, but they forgot a good part of the message that was sent them: so We estranged them, with enmity and hatred between the one and the other, to the Day of Judgement. And soon will Allah show them what it is they have done.[79]

> Then, in their wake, We followed them up with (others of) Our messengers: We sent after them Jesus the son of Mary, and bestowed on him the gospel; and We ordained in the hearts of those who followed him compassion and mercy, but the monasticism which they invented for themselves, We did not prescribe for them: (We commanded) only the seeking for the good pleasure of Allah; but that they did not foster as they should have done. Yet We bestowed, on those among them who believed, their (due) reward, but many of them are rebellious transgressors.[80]

(As a brief digression, it is interesting to note how the second passage above, with its emphasis on the "enmity and hatred between the one and the other" Christian groups appears to predict so accurately the abuses and barbarities perpetrated by Christians upon Christians during the Protestant Reformation, the origins of the Anabaptist movement, and the infamous Inquisition.)

Muhammad and the Final Revelation of Islam

Muhammad did not originate or create Islam, nor was Islam originated based on the revelations given to Muhammad by Allah.[81] Rather, Muhammad was the Seal of the Prophets, i.e. the last in the line of Allah's prophets, just as a seal at the end of a document is the last thing affixed to that document. It may be noted that Westerners and adherents to the Judeo-Christian perspective frequently attribute hierarchical significance to the title "Seal of the Prophets", as though Muslims claim that Muhammad was the greatest or best of the prophets of Allah. This type of thinking is contrary to Islam, and is specifically prohibited by the *Qur'an*, which states that Muslims are to make no hierarchical distinctions among the prophets of Allah.[82] Like all the prophets before him, Muhammad was not divine, but was only a man endowed with the message of Allah.[83]

However, it was through the progressive revelation given to Muhammad that Islam was perfected and completed. This revelation abrogated, elaborated, and altered parts of the revelations given to earlier prophets, was memorized and written down by the early companions of Muhammad, and became known as the *Qur'an*. Thus, Islam finds its final evolution in the message of Muhammad, not its genesis. Further, as the Seal of the Prophets, Muhammad was the "international" prophet, bringing Allah's message not only to the people of Muhammad, whether defined as Makkans, the members of the Quraish tribe, or Arabs, but to the people of the world at large.

> Say: "No reward do I ask of you for this (*Qur'an*), nor am I a pretender. This is no less than a message to (all) the worlds."[84]

Summary

The Islamic perspective affirms the following evolution of Islam, Judaism, and Christianity. Islam began with Adam, and has evolved in accordance with the progressive revelations given by Allah to His various prophets. This evolution of Islam finds its perfect culmination in the final revelations of Allah, which were bestowed upon Prophet Muhammad. Early on, among the descendants of Prophet Jacob, distortions of the basic message of Islam were codified and ritualized, giving rise to the religion of Judaism. Subsequent prophets to the house of Israel continually warned the Israelites and Jews to return to Islam, and to forsake their deviations, which included Judaism, and their unbelief. Among those prophets, whose ministry was limited to the Israelites and Jews, was Jesus (the Messiah or Christ, and the son of the virgin Mary). However, Jesus' message and ministry were also distorted, giving rise to such concepts as the begotten son of God, the crucifixion of Jesus, and the trinitarian concept of God. This distortion of the message of Jesus by Paul of Tarsus and others became codified as Christianity. This brief summary is presented graphically in Table 2 below:

Conclusions

Words are sometimes deceiving in their ability to mislead others. This is especially the case when words are used to represent abstract concepts or complex systems or thoughts. As has been shown in the above discussion, words such as "revelation", "covenant", "Judaism", "Christianity", and "Islam" have radically different meanings for Muslims, than they do for adherents to the traditional Judeo-Christian perspective, which typically is the only viewpoint expressed in Western academia. Likewise, names such as Jesus, Muhammad, Moses, Abraham, etc., convey different images and associated concepts, depending upon the religious orientation of the individual. By contrasting the Judeo-Christian and Islamic perspectives on the origins of Judaism, Christianity, and Islam, some of these differences have been identified and discussed. Allah willing, this endeavor may contribute to better and heightened communication among the adherents of these three religious traditions.

Table 2
The Islamic Perspective: the Origins of Judaism, Christianity and Islam

Adam
(Initial revelation of Islam)

The Prophets
(Called the people back to Islam)
(A covenant established by Allah with each)
(Received a progressive revelation from Allah,
resulting in the evolution of Islam)

Prophets to Israel
(Isaac, Jacob, Aaron, Moses, etc.)
(Called the people back to Islam)
(Each with a covenant and a
progressive revelation)
(Islam continues to evolve according
to revelation from Allah)

Prophets to other people
(Called the people back to Islam)
(Each with a covenant and a
progressive revelation)
(Job, Hud, Salih,
Shuayb, etc.)

Distortion of the message   **Additional prophets**
(John the Baptist etc.)
(Preservation and evolution of Islam)

Judaism

Jesus Christ
(Prophet of Allah)
(Preservation and evolution of Islam)

Distortion of the message Preservation of the message
(Paul of Tarsus and others)

Christianity

Muhammad
(Seal of the Prophets)
(Islam in perfect evolutionary completion)

Chapter 3

The Books of Revelation and Scripture

– A Comparison of Judaism, Christianity and Islam

Judaism, Christianity, and Islam all claim to be based on a book or books of divine revelation and scripture, which comprise the words (whether literally or figuratively understood) of Allah[1]. While there is substantial overlap in the contents of these books, there are also certain obvious differences. An attempt has been made in this chapter to introduce and compare the structural aspects and provenance of these books of revelation and scripture. The book of revelation adhered to by Islam is a single book of revelation, i.e. the *Qur'an* in contrast to the division of books found in the Christian *Bible*. The books of scripture adhered to by Judaism number 39 (as counted in the Christian *Bible*), whereas the scriptures propounded by Christianity include these 39 books of Judaism besides 27 additional books[2] that comprise the *New Testament* of the Bible.

The Jewish Scriptures

The Jewish books of scripture, i.e., the *Tanakh*,[3] are traditionally organized into three categories known as: the *Torah*, i.e. "the law" or "the teaching"; the *Nevi'im*, i.e., "the prophets"; and the *Ketuvim*, i.e. "the writings". This three-fold division serves as a rough chronological sequence, corresponding to the time, in which these books were accepted as canonical scripture by Judaism. This means that the *Torah* was probably accepted as a closed canon of scripture early in the fourth century BCE during the time of Ezra. The *Nevi'im* received acceptance perhaps after the schism separating Samaritans and Jews somewhere in the fourth century (BC) or by the second century BCE. Finally, the *Ketuvim* became recognized as a category of scripture during the second century BCE, but the canon of the *Ketuvim,* and hence the *Tanakh,* was not officially closed until around the end of the first century CE, i.e., the council of Jamnia circa 85-90 CE.[4]

Of the 39 books comprising the *Torah, Nevi'im,* and *Ketuvim,* the *Qur'an* specifically mentions the *Zabur* (or *Psalms*) of David[5], peace be upon him[6] and the *Torah* (or Law) of Moses.[7] These six books, viz., the five books of the *Torah (Genesis, Exodus, Leviticus, Numbers,* and *Deuteronomy)* and the one book of *Psalms,* are the only ones of the 39 books of Jewish scripture that are mentioned in the *Qur'an.* It's beyond the scope of this book to discuss each and every one of the 39 books referred to above. However, a list of the books comprising the *Torah,* the *Nevi'im* and the *Ketuvim* appears below only as a ready reckoner.

Table 1: The composition of the *Torah, Nevi'im* and *Ketuvim*

TORAH	NEVI'IM	KETUVIM
Genesis	Joshua	Psalms
Exodus	Judges	Proverbs
Leviticus	I Samuel	Job
Numbers	II Samuel	Song of Solomon
Deuteronomy	I Kings	Ruth
	II Kings	Lamentations
	Isaiah	Ecclesiastes
	Jeremiah	Esther
	Ezekial	Daniel
	Hosea	Ezra
	Joel	Nehemiah
	Amos	I Chronicles
	Obadiah	II Chronicles
	Jonah	
	Micah	
	Nahum	
	Habakkuk	
	Zephaniah	
	Haggai	
	Zechariah	
	Malach	

The Christian Scriptures

The 27 books comprising the *New Testament* of the *Bible* represent those books of scripture that are exclusive to Christianity. Of these 27 books, one is an apocalypse[8], one is an early church history[9], 21 are epistles of one sort or another[10], and four are labeled as being gospels.[11] It is highly improbable that any of these 27 books were written by anyone who had first-hand contact with Jesus, peace be upon him[12], though each of the four gospels purports to be a history of the teaching and ministry of Jesus.

It is very likely that the canon of the *New Testament* evolved gradually over several centuries. Initially, during the first three centuries of the so-called Christian era, there was no concept of an authorized and closed canon of *New Testament* scripture. Various books were viewed as scriptural on the sheer strength of their self-stated claim of being divinely inspired. Their circulation and popularity among the various Christian churches gave them a further impetus in this direction. As a result of this, what was regarded as holy scripture at one place was not necessarily regarded so in another.

However, in the early fourth century CE, the situation began to change. In his *Ecclesiastical History*, Eusebius Pamphili, the fourth century CE bishop of Caesarea, proposed a canon of *New Testament* scripture in which he omitted many books currently found in the *New Testament*. In 367 CE, Athanasius, the bishop of Alexandria, circulated an Easter letter, which included the first listing of *New Testament* scripture in conformity with the current *New Testament*, although, only a few years earlier , he had been championing *The Shepherd of Hermas* as being accurate, canonical scripture. The *New Testament* scripture was later ratified at the Council of Hippo in 393 CE, the Synod of Carthage in 397 CE, and the Carthaginian Council in 419 CE. However, not all the Eastern churches agreed with this proposed canon until the time when the Syriac translation of circa 508 CE finally conformed to this canon.[13]

It took three to five centuries following the completion of the ministry of Jesus before early Christian churches formulated the final canon of the 27 books, presently comprising the *New Testament*. Of these 27 books, the *Qur'an* refers only to the *Gospel* (*Injil*) of Jesus, a book of revelation that was given to Jesus Christ.[14] However, the four canonical gospels of Christianity are definitely not this book of revelation, although they may include parts of this book in their alleged recordings of "sayings" of Jesus. For understanding the crux of the subject, this chapter, instead of going into the details of all the 27 books, confines itself only to the   structural composition of the *New Testament* gospels.

Analysis of Structure and Provenance

Having necessarily limited the scope of inquiry to the *Qur'an*, the *Torah*, and the canonical gospels of the *New Testament*, the issues of structural analysis and provenance becomes apparent. The chapter focuses on four considerations. First, is the book under consideration a unitary compilation? Second, is it a cut-and-paste work, which pieces together bits from more than one earlier written source, without apparently using the entirety of the earlier sources? Third, is the book a layered composition, with later material being layered onto and added to earlier material? Fourth, has the book undergone significant editorial redaction or glosses in an evolutionary development?

The answers to the second, third and fourth questions are not mutually exclusive. A book's structural form could be simultaneously cut-and-paste, layered, and redacted. In contrast, if the book were a single, unitary composition, this obviates the possibility of cut-and-paste, layering, and redacting.

With regard to provenance, the following questions loom large. First, can the book be directly attributed to the person who allegedly received the revelation?[15] Second, what is the time lag between the revelation and first compilation of the book? Third, do variant versions of the book exist, or did they exist at any given point of time? Fourth, what is the time lag between the revelation and "final" compilation of the book? Fifth, is the provenance of the revelation complete and unbroken, i.e., is there historical assurance that the original revelation was accurately and completely encapsulated by the original compilation of the book? Sixth, is there an historical assurance that the book, as it exists today, is the same as the book originally compiled?

The Book of Revelation given to Muhammad

A structural analysis of the *Qur'an* is a fairly straightforward and simple task. The *Qur'an* consists of only one book of revelation, all of which was revealed to Prophet Muhammad, peace be upon him, from Allah through the angel Jibril (Gabriel). However, a crucial distinction needs to be understood between: the *Qur'an*, i.e., the revelation of Allah given to Muhammad; and the *Ahadith* (singular = *Hadith*), i.e., the recorded sayings of what Muhammad said and did.

The *Qur'an*

Prophet Muhammad reportedly received his first revelation in the year 610 CE. Thereafter, revelations continued on an episodic basis until the close of his life in 632 CE. As such, the *Qur'an* can be said to have an earthly birth during the years 610 through 632 CE. Throughout these 22 years, the companions of Prophet Muhammad listened to his recitations of the revelations, memorized them, and wrote them down on stones, palm leaves, and whatever other writing surface on which they could lay their hands. Those companions who successfully memorized the entire *Qur'an* were known as "*Hafez*".

Upon the death of Prophet Muhammad in 632 CE, Abu Bakr was chosen as the first Caliph[16] of Islam. Approximately a year later, i.e. circa 633 CE, Abu Bakr appointed Zayd ibn Thabit to produce a written copy of the entire *Qur'an*, as revealed to Prophet Muhammad by Allah. Zayd ibn Thabit, himself an *Hafez*, and one who had served as the principle secretary to the Prophet produced a complete copy of the *Qur'an* just about a year after the demise of the Prophet. Zayd completed this task by using: his own memorization of the entire set of revelations, as well as those of other *Hafez*; and the available written fragments of the revelations.

This single, authenticated copy of the *Qur'an* was preserved dearly by Abu Bakr until his death in 634 CE. Soon thereafter, the possession passed to 'Umar ibn Al-Khattab, the second Caliph of Islam. 'Umar entrusted this copy of the *Qur'an* to his daughter, Hafsah, who was one of the widows of Prophet Muhammad. After 'Umar's death in 644 CE, the third Caliph of Islam, 'Uthman ibn 'Affan, directed Zayd ibn Thabit to utilize the copy of the *Qur'an* that had been entrusted to Hafsah, and to make a final recension of the *Qur'an*. This final recension consisted primarily of standardizing minor differences in dialect among the various Arab-speaking Muslims of the time.

Within the *Qur'an*, there are divisions into *Surat* (chapters) and *Ayat* (signs or verses). Further, with some degree of accuracy, one can separate the *Qur'an* into earlier revelations and later revelations, into revelations received at Makkah and revelations received at Madinah, and into content areas such as sacred history, community rules and laws, and instruction on the proper belief in and worship of Allah. Nonetheless, the *Qur'an* remains a single, unitary book of revelation, i.e., a verbatim recording of Muhammad's recitation of the revelations he received.

It is thus clear that the *Qur'an* is a single document, representing a single source, which is dependent only on the revelations received by Muhammad. There has been no cut-and-paste compiling, layering of diverse material from different times, or editorial re-writes or redactionistic revisions of the *Qur'an*. In this regard, the provenance of the *Qur'an* as tracing solely to the Prophet Muhammad is historically indisputable. Whether or not Muhammad's statements of received revelation are seen by contemporary readers as being divine revelations from Allah through Jibril is a religious verdict. However, the strictly historical verdict is unambiguously clear. The provenance of the *Qur'an* traces only to Prophet Muhammad.

Ahadith and *Sunnah*

A sharp distinction needs to be made between the sayings of Muhammad, whether on religious or non-religious issues, and his recitation of the revelations he received. The former are *Ahadith,* while the latter is the *Qur'an*. Within Islam, only the *Qur'an* has the status of canonical scripture. However, as a source of religious information and instruction, Muslims rank the *Ahadith* of Muhammad as second in authority only to the *Qur'an*. If the *Qur'an* is a Muslim's primary textbook for the final examination of life, the Ahadith, on the other hand represent the practical, supplemental reading, which may well help make the difference between passing and failing that all important examination.

Each *Hadith* is comprised of two parts: an *Isnad*; and a *Matn* (i.e., narrative). The *isnad* consists of a complete listing of the narrators of the *Hadith*, and is an attestation as to the provenance of the *Hadith*. As a hypothetical example, an *isnad* might state that the written recorder of the *Hadith* received the narration from X, who received it from Y, who received it from Z, that the Prophet Muhammad said... No *Hadith* is accepted as authoritative without a complete and unbroken *isnad*. Furthermore, each *isnad* is minutely examined in order to make sure: that X actually met Y; that Y actually met Z; that Z actually met the Prophet Muhammad; that X, Y, and Z had excellent memory skills; and that X, Y, and Z were individuals of high moral character and religious repute. Only if the *Isnad* passes this rigorous test is the *Hadith* accepted as authoritative.

The second part of the *hadith* consists of the *matn* or narrative content of what the Prophet Muhammad reportedly said or did. This narrative content is also minutely examined to assure consistency with the *Qur'an*, and compliance with other, already verified, *Ahadith*. Assuming that the *Hadith* has already passed muster in regard to an examination of its *isnad*, it is still not accepted as authoritative unless this narrative examination is also satisfactorily cleared.

Summary

Islam makes a sharp distinction between its canonical scripture, i.e., the *Qur'an*, and its supplementary books of religious instruction, i.e., the *Ahadith*. The *Qur'an* is primary, the *Ahadith* are secondary, but both are religiously authoritative.

In regard to the structural composition of the *Qur'an*, it is a single, unitary document, which was revealed over a time span of about 22 years between 610 and 632 CE. As stated earlier, there is no cut-and-paste composition, no layering, and no editorial redaction. It has a single source, and a complete, unbroken, and unambiguous provenance back to the Prophet Muhammad. Furthermore, it was compiled into a single, written document within one year of the death of the person who had originally received the revelations, viz. Prophet Muhammad. No variant versions of the *Qur'an* exist, resulting in the time interval between revelation and "final" compilation being the same. (The 'Uthman recension of the *Qur'an* merely standardized dialectic differences, and the chain of possession of the *Qur'an* reiterates the fact that the first compilation of the *Qur'an* also happens to be its last compilation.) The short time interval between revelation and the first compilation of the *Qur'an*, and the care exercised by Zayd ibn Thabit and other *Hafez* involved in producing the complete written text, make it amply clear that there is complete and unbroken provenance between the original revelation and the initial compilation of the *Qur'an*. Further, as the first compilation of the *Qur'an* was also its last, the provenance of this book is totally complete and indisputably unbroken.

The Book of Revelation given to Moses

The Jews, Christians and Muslims agree that a book of revelation was given to Moses, by Allah, and that this is called the *Torah*. However, there is some scholarly debate within the Judeo-Christian tradition regarding the era of Moses, with some scholars placing Moses as leading the Israelite exodus from Egypt as late as 1250 BCE[17] (or even 1220 BCE[18]). However, the internal evidence from the *Bible* states that the exodus from Egypt occurred 480 years prior to the start of the construction of the

Solomonic Temple in the fourth year of the reign of King Solomon, peace be upon him.[19] As there is more or less unanimous agreement among the scholars that the reign of King Solomon began at about midway of the first half of the 10th century BCE[20], this places the Israelite exodus from Egypt at about 1446 BCE. Thus, if one were to accept the Biblical dating process, the life of Moses and the book of revelation given to him would be no later in time than the 15th century BCE.

The Received *Torah*

A distinction needs to be made between the *Torah* that was given to Moses, and the *Torah* that is found in the contemporary *Bible*. The former, which can be termed the original *Torah*, was a single and unitary composition, although it may well have been divisible into parts in much the same way as the *Qur'an*. The latter, which can be termed the received *Torah*, and in the contemporary *Bible* is a composite, cut-and-paste compilation, which originated in something approaching its current form late in the fifth or early in the fourth century BCE, fully 10 centuries after the lifetime of Moses. Moreover, the compilation of the received *Torah* took place over a time period of at least five centuries, if not more.[21]

The received *Torah* consists of five Biblical books, which together are known as the *Pentateuch*, and which individually are known as *Genesis, Exodus, Leviticus, Numbers,* and *Deuteronomy.* Not only are these five books not a single, unitary composition, but they themselves are frequently cut-and-paste compilations from earlier written records or literary strands, known to the world of Biblical scholarship as *J, E, P,* and *D.* In addition, some unidentifiable and undated source material (identified with a question mark "?" in this chapter) has been occasionally used in constructing the received *Torah.* The nature of this cut-and-paste compilation of the received *Torah* is succinctly summarized in Table 2 below.

Table 2: Compilation of the Received *Torah* [22]

BOOK	SOURCES USED
Genesis	J, E, P, ?, plus editorial glosses
Exodus	J, E, P, D, ?, plus editorial glosses
Leviticus	P, plus editorial glosses
Numbers	J, E, P, plus editorial glosses
Deuteronomy	P, D, ?, plus editorial glosses

The Literary Strands

The nature of the cut-and-paste compilation of the received Torah does not end with the information presented in Table 2 above. Each of the literary strands, i.e., *J, E, P,* and *D*, is in itself a cut-and-paste compilation from earlier sources, whether written or oral, that can no longer be clearly demarcated and identified. Further, at least with *P* and *D*, these literary strands evolved over a considerable stretch of time before arriving at their final form, and thus indicate a compilation process of layering.[23]

It is usually relatively easy to identify and contrast these four literary strands on the basis of their distinct literary characteristics. *J* consistently refers to: Allah as Yahweh; Isaac's second son as Israel, peace be upon them; the mountain of Moses as Mount Sinai; northern Mesopotamia as Aram-naharaim; the inhabitants of Palestine as Canaanites; and the first person with the Hebrew pronoun "Anokhi". In contrast, *E* typically refers to: Allah as Elohim; Isaac's second son as Jacob; the mountain of Moses as Mount Horeb; and the inhabitants of Palestine as Amorites. Meanwhile, *P* refers to: Allah as Elohim; northern Mesopotamia as Paddan-aram; the mountain of Moses as Mount Sinai; and the first person with the Hebrew pronoun "Ani". Finally, *D*, which shows certain affinities with E, typically refers to: Allah as Elohim; and to the inhabitants of Palestine as Amorites.[24]

The four literary strands comprising the received *Torah* originated and were combined across a time period of over five centuries. Further, the four literary strands have different geographical points of origin, with *J* being a Judean document, while *E* and *D* appear to have initially originated within the northern Kingdom of Israel. This process of origination and combination is summarized in Table 3 below, and illustrates that the received *Torah* did not come into anything even resembling its current form until approximately 1,000 years after the life of Moses.

Table 3: Chronology of the Strands of the Received *Torah* [25]

TIME	EVENT
Circa 950 BCE	Composition of *J*
Circa 750 BCE	Composition of *E*

Late 8th century BCE   *J* and *E* combined
7th century BCE   Final composition of *D*
6th through 5th centuries BCE Composition of *P*
Circa 400 BCE   Composition of the received
                               Torah

The cut-and-paste nature of the combining of the various literary strands underlying the received *Torah* has resulted in some interesting inconsistencies. One such example concerns the discrepancies between the creation story in *Genesis* 1:1-2:4a (*P* strand material), and the creation story in *Genesis* 2:4b-25 (*J* strand material). A second example is the subtle inconsistency between the *Exodus* 20:1-17 version of the Ten Commandments and the *Deuteronomy* 5:6-22 version of the Ten Commandments (*D* strand material). The two accounts give radically different justifications for the keeping of the Sabbath as a day of rest. In the *Exodus* account, this is tied to the story of the creation. In the *Deuteronomy* account, this is tied to the story of the enslavement of the Israelites in Egypt.

A third and more obvious example concerns the inconsistencies in the story of Sarah being taken from Abraham, peace be upon him, by a wicked monarch (*J* strand account of *Genesis* 12:10-20 versus the *E* strand account of *Genesis* 20:1-17). In both stories, Abraham is portrayed as having pretended that Sarah was his sister, instead of his wife. While the compiler of *Genesis* has attempted to resolve these discrepancies by positioning the two accounts as though they were two separate events. These are merely two different and inconsistent accounts of the same story.[26] The *J* strand account has the pharaoh of Egypt abducting Sarah, while the *E* strand account has King Abimelech (Abimelech literally means "my father, the king") of Gerar abducting Sarah. To further complicate matters, the *J* strand narrative of *Genesis* 26:6-11 indicates that a situation did occur with Isaac and his wife, Rebekah, which involved King Abimelech of Gerar, and in which Isaac reportedly pretended that Rebekah was his sister. Thus it can be seen that the *E* strand narrative is a fusing of two separate stories from *J*, one involving Abraham, Sarah, and the pharaoh, and one involving Isaac, Rebekah, and King Abimelech. Incredibly, the compiler of the cut-and-paste creation of the book of *Genesis* has retained all three stories as though they were three separate events.

However, an even more dramatic example of the cut-and-paste nature of *Genesis* can be presented, i.e., the story of the selling of Joseph[27], peace be upon him, into slavery in Egypt, after he had been thrown into a pit by his brothers. The compiler of *Genesis* used his cut-and-paste technique in an attempt to integrate two very different versions of Joseph being sold into captivity. The *J* strand narrative maintains that, for 20 pieces of silver, the brothers of Joseph sold him to a caravan of Ishmaelites, i.e., descendants of Abraham's son Ishmael[28], peace be upon him, who then re-sold Joseph into captivity in Egypt. In contrast, the *E* strand narrative states that a band of wandering Midianites, i.e., descendants of Abraham's son Midian[29], found Joseph in the pit, removed him from the pit, and then sold him into slavery in Egypt. The cut-and-paste merging of the two strands makes for some obvious inconsistencies, which are demonstrated in the following quotation from *Genesis*, in which the *J* strand narrative is presented in boldface type, and in which the *E* strand narrative is presented in italics. The following quotation also highlights just how much of a cut-and-paste job was done at times in compiling the book of *Genesis*.

Then they sat down to eat, **and looking up they saw a caravan of Ishmaelites coming from Gilead, with their camels carrying gum, balm, and resin, on their way to carry it down to Egypt. Then Judah said to his brothers, "What profit is it if we kill our brother and conceal his blood. Come, let us sell him to the Ishmaelites, and not lay our hands on him, for he is our brother, our own flesh." And his brothers agreed.** *When some Midianite traders passed by, they drew Joseph up, lifting him out of the pit,* **and sold him to the Ishmaelites for twenty pieces of silver.** *And took Joseph to Egypt. When Reuben returned to the pit and saw that Joseph was not in the pit, he tore his clothes. He returned to his brothers, and said, "The boy is gone; and I, where can I turn...Meanwhile the Midianites had sold him in Egypt to Potiphar, one of Pharaoh's officials, the captain of the guard...* **Now Joseph was taken down to Egypt, and Potiphar, an officer of Pharaoh, the captain of the guard, an Egyptian, bought him from the Ishmaelites who had brought him down there.**[30]

Recensions of the Received Torah

By circa 400 BCE, the evolutionary process that eventually resulted in the received *Torah* was well on its way. *J, E, P, D,* and additional source material had been combined into a recognizable unit of scripture. However, various versions of this unit of scripture continued to evolve over the following centuries. By the time of Jesus in the first century CE, there were at least four versions of the *Torah* in circulation, including, the proto-Masoretic, the Samaritan, the Alexandrian, and the Palestinian.

The proto-Masoretic text probably dates to around 400 BCE, and appears to have had a Babylonian origin, or was at least heavily associated with those Jews whose ancestors were involved in the Babylonian exile of the sixth century BCE. This text, which no longer exists, evolved into the Masoretic text under the influence of the Pharisaic sect of Judaism beginning sometime after the fall of Jerusalem in 70 CE. It was not completed until the development of the Tiberian system of vowel markings between 780 and 930 CE. The oldest existing manuscript of the Masoretic text is the one by Moses bar Asher in Tiberias, Palestine, circa 895 CE, which is approximately 24 centuries after the life of Moses. It is the Masoretic text that is used by contemporary Jews as their version of the *Torah*.[31]

The Samaritan text can be dated no earlier than the fourth century BCE, to the time of the schism between the Samaritans and the Jews. However, many Biblical scholars suggest that the second century BCE is a more likely point of origin. The variations between the Masoretic and Samaritan texts are dramatically illustrated by the fact that they differ from each other in some 6,000 places, with the Samaritan text agreeing with the Alexandrian text (see below) in about one third of those places. Most of the ancient manuscripts of the Samaritan text that still exist can be dated no earlier than the 13th century CE, which is approximately 28 centuries after the life of Moses.[32]

The Alexandrian text was the Hebrew text that was translated into Greek, in order to create the Greek *Septuagint* beginning in the third century BCE. The original Alexandrian text no longer exists, nor does the initial Greek translation. Later versions of the *Septuagint* were preserved by the early Christian churches, and demonstrate that numerous revisions were being made in the text during the first 1,000 years of its existence. All of these copies of the *Septuagint* differ in some important details from the Masoretic, Samaritan, and Palestinian texts, and all these copies of the *Septuagint* differ among themselves.[33]

The Palestinian text no longer exists in its entirety, and was not even known to have existed until the discovery of the Dead Sea Scrolls at Khirbet Qumran, beginning in the 1940s. The archaeological finds at Qumran have revealed a number of fragments of the Palestinian text, which differs in places from the Masoretic, Samaritan, and Alexandrian texts. The Palestinian text occasionally agrees with the Samaritan, and occasionally agrees with the Alexandrian.[34]

In providing the received *Torah* in a contemporary English *Bible,* e.g. the New Revised Standard Version, Biblical scholars have recourse to all four texts. The English translation that is read by the modern laity represents the Biblical scholars' attempt to reconstruct the "original" received *Torah,* i.e. the received *Torah* of approximately 400 BCE. This hypothetical reconstruction is based on a process that makes use of all four texts, occasionally following this text and occasionally following that text, with selection of text based upon historical, linguistic, and "best guess" considerations.

Summary

The received *Torah* is not a single, unitary document. It is a cut-and-paste compilation (primarily *J* and *E*) with additional layering (primarily *D* and *P*). While Moses, the person who received the original revelation, which the *Torah* is supposed to represent, lived no later than the 13th century BCE, and probably lived in the 15th century BCE, the received *Torah* dates to a much later epoch. The oldest identifiable substrata of the received *Torah,* i.e., *J,* can be dated no earlier than the 10th century BCE. Other substrata of the received *Torah* can be dated to the eighth century BCE, i.e., *E,* the seventh century BCE, i.e., *D,* and the sixth through fifth century BCE, i.e., *P.* Further, these different substrata were not combined into a received *Torah* until approximately 400 BCE, which would be approximately 1,000 years after the life of Moses. Still further, the received *Torah* was never totally standardized, with at least four different texts existing in the first century CE, which was approximately 1,500 years after the life of Moses. Additionally, if one adopts the Masoretic text as the most "official" text of the received *Torah,* then the oldest existing manuscript dates to circa 895 CE, which is about 2,300 years after the life of Moses. In short, although the received *Torah* may well contain some portions of the original *Torah,* the provenance of the received *Torah* is broken, largely unknown, and can in no way be traced to Moses.

The Book of Revelation given to David

David became king of the Israelite tribe of Judah circa 1013 to 1008 BCE, and was anointed king of Israel, i.e., of all 12 tribes, circa 1006 to 1001 BCE. He continued his rule as the second king of Israel until his death in circa 973-969 BCE.[35] Biblical tradition and the *Babylonian Talmud* attribute the Biblical book of *Psalms* to David.[36] As the *Qur'an* refers to a book of revelation, i.e., *Zabur*, given to David[37], the equation is often made that *Psalms* is *Zabur*. However, this equation appears to be erroneous, even though *Psalms* may well include some portions of *Zabur*.

David and Iron Chain Mail

As a slight digression before looking into the structural integrity of the *Psalms*, it is noted that the *Qur'an* specifically refers to Prophet David as being the originator of iron chain mail, i.e., a type of defensive body armor.[38] The traditional chronology of Middle Eastern archaeology is in conflict with that claim, as the traditional chronology places the reign of David on the borderline between Iron Age IB and Iron Age IIA, suggesting that the use of iron was well established by the time of David. However, the traditional chronology of Middle Eastern archaeology is under significant intellectual assault by a new generation of scholars, and it is now hypothesized that the reign of David corresponds with the borderline between Late Bronze Age IIA and Late Bronze Age IIB.[39] This recent scholarly revision in the chronology of Middle Eastern archaeology is consistent with the Prophet David having been the originator of iron chain mail and body armor, thus providing circumstantial, archaeological support for the *Qur'anic* statements in that respect.

Structure of the *Psalms*

As presently constituted in the contemporary English *Bible*, *Psalms* consist of five "books". The first "book" corresponds to the first 41 chapters or individual hymns. The second "book" includes chapters 42 through 72. The third "book" includes chapters 73 through 89. The fourth "book" includes chapters 90 through 106. Finally, the fifth "book" includes chapters 107 through 150. Each of the 150 chapters is further divided into individual verses. Scattered across these five books, one finds hymns of praise[40], hymns of Zion[41], enthronement hymns[42], individual laments[43], community laments[44], hymns of confidence[45], hymns of thanksgiving[46], royal hymns[47], hymns of wisdom[48], liturgies[49], pilgrim hymns[50], etc.

The basic division into five "books", coupled with a later editor's attribution of authorship for individual hymns[51], provides significant clues for deciphering the original compilation process of the book of *Psalms*. Given these clues, one can identify four different hymnbooks, i.e. collections of individual hymns[52], which were combined in an initial stage of compiling the *Psalms*. These four hymnbooks included: 1) a hymnbook attributed to Davidic authorship[53], which refers to Allah as Yahweh, thus following the tradition of the *J* source of the received *Torah*; 2) a hymnbook attributed to the descendants of Korah[54]; 3) a second hymnbook attributed to Davidic authorship[55], which refers to Allah as Elohim, thus following the *E* source of the received *Torah*, and thus indicating a different author from the author of the first hymnbook attributed to Davidic authorship; and 4) a hymnbook attributed to Asaph.[56] That these four different hymnbooks existed can be seen from the fact that the first and second hymnbooks attributed to Davidic authorship overlap, with *Psalms* 14 being repeated as *Psalms* 53, and with *Psalms* 40:13-17 being repeated as *Psalms* 70. Given the above, one can now see that the first "book" of *Psalms* basically conforms to the first hymnbook attributed to David, coupled with the addition of a later prologue, i.e., *Psalms* 1. The second "book" of *Psalms* basically conforms to the combination of the hymnbook of the descendants of Korah and the second hymnbook attributed to David. Finally, the majority of the third "book" of *Psalms* consists of the hymnbook of Asaph.[57]

This initial stage in the compilation of *Psalms* produced a book basically conforming to *Psalms* 2-83. Subsequently, in an undated, second stage of compilation, *Psalms* 84-89 were added as an appendix of presumably popular hymns, which had not yet been incorporated into the evolving book of *Psalms*. This second stage of compilation completed the third "book" of the *Psalms*. At yet a third stage of compilation, *Psalms* 90-149 were added, creating the fourth "book" and all but the final chapter of the fifth "book" of the *Psalms*. By grouping *Psalms* 90-149 into two "books", the unknown editor created an historical illusion to the five books of the received *Torah*, indicating that this stage of the compilation process was not completed until after the initial compilation of the received *Torah* circa 400 BCE. At still a fourth stage of compilation, an unknown editor added a prologue (*Psalms* 1) and a closing doxology (*Psalms* 150). In short, the compilation of this initial recension of the complete book of *Psalms* was not finished until between 400 and 200 BCE, i.e., around 570 to 770 years after the death of David.[58]

Summary

Quite clearly, *Psalms* is not a single, unitary document. While evidence of cut-and-paste cannot be demonstrated in the same unambiguous fashion as with the received *Torah,* the possibility cannot be dismissed that a cut-and-paste procedure was used. However, the structural analysis of *Psalms* reveals clear evidence of layering and of the combining of prior documents. Further, editorial redaction and glosses, e.g., *Psalms* 1 and 150, are clearly demarcated.

The structural analysis of the *Psalms* indicates that the book as a whole certainly cannot be attributed to Davidic authorship. Further, the two main sections of *Psalms* that are attributed to Davidic authorship are clearly written by different people, as indicated by the first hymnbook referring to Allah as Yahweh and the second hymnbook referring to Allah as Elohim. Thus, while isolated and individual hymns may actually have a Davidic authorship, the structural analysis of *Psalms* clearly refutes Davidic authorship for the book as a whole. Further, there is a 570 to 770 year time lag between the death of David and the initial compilation of the completed book. Still further, different versions of Psalms, e.g., Masoretic vs. Alexandrian text, existed in the centuries after the initial compilation of the complete book. If one takes the Masoretic text of circa 895 CE as the final "authoritative" version of *Psalms*, there is a time lag of around 1,865 years between the death of David and the "final" version of *Psalms*. Clearly, the provenance of the book of *Psalms*, is largely unknown, incomplete, and grossly broken.

The Book of Revelation given to Jesus

Most people probably think that the dating of the life of Jesus is a relatively simple and straightforward procedure. While it is certainly possible to date the mission and ministry of Jesus to the first half of the first century CE, precise dating is not always possible. For example, *Matthew* 2:1 states that Jesus was born during the reign of King Herod. As history chronicles that the only Herod who bore the title of king was Herod the Great, an Idumean (Edomite) vassal of Rome, and that he died sometime in April of 4 BCE[59], *Matthew* initially dates the birth of Jesus to 4 BCE at the latest.[60] However, *Luke* 2:1-7 indicates that Jesus was born during a census when Quirinius was serving as governor of Syria for Caesar Augustus of Rome. Publius Sulpicius Quirinius was governor of Syria only during 6-7 CE, and a Palestinian census did occur during that time.[61] Following this information the birth of Jesus should be placed in 6 CE, fully 10 to 12 years after the dates implied by *Matthew*.

Luke 3:1 offers additional information for historical dating, by claiming that John the Baptist (Yahya, peace be upon him) began his ministry in the 15th year of the reign of Tiberius, when Pontius Pilate was governor of Judaea. Pontius Pilate was governor (prefect) of Judaea from 26 through 36 CE, and Tiberius succeeded Caesar Augustus in 14 CE.[62] All this suggests that John began his ministry in 28 or 29 CE, and that shortly thereafter Jesus was baptized by John, and began his own ministry.

Whatever the probable dates of Jesus' life on earth, Muslims and Christians are in agreement that Jesus brought a revelation from Allah to mankind. While Muslims see this revelation as being verbal and on the order of revelations given to other prophets, Christians sometimes tend to see the revelation as being the actual existence and person of Jesus.[63] Nonetheless, both Muslims and Christians maintain that Jesus brought a gospel message or "good tidings".[64] Christians typically maintain that this revelatory good news was encapsulated within the four canonical gospels of the *New Testament*. In contrast, Muslims maintain that the original book of revelation, i.e., the *Injil*, has been altered and largely lost. This leads us to an analysis of the canonical gospels.

The Gospels in Context

It may come as a shock to most Christians to realize that the earliest Christian writings pay little attention to the sayings and actions of Jesus. For example, the epistles of Paul (Saul of Tarsus) provide only the barest of allusions to the historical Jesus. Quite simply, within that portion of the early Christian church that produced the earliest preserved Christian literature, i.e. that aspect of the early church usually identified as Pauline or gentile, the historical Jesus was basically incidental to what was believed to be a process of ongoing inspiration and revelation. What the historical Jesus said, did, or revealed was therefore largely superfluous. What was important was that any individual could claim divine authority for pronouncements and writings, by appealing to ongoing inspiration and revelation through the allegedly "risen" Jesus. In fact, Paul's entire claim to apostolic authority is based upon such a self-aggrandizing assertion.[65] As such, the gospels, which purport to relate the life, history, and sayings of Jesus, were a relatively late development in early Christian literature.[66]

It is usually maintained by Biblical scholars that, at the earliest, the gospels came into being as a literary art form during the last quarter of the first century CE.[67] Furthermore, it was not until circa 130 CE that one of the apostolic fathers, i.e., Papias, the bishop of Hierapolis, actually referred to a gospel by name.[68] Additionally, even after gospels began to appear on the scene as a literary form, they were only infrequently cited as authoritative by the early church fathers. In fact, throughout the first half of the second century CE, the alleged words of Jesus as recorded in the various gospels were seldom regarded as authoritative. It was only towards the end of the third quarter of the second century CE that the gospels began to assume the role of authoritative scripture in the early Christian churches.[69]

The gospels were accepted as authoritative scripture late in the chronicle of events, secondary to the slow development of interest in the words and actions of the historical Jesus by the Pauline branch of the early Christian church. However, gospel writing eventually began to take form as a mode of literary art, and this finally led to a veritable plethora of gospels. While only four such gospels were finally entered into the *New Testament* canon, over 40 so-called "apocryphal" gospels can be identified through references found in the writings of early church fathers or with the help of extant copies.[70] Interestingly, almost all the events relating to Jesus that are mentioned in the *Qur'an* (some of these have been noted in an earlier chapter) and that are not recorded in the four canonical gospels, can be readily identified in the so-called "aprocryphal" gospels.

The evolutionary process by which the *New Testament* canon came into existence across the span of over five centuries has already been referred to earlier on in the chapter. It would suffice to say here that the final *New Testament* canon eventually came to include only four gospels, i.e., *Mark, Matthew, Luke*, and *John*, at the expense of numerous other "apocryphal" gospels that were regarded as authoritative and scriptural by many of the early Christian churches. Of these four, the first three have certain commonalties, which have led to their designation as synoptic gospels, and which allow them to be analyzed as a unit. In contrast, *John* frequently represents a different tradition within the early Christian churches. However, it is necessary at this juncture in the chapter to shed light on the literary forms that arose in the early Christian milieu prior to the gospels and upon which the canonical gospels are also based.

The Gospels and the Literary Forms

The school of higher Biblical criticism known as Formgeschichte, i.e., form criticism, has successfully identified at least five types of oral literary forms behind the composition of the gospels. These literary forms, which are summarized in Table 4 (see below), were supposedly gathered into written collections, which continued to preserve this inherent literary form. Therefore, Table 4 can be presumed to summarize both the initial development of oral literary forms, and the later, gradual emergence of written collections of individual pericopes or literary units.

Table 4: Literary Forms underlying the *Gospels*[71]

A. Old Testament prophecy or passages allegedly referring to Jesus.
B. Narratives culminating in an alleged saying of Jesus.
C. Detailed narratives, primarily focused on the miracles of Jesus.
D. Special narrative traditions.
    1. The baptism of Jesus by John the Baptist.
    2. The temptation of Jesus by Satan.
    3. The alleged transfiguration of Jesus.
    4. Peter's confession as to Jesus' alleged identity.
    5. The alleged passion of Jesus, although it has been argued
       that this is a Markan creation and is synonymous with the
       construction of Mark.[72]
E. Alleged sayings and parables of Jesus.

By the foregoing analysis, it becomes apparent that any actual revelation that was given to Jesus would find primary expression only in literary form E. Literary form A was obviously a literary creation of certain segments of the early Christian churches, which was designed to justify the churches' evolving theology and separation from Judaism. However, literary forms B through D, and probably numerous of the pericopes found in literary form E, represent something different. Here, one is confronted with alleged actions and sayings of Jesus. One is decidedly not dealing with the verbal and verbatim revelation given by Allah to Jesus, but rather with what Jesus as a person allegedly said and did. In other words, to use the distinction previously presented when analyzing the *Qur'an* and the *Ahadith*, literary forms B through D, and most likely many of the pericopes found in literary form E, are alleged

Ahadith of Jesus, whether fabricated or actual.

The type of careful and meticulous distinction, made by Islam between the *Qur'an* and the *Ahadith*, was totally and consistently ignored in the early Christian formation of the literary forms pertaining to Jesus. To whatever extent actual revelation was preserved, it was hopelessly intertwined with the alleged *Ahadith* of Jesus. Furthermore, while Islamic tradition has carefully preserved the two component parts, i.e., *isnad* and narration, of every acceptable *Hadith* of Prophet Muhammad, the early Christian tradition totally failed to record any *isnad*, i.e., chain of transmission of the narration, and thus failed to provide any provenance for these alleged *Ahadith* of Jesus. This makes any attempt to separate authentic from fabricated *Ahadith* of Jesus totally dependent upon an analysis of the content of the narration. The provenance, i.e., the *isnad*, of the narration is totally absent in this case.

As portrayed in Table 4, these initial written collections were rather primitive literary attempts. In literary form D in Table 4, it is noted that many Biblical scholars posit a specific, written miracles or signs source behind the canonical gospels. Likewise, with regard to literary form E in Table 4, Biblical scholarship has successfully identified a written "sayings" source, which is known as *Q*.[73] (*Q* stands for the German word "*Quelle*", which may be translated as "source".) *Q* was originally defined as that material which is common to *Matthew* and *Luke*, while being absent from *Mark*.[74] However, the archaeological discovery of the gospel of *Thomas* at Nag Hammadi, Egypt, in 1945, suggested that this initial definition of *Q* needs revision. Without question, *Thomas* is a *Q* related document[75], which is interspersed with Gnostic interpolations and alterations. In fact, about one third of the sayings in *Thomas* have direct parallels in the traditionally defined *Q* material of *Matthew* and *Luke*.[76] *Q* may therefore be better defined as: that material which is common to *Matthew* and *Luke*, while being absent from *Mark*; material found in *Matthew* and *Thomas, Luke* and *Thomas*, or *Matthew, Luke*, and *Thomas*, whether or not found in *Mark*.

The *Q* and Miracles Source

Having finally identified two of the written sources, i.e., *Q* and the miracles or signs source, standing behind the canonical gospels, it is imperative to realize that these documents were not, even in themselves, unitary constructions. First of all, they were collections of individual pericopes or literary units. Second, modern Biblical scholarship has identified three different layers of Q. The earliest layer of Q, identified as $Q1$, appears to have been collected as a written document circa 50 CE. In contrast, $Q2$ appears to have been formulated circa 65 CE, and $Q3$ circa 75 CE.[77]

In view of this, it can be assumed that many of the sayings attributed to Jesus in Q cannot possibly be linked directly with Jesus. One can posit that many of the best loved sayings from the so-called Sermon on the Mount pre-existed Jesus' ministry. This hypothesis is proven by these sayings being found almost verbatim in the so-called pseudepigraphical and non-canonical Jewish literature of the third though second centuries BCE, i.e., they existed as written sayings 100 to 200 years before the birth of Jesus. In that respect, the *Testaments of the Twelve Patriarchs* are particularly rich in quotations attributed a few centuries later to Jesus.[78] Allowing for translations from one ancient language to another, the "almost verbatim" qualifier can largely be dismissed as being secondary to the process of translation. As such, in those instances in which Q places quotations from these earlier pseudepigraphical books into the mouth of Jesus, one must conclude that either: Q is wrong in attributing these quotations to Jesus; or that Jesus quoted rather extensively from these earlier writings.

Structural Analysis of the Canonical Gospels

A structural analysis of the earliest of the canonical gospels, i.e., *Mark,* demonstrates that *Mark* made extensive cut-and-paste use of the miracles or signs source, various pronouncement stories in circulation, and some probable use of Q.[79] The initial author of *Mark* arranged the individual pericopes from these sources into some, perhaps arbitrary, chronological order, and then linked them with his own editorial glosses. The resulting document may be termed proto-*Mark*. Later revision by unknown redactors, probably coupled with the addition of material not originally included in proto-*Mark*, resulted in the gospel of *Mark*, dating to some point around 75 CE.[80] For purposes of determining historical provenance, one can date the initial compilation of the book of *Mark* to this date of circa 75 CE.

Matthew is typically credited as being the second of the canonical gospels, and is usually dated to circa 85 CE.[81] A structural analysis of

Matthew indicates that it was composed in a cut-and-paste fashion from *Mark* (or possibly proto-*Mark*), *Q*, and oral or written sources unique to *Matthew*, which may be termed *M*.[82] Likewise, a structural analysis of *Luke* demonstrates that it was composed in a cut-and-paste procedure from *Mark* (or possibly proto-*Mark*), *Q*, and oral or written sources unique to *Luke*, which may be termed *L*.[83] The compilation of *Luke* is frequently dated to circa 95 CE.[84]

As noted previously, *John* does not share the same commonalties that are found in *Matthew*, *Mark*, and *Luke*. To a great extent, the prior sources utilized by the author of *John* are veiled in mystery.[85] Certainly, the author of *John* was dependent upon the same literary forms, whether oral or written, that are detailed in Table 4. Furthermore, as it is generally agreed that *John* was the last of the four canonical gospels to be written, probably around 110 CE[86], it is very likely that most of the time the author of *John* used literary forms that were compiled already into written collections, especially the miracles or signs source[87], and perhaps also used the synoptic gospels. Further, although it remains a debatable point, it's worth noting that Clement of Alexandria[88], writing circa 190 CE, specifically stated that the author of *John* was familiar with the synoptic gospels[89], implying that *John* may be based in part, on *Mark*.[90] Regardless, it is clear that *John* is a cut-and-paste compilation from earlier sources. Further, the internal testimony of *John* 21:24-25 clearly identifies an original "author" and a later "editor", which necessitates that *John* also be seen as a layered composition, with *John* 21 serving as a later appendix to the gospel[91] and *John* 1:1-18 serving as a later prologue to the gospel.[92]

However, the story of the gospels does not end with their initial compilations. They continued to undergo editorial revision and glosses, as demonstrated by the later addition of *Mark* 16:9-20, the alteration of *Luke* 3:21-22[93], the addition to the so-called Lord's Prayer in *Matthew* 6:13[94], the rather obvious editorial revisions of *John* 2:21-22 and 4:2[95], the later reversal of the original order of *John* 5 and 6[96], and other such occurences. In fact, the process of editorial revision continues to date, as witnessed by changes in the synoptic gospels across the King James Version, the Revised Standard Version, and the New Revised Standard Version.

There are numerous, ancient versions of the *New Testament,* none of which can be said to be original. Without getting into an overly technical discussion, it suffices to note that there were various Greek

(Koine) versions, Syriac versions, Coptic versions, and Latin versions. While the *New Testament* is believed to have been initially written in Koine Greek, it is not necessarily the case that Greek versions should always take precedence over the other available versions. In that regard, it is noted that one of the Syriac versions, e.g., the *Sinaitic Syriac*, traces back to the fourth century CE, and predates most Greek versions. As such, these non-Greek versions can bear important witness to later insertions and interpolations within the Greek versions. It must be noted that the *Sinaitic Syriac* does not include the alleged words of Jesus as recorded in *Matthew* 16:17-20[97], indicating that these verses were not included in the ancient manuscript from which the *Sinaitic Syriac* was copied, and suggesting that these verses were later additions.[98]

Summary

The structural analysis of the four canonical gospels clearly indicates that none of them is a single, unitary document. All four are cut-and-paste compilations from earlier sources, of which at least one, i.e., *Q*, was a layered composition in its own right. Further, all four canonical gospels have undergone their own process of layering and/or of later editorial revision.

The actual provenance of the four canonical gospels dramatically refutes any claim of being the revelation given by Allah to Jesus, though some actual revelation may be preserved in pieces in parts of these four gospels, their provenance basically remains unknown. However, the bulk of these gospels clearly consists of alleged *Ahadith*, i.e., sayings and actions, of Jesus as a person. Further, the gospels make no attempt to distinguish between *Ahadith* and revelation, and make no attempt to provide an *Isnad*, i.e., a chain of transmission, for the alleged *Ahadith* that are being recorded. Hence, in each individual case, the provenance for an alleged *Hadith* is basically nonexistent. As such, the task of separating authentic from fabricated *Ahadith* is highly complicated, and is totally reliant upon a content analysis of the narrative. Still further, in many cases, it can be shown that the sayings attributed to Jesus actually existed in written form in the pseudepigraphical literature of Judaism prior to the time of Jesus. Finally, it is noted that the canonical gospels did not even exist in their initial composite forms until around 40 to 70 years after the ministry of Jesus. Thereafter, they kept appearing in variant versions, leaving the provenance of the books themselves, not to mention the revelation of Jesus, in a very fragmented and disjointed state.

Conclusion

An analysis of literary structure and provenance has allowed numerous and significant contrasts to be drawn among the *Qur'an,* the received *Torah,* the *Psalms,* and the canonical gospels of the *New Testament.* Of these four sources of scripture, only the *Qur'an* is a single, unitary document, and only the *Qur'an* has a known and proven provenance. The significant contrasts regarding structure and provenance of these four sources of scripture are summarized in Table 5 below.

Table 5: The Books of Scripture

STRUCTURE

	Qur'an	*Torah*	*Psalms*	*Gospels*
Single, unitary	Yes	No	No	No
Cut-and-paste	No	Yes	?	Yes
Layered	No	Yes	Yes	Yes
Editorial redaction	No	Yes	Yes	Yes

PROVENANCE

	Qur'an	*Torah*	*Psalms*	*Gospels*
Attribution to "author" [99]	Yes	No	No	No
Time lag #1 [100]	1 yr.	1,000 yrs.	570-770 yrs.	40-70 yrs.
Variant versions	No	Yes	Yes	Yes
Time lag #2 [101]	1 yr.	2,300 yrs.[102]	1,865 yrs.[103]	Uncertain[104]
Provenance of revelation	Yes	No	No	No
Provenance of book	Yes	No	No	No

Chapter 4

The Baptism of Jesus
– The origin of the "sonship" of Jesus

Say: He is Allah, the One and Only; Allah, the Eternal, Absolute; He begetteth not, nor is He begotten; and there is none like unto Him.[1]

They say: (Allah) Most Gracious has begotten a son! Indeed ye have put forth a thing most monstrous! As if the skies are ready to burst, the earth to split asunder, and the mountains to fall down in utter ruin. That they should invoke a son for (Allah) Most Gracious. For it is not consonant with the majesty of (Allah). Most Gracious that He should beget a son. Not one of the beings in the heavens and the earth but must come to (Allah) Most Gracious as a servant.[2]

The earliest of the four canonical gospels, i.e.,*Mark*, which was compiled about 65-80 CE[3], begins with a brief introduction of John the Baptist (Yahya, peace be upon him[4]), and then immediately goes on to report the baptism of Jesus, peace be upon him, by John. It is enlightening to note that *Mark* sees no reason to report anything about the life of Jesus prior to his baptism. Apparently, what came before the baptism is of no concern to the author of *Mark*. Rather, according to *Mark*, the gospel, i.e., good news, begins only with the baptism of Jesus.

A Temporal Trajectory

The gospel of *Matthew*, which was compiled about 80-90 CE[5], begins with the nativity and infancy of Jesus, recounting the virgin birth of Jesus, and then directly introduces the reader to the baptism of Jesus. The gospel of *Luke*, which was compiled about 80-110 CE[6], starts with a nativity narrative of John the Baptist, which is immediately followed by a nativity narrative of Jesus, recounting the virgin birth of Jesus. After the infancy stories of Jesus, *Luke* adds one event regarding Jesus at age 12[7], and then moves directly to the baptism of Jesus. The gospel of *John*[8], which was compiled about 85-115 CE[9], begins with a prologue heavily influenced by Greek philosophy and later church theology, recounting the meeting of John the Baptist and Jesus.

This may be due to some disparity in thoughts about the revered status of the two prophets, viz., Jesus and John the Baptist, amongst the early churches, the baptism of Jesus by John the Baptist, is never directly mentioned in the gospel of *John*, although the baptism is readily inferred by the reader. A second reason for John's relative silence in directly stating that Jesus was baptized by John the Baptist may relate to the nascent conflict between the early Mandaean community, which claimed its origin from John the Baptist, and the early Christian churches.

In short, all four canonical gospels make the baptism of Jesus a central and crucial starting point for understanding the life and public ministry of Jesus. However, this central role for the baptism begins to get somewhat obscured with the passage of time, and as individual gospel compilation becomes further and further removed in time from the actual life of Jesus. This can be illustrated via a chronological, timeline analysis of the four canonical gospels.

Assuming the compilation of *Mark* around 75 CE, of *Matthew* around 85 CE, of *Luke* around 95 CE, and of *John* around 110 CE, assumptions which are well within the limits set by contemporary Biblical scholars[10], one sees a progressive shift away from the baptism of Jesus as the crucial starting point of Jesus' religious life and ministry. This shifting over time represents a trajectory within one segment of the early Christian churches in their attempt to "theologize" the life and ministry of Jesus, simply to make his life and ministry fit with their evolving theology and dogma. This temporal trajectory is illustrated in Table 1 below

Gospel	Date	Starting Point
Mark	75 CE	Baptism by John the Baptist[11]
Matthew	85 CE	Virgin birth and infancy of Jesus[12]
Luke	95 CE	Virgin birth and infancy of Jesus[13] and then teaching in the Temple at age 12[14]
John	110 CE	Pre-existence of Jesus from time immemorial[15]

Table 1: Temporal Trajectory in theologizing
the start of the "Ministry" of Jesus

It is really quite amazing! In the course of just 35 years, one moves from: all one needs to know about the life of Jesus can be told by beginning at the baptism; through a need to emphasize the virgin birth and an infancy story or two; through a need to add an account of Jesus at age 12; to Jesus existed since the beginning of time. The Christology and theology within one branch of the early Christian churches were developing at a rapid pace, and the canonical gospels dramatically reflect that evolutionary trajectory through time.

However, in presenting this evolution of the gospel message as a trajectory through time, which reflects the developing Christology and theology within one segment of the early Christian churches, the author wishes to make clear that he is in no way suggesting that the virgin birth of Jesus is a later fabrication of the early Christian churches. Rather, the point is that within the short span of just 10 years, from around 75 to 85 CE, this evolutionary trajectory began to emphasize the virgin birth, as demarcating the start of the public ministry of Jesus as the "begotten" son of God (hereinafter, usually the term "Allah" is used[16]).[17] This trajectory then continues over the course of the next 25 years, from 85 CE to 110 CE, and ends up claiming that Jesus pre-existed his own birth, had lived since the very beginning of time, was neither created nor begotten, and was one with Allah.[18]

The Baptism: The Setting

Luke places the baptism of Jesus in the 15th year of the reign of the Roman Emperor Tiberius, and during the time when Pontius Pilate was governor (prefect) of Judaea.[19] In that regard, it is noted that Pontius Pilate was prefect of Judaea from 26 through 36 CE, and that Tiberius succeeded Caesar Augustus in 14 CE[20]. Therefore, if one accepts the Lukan chronology, Jesus was baptized by John the Baptist in 29 CE. The location of the baptism is, however, subject to some debate. Nonetheless, the four canonical gospels are unanimous in declaring that John conducted his preaching and baptisms in the vicinity of the Jordan River[21], apparently ranging as far north as the Sea of Galilee (Lake Tiberias) and as far south as the Dead Sea[22]. Further, *John* suggests that Jesus met John "in Bethany across the Jordan"[23], suggesting that the baptism took place just north of the Dead Sea, and either on the Jordan side of the river or at the spring of John the Baptist, which drained into the Jordan River down a valley about one mile long.

The Baptism

As previously noted, the baptism of Jesus is explicitly reported in each of the synoptic gospels, i.e. *Matthew, Mark,* and *Luke.* Of these three reports of the baptism, this chapter will follow that of *Luke,* because some ancient texts of *Luke* preserve what is apparently the oldest version of the baptismal story. Leaving aside the issue of later amendments to the story, by early Christian churches to insure that Jesus was portrayed in a superior position than John, the heart of the matter is that Jesus was baptized by John, and then reportedly experienced a revelation from Allah.

> When all the people were baptized, and so too, Jesus, the Holy Spirit descended upon Jesus in bodily form like a dove. And a voice came from heaven, "You are my Son, the Beloved; with you I am well pleased." [24]

The "Sonship" of Jesus

The above passage from *Luke* clearly indicates why the baptism of Jesus assumed a central place in the canonical gospels. It was with the baptism that Jesus' "sonship", to utilize a neologism, was acknowledged (refer Table 1). The trajectory that is being mapped here is only to understand the evolution of the concept of the "sonship" of Jesus. In the earliest gospel, i.e., *Mark,* the "sonship" was first acknowledged at the time of baptism, the very nature of the "sonship" was intricately intertwined with the baptism, and the "sonship" was somehow dependent upon it. In short, Jesus was the "created son" of Allah, being, as it were, "adopted" by Allah during the time of baptism. However, by the time of *Matthew* and *Luke,* the "sonship" had been pushed back in time to the birth of Jesus, and got associated with the virgin birth. This gave rise to the "false" notion of the "begotten son". The "sonship" as can be seen from the narration had become dependent on the miraculous conception and birth of Jesus. The emergence of this concept was not from Judaism nor for that matter, from the nascent Judeo-Christian church[25], but was a result of polytheism, e.g., the birth stories of Hercules.

Still later, by the time of *John,* the "begotten sonship" had evolved into the concept of the pre-existence of Jesus, and the oneness of Jesus with Allah. This concept was, however, blasphemous according to the dictates of Judaism, Islam, and many branches of early Christianity, particularly the early church at Jerusalem, whose members had personally known Jesus. Judging by the chronological dates of the compilation of the four gospels, it can be seen that that this evolution in Christology occurred very rapidly, within the confines of at least one segment of the early Christian churches, and within a course of only 35 years. This trajectory, being as it was the formulation of one of the branches of the early churches, was outrightly rejected by other segments of the early Christian churches for centuries, and these other branches of early Christianity continued to define the "sonship" of Jesus only secondary to the baptism of Jesus. These churches which rejected the thesis of "sonship" were labelled by the evolutionary Christians as "adoptionists", "subordinationists", "Arians", etc.

If that were the sum total of the story, it would be most enlightening. However, the story does not end with this, and there is more to it. The continuation of the "sonship" story is found in certain ancient Greek manuscripts and quotations of *Luke*, long known to *Bible* scholars, but only accessible to the Christian laity during the last half century. Nestled into an obscure footnote, the 1946 Revised Standard Version and the 1989 New Revised Standard Version of the *New Testament* reveal only what has already been known for quite some time by the scholars and researchers on the topic in question. Utilizing the information given in those footnotes, it can be seen that the *Lukan* account actually reads as follows (with italics added by the present author for emphasis).

Now when all the people were baptized, and when Jesus also had been baptized and was praying, the heaven was opened, and the Holy Sprit descended upon him in the form like a dove. And a voice came from heaven, "You are my son; *today I have begotten you.*"[26]

"(T)oday I have begotten you." The original Lukan narrative clearly documented that the "sonship" of Jesus began only with the baptism. Despite the use of the word "begotten" in the text, this was clearly a "created sonship", which began only secondary to Allah granting a special relationship with Him to Jesus, at the time of the baptism. Clearly, those among the early churches who supported the concept of a "begotten sonship" could not afford to have this text of *Luke* remain within the domain of canonical scripture. As a result, the process of altering the *Lukan* text began. The fact that this altering process was not systematically completed with other *New Testament* books is clear from the original word-for-word quotation from *Luke* 3:22b remaining unaltered in *Hebrews* 1:5b.

It may be noted that the earlier wording of Allah's reported message to Jesus did not just exist in *Luke*. It is also to be found in the *Gospel of the Ebionites* (an apocryphal *gospel* harmony) dating back to the middle of the second century CE, based upon references to it in the writings of Irenaeus.[27] (Irenaeus was the late second century CE bishop of Lyon who authored the five-volumes of *Adversus Haereses* and was subsequently canonized as a saint by the Roman Catholic Church.[28]) Unfortunately, those segments of the early churches, which supported the concept of the "begotten sonship" of Jesus, were quite successful in destroying the *Gospel of the Ebionites*. Thus, only fragments of this gospel were preserved as quotations by Epiphanius[29], who was canonized by the Roman Catholic Church, and who lived from around 315 to 403 CE. Epiphamius was born in Palestine, studied and entered the priesthood in Egypt, and later went on to set up a monastery in Palestine, subsequently becoming the bishop of Constantia (Salamis), Cyprus.[30] Fortunately, Epiphanius quoted the relevant passage about the baptism of Jesus from the *Gospel of the Ebionites* in his *Panarion*.

> When the people were baptized, Jesus also came and was baptized by John. And as he came up from the water, the heavens were opened and he saw the Holy Spirit in the form of a dove that descended and entered into him. And a voice (sounded) from heaven that said: "Thou art my beloved Son, in thee I am well pleased". And again: "I have this day begotten thee".[31]

The origins of the "Created Sonship"

Within the confines of the greater Judeo-Christian tradition, the concept of the "created sonship" does not begin with the canonical gospels, nor even with the baptism of Jesus. Its origins can be traced back through the centuries to the ancient Israelites. While examining the canonical and non-canonical scripture of the Israelites, numerous examples of the concept of the "created sonship" get applied to various people, such as the Israelite people as a whole, and especially to the Israelite sub-tribe of Ephraim (Ephraim was one of the two sons of Joseph, peace be upon him, and thus represented one branch of the Joseph tribe).

> Then you shall say to Pharaoh, "Thus says the Lord: 'Israel is my firstborn son'. I said to you, 'Let my son go that he may worship me.'"[32]

When Israel was a child, I loved him, and out of Egypt I called my son. The more I called them, the more they went from me; they kept sacrificing to the Baals, and offering incense to idols. Yet it was I who taught Ephraim to walk, I took them up in my arms; but they did not know that I healed them...They shall go after the Lord, who roars like a lion; when he roars, his children shall come trembling from the west. They shall come trembling like birds from Egypt, and like doves from the land of Assyria; and I will return them to their homes, says the Lord.[33]

With weeping they shall come and with consolations I will lead them back, I will let them walk by brooks of water, in a straight path in which they shall not stumble; for I have become a father to Israel and Ephraim is my firstborn.[34]

Is Ephraim my dear son? Is he the child I delight in? As often as I speak against him, I still remember him. Therefore, I am deeply moved for him; I will surely have mercy on him, says the Lord.[35]

In addition, the concept of the "created sonship" was also applied to the Israelite kings, especially to those kings who were also prophets, e.g., David and Solomon, peace be upon them. The following Biblical quotations substantiate this point.

I will tell of the decree of the Lord: He said to me, "You are my son; today I have begotten you".[36]

He shall cry to me, "You are my Father, my God, and the Rock of my salvation!" I will make him the firstborn, the highest of the kings of the earth. [37]

He shall build a house for my name, and I will establish the throne of his kingdom forever. I will be a father to him, and he shall be a son to me. When he commits iniquity, I will punish him with a rod such as mortals use, with blows inflicted by human beings.[38]

The concept of the "created sonship" was also applied to the angels, as can be seen when we realize that the Hebrew words, translated as "heavenly beings" in *Job* 1:6, meant "sons of God" [39], and this substitution of words does appear in the following quotation:

One day the sons of God came to present themselves before the Lord, and Satan also came among them.[40]

Further, the concept of the "created sonship" was also applied to all of the faithful Israelites.

You are children of the Lord your God. You must not lacerate yourselves or shave your forelocks for the dead.[41]

Finally, the concept of the "created sonship" was also applied to the righteous, individual man.

Be as a father to orphans, and in place of a husband to widows; then God will call thee "son", and will be gracious to thee, and deliver thee from the pit.[42]

The above illustrations make it very clear that the "created sonship" was seen as an act of "adoption", whereby the "son" moved into a special relationship with Allah[43]. In no way did this imply physical begetting by Allah or a physical incarnation of Allah.[44]

Of the various *Old Testament* quotations noted above, one in particular deserves special attention. –The quotation from *Psalms* 2:7b, originally meant to apply to David, states, "You are my son; today I have begotten you". This wording is identical to the original wording in *Luke* 3:22b, thus establishing that Jesus was the "created son" or "adopted son" of Allah in the same way as David was. Their "sonships" were the result of Allah creating a special relationship between Him and them. They had been publicly confirmed by Allah in their prophetic offices, even if their status as prophet had pre-existed this public confirmation.[45] They had moved into a special relationship with Allah, a relationship that was to be interpreted as being that of "an adopted son."

From Servant to Son?

As has been seen, the statement recorded in *Luke* 3:22b is identical with that recorded in *Psalms* 2:7b. In fact, Biblical scholars[46] have long argued that the whole of *Luke* 3:22 is primarily based upon *Psalms* 2:7b, and to a lesser extent on *Isaiah* 42:1, quoted immediately below.

Here is my servant, whom I uphold, my chosen, in whom my soul delights; I have put my spirit upon him; he will bring forth justice to the nations.

However, while *Psalms* 2:7b emphasizes the "adopted" or "created sonship", *Isaiah* 42:1 emphasizes the concept of "servant" or "slave". Given this discrepancy, and given the results of highly technical linguistic analysis, several Biblical scholars have proposed that the original, pre-Greek, Palestinian, oral tradition of the baptism of Jesus was more heavily based on *Isaiah* 42:1 than on *Psalms* 2:7, and thus used the Aramaic word "*'Abhdi*", meaning "servant".[47] If the results of this linguistic and literary form analysis were accepted, the original, pre-Greek, Palestinian, oral tradition would have been something akin to the following quotation:.

> Now when all the people were baptized, and when Jesus also had been baptized, the heaven was opened, and Allah placed his spirit upon him. And a voice came from heaven, "You are my servant, whom I uphold, and whom I have chosen."

The above analysis posits a new starting point for the trajectory originally presented in Table 1, and Table 2 at the end of the chapter incorporating this new hypothesis for a clear understanding of the topic.

Summary and Conclusions

Solely on the basis of the existing texts of the canonical gospels of the *New Testament*, we are able to trace a temporal trajectory, thereby mapping the evolution of the concept of the "sonship" of Jesus. Utilizing these texts, we can trace within at least one segment of the early Christian churches, the evolution from the concept of the "adopted" or "created sonship" to that of a "begotten sonship", and arrive at the concept of a "pre-existent sonship". The accuracy of the mapping of this trajectory is confirmed by the original Greek version of *Luke* 3:22, as well as by *Psalms* 2:7, the *Gospel of the Ebionites*, and the *Old Testament* concept of the "adopted" or "created sonship."

However, linguistic and literary form analysis of the canonical gospel accounts of the baptism of Jesus suggests the original influence of *Isaiah* 42:1 in a pre-Greek, Palestinian, oral tradition, in which the concept of a later "adopted" or "created sonship" was initially preceded by the concept of the "servant" or "slave". (It is worth noting that in the process, we are able to arrive at the exact wording of one of the titles frequently given to Prophet Muhammad, peace be upon him, i.e., "slave of Allah". And this is exactly one of the titles, the *Qur'an* gives to Jesus.[48]) Given the theology of *Paul*[49], such a pre-Greek, Palestinian core to the stories of Jesus' baptism must be posited to precede the *Pauline* epistles of the *New Testament*, resulting in a hypothesized date for the concept of "servant" at around 45 CE at the latest.

However, we must realize that these linguistic and literary form analyses are merely hypotheses and they do not and cannot have the measure of certainty that is associated with actual text. Hence, in presenting Table 2 below, the author notes that while the "stage 1" entries are hypothetical, the remaining entries are clearly verified by the texts themselves.

Table 2: The Temporal Trajectory of the "Sonship" of Jesus

Stage	Date	Nature of Sonship	Defining Event
1	45 CE	Servant or slave, not son	Baptism of Jesus
2	75 CE	Adopted or created	Baptism of Jesus.
3	85 CE	Begotten sonship	Virgin birth of Jesus
4	110 CE	Pre-existent sonship	No longer applicable

All said and done, the above analysis demonstrates that: the original concept of the "sonship" of Jesus was in line with Islamic belief and thought; with the passing of time, the "sonship" concept started deviating and oscillating from the Islamic perspective, presumably under the influence of Roman and Greek polytheism; and this deviation began quite early within the development of the Christian churches, and proceeded at a rapid pace. In contrast to this evolutionary trajectory regarding the "sonship" of Jesus within the early Christian churches, the religion of Islam has consistently maintained that Allah has no begotten son. In this respect, the Islamic doctrine is far closer to that of the foundations of Christianity than is modern Christian doctrine. With this in mind, the following passages from the *Qur'an* are worth noting.

O People of the Book! Commit no excesses in your religion: nor say of Allah aught but the truth. Christ Jesus the son of Mary was (no more than) a Messenger of Allah, and His word, which He bestowed on Mary, and a spirit proceeding from Him: so believe in Allah and His messengers. Say not "trinity": desist: it will be better for you: for Allah is One God: glory be to Him: (Far exalted is He) above having a son. To Him belong all things in the heavens and on earth. And enough is Allah as a disposer of affairs.[50]

They say, "Allah hath begotten a son!"—glory be to Him! He is self-sufficient! His are all things in the heavens and on earth! No warrant have ye for this! Say ye about Allah what ye know not?[51]

Blessed is He Who sent down the criterion to His servant, that it may be an admonition to all creatures—He to Whom belongs the dominion of the heavens and the earth: no son has He begotten, nor has He a partner in His dominion: it is He Who created all things, and ordered them in due proportions.[52]

When (Jesus) the son of Mary is held up as an example, behold thy people raise a clamor thereat (in ridicule)! And they say, "Are our gods best, or he?" This they set forth to thee, only by way of disputation: yea, they are a contentious people. He was no more than a servant: We granted Our favor to him, and We made him an example to the children of Israel.[53]

Chapter 5

The Crucifixion
– A Question of Identity

That they said (in boast), "We killed Christ Jesus the son of Mary,
the messenger of Allah"—but they killed him not, nor crucified him,
but so it was made to appear to them, and those who differ therein
are full of doubts, with no (certain) knowledge, but only conjecture
to follow, for of a surety they killed him not—nay, Allah raised him
up unto Himself; and Allah is exalted in power, wise— [1]

There are very few issues, which separate Muslims from
Christians as sharply as that of an alleged crucifixion, which
reportedly occurred on the outskirts of Jerusalem in the first
half of the first century CE. That the crucifixion was little noted at the
time, cannot be doubted. Besides the books of the *New Testament* of the
Bible (authored during the second half of the first century and the first
half of the second century CE), as well as other early Christian literature,
the only near-contemporary mention of the crucifixion is found in just
two places. A mention of the event occurs briefly in the works of the
Jewish historian, Josephus bin Matthias, (during the second half of the
first century) who wrote:

> At this time there was a wise man called Jesus, and his conduct was
> good, and he was known to be virtuous... Pilate condemned him to
> be crucified and to die. But those who had become his disciples did
> not abandon his discipleship. They reported that he had appeared to
> them three days after his crucifixion and that he was alive.
> Accordingly, he was perhaps the Messiah, concerning whom the
> prophets have reported wonders.[2]

The other writer who reported the event in passing was the Roman
historian, Tacitus, who lived from around 55 to 115 CE. He stated:

Christus...had undergone the death penalty in the reign of Tiberius,
by sentence of the procurator Pontius Pilate...[3]

Certainly, there are other issues, that separate and divide Islamic from
Christian belief, most conspicuously the Christian doctrine of the trinity.
However, the doctrine of the trinity is so ephemeral and so complex that
the average Christian does not even begin to understand the doctrine.
If asked to define it, he would probably provide a definition of the
trinity, which the church has long since declared to be heresy. But, the
crucifixion is an issue that does matter to the average Christian, who sees
the crucifixion of Jesus, peace be upon him[4], as an historical event about
which there really can be no doubt. Indoctrinated throughout childhood
by years of listening to *Bible* stories of the crucifixion, and by instruction
in how the *Bible* is to be read and understood, the average Christian is
often rather incredulous that anyone can even doubt that Jesus Christ was
crucified. Most Christians believe that one can question the virgin birth,
one can question the post-crucifixion resurrection of Jesus, one can question the trinity, but how can one even start to question the historical event
of the crucifixion of Jesus?

In marked contrast, the *Qur'an* explicitly states that "they killed him
not, nor crucified him". However, the *Qur'an* does not say that there was
no crucifixion. Rather, the *Qur'an* states that it was not Jesus Christ who
was crucified, even though it was made to appear that he was. In short,
the chasm, which separates Islam and Christianity in regard to the crucifixion, is not whether or not there was a crucifixion at the time and place
the *New Testament* maintains, but only whether the person so crucified
was Jesus. Given this consideration, the present chapter ignores the
myriad of debates within Christianity as to the place[5] and actual date[6] of
crucifixion. Instead, it focuses on just one point, i.e., was it Jesus who
was crucified?

In raising this question, the author proposes to show that the Christian
literature and scripture, in and of itself, provide several reasons to accept
the Qur'anic statement that it was not Jesus, the prophet of Allah[7],
who was crucified. In so doing, it is readily acknowledged that one is
traveling down a path "with no (certain) knowledge", and with only the
signposts of "conjecture to follow". However, it is not the purpose of this
essay to show what really took place that long ago day in Jerusalem.
Rather, it is to demonstrate that the early Christians were quite confused
and uncertain about what actually happened during the crucifixion event.

The very fact that such confusion existed is sufficient evidence, to doubt the crucifixion of Jesus, and should cause Christians to ponder on the Qur'anic statement that Jesus Christ was not crucified; and the essential similarity between the *Qur'an* and various branches of the early Christian church.

The Evidence

Three basic classes of information are utilized in what follows. First, information regarding the crucifixion is presented from the so-called apostolic fathers of the early Christian churches. Second, information is taken from the so-called apocryphal books of the *New Testament* of the *Bible*. Third, information regarding the crucifixion is based on the so-called canonical gospels of the *New Testament*. Hence, it can be seen that all the evidentiary information is from early Christianity, and not from Islam. Thus, early Christian literature and scripture is used to cast doubt on official Christian doctrine.

The Apostolic Fathers

Before proceeding to examine apocryphal books, a brief word ought to be mentioned about the evidence to be found in the writings of the so-called apostolic fathers of the early Christian churches. The apostolic fathers frequently noted that there were "heretical" sects (i.e., Christian sects, which did not agree with the particular dogma being espoused by the apostolic father in question), which taught that the "passion" or suffering of Jesus on the cross was untrue and/or illusory. In that regard, such references are found in the writings of Ignatius, Polycarp, Justin, Irenaeus, Tertullian, and Hippolytus. Together, these apostolic fathers form a veritable *Who's Who* of the early Christian churches.[8]

A particular example may be of interest.

In his *Trallians*, Ignatius, the bishop of Antioch (who died around 110 CE, and who wrote during the first decade of the second century CE), was quite eloquent in his attack against the early Christians who denied that the crucifixion of Jesus was anything more than an illusion. The following quotation from Ignatius (italics added for emphasis by the present author) is directly to the point:

> But if, as some say...*his suffering was only an appearance*, then why am I a prisoner, and why do I long to fight with the wild beasts? In that case, I am dying in vain.[9]

One cannot attack as heresy a belief or doctrine that does not yet exist. The theology of Ignatius not withstanding, his attack against those early Christians who believed that Jesus' crucifixion was only illusory, demonstrates the existence of that belief among the early Christians. Further, the fact that Ignatius even bothered to attack this doctrine suggests that the belief in the illusory nature of the crucifixion was quite widespread by 110 CE. Clearly, the doctrine of or belief in the illusory nature of the crucifixion was perceived by Ignatius to be a threat to what would much later become the orthodox position of the Christian church regarding the crucifixion. As it would take some years for such a belief to become widespread across the vastness of the Roman Empire, it can be deduced that the origin of the doctrine of the illusory nature of the crucifixion must be dated well back into the first century CE, and quite possibly right back to the time of the crucifixion itself.

When considering the above, it must be remembered that Ignatius was attacking Christians, not non-Christians, although the particular Christians being attacked shared a specific belief system at odds with that of Ignatius when it came to the particulars of the doctrine of the crucifixion. To millions of Christians raised with a Sunday School interpretation of Christianity, the above may come as something of a shock. However, for those Christians, the shocks are only just the beginning. Indeed, the shocks dramatically increase in voltage when one considers the early Christian scriptures, both apocryphal and canonical.

Apocryphal Books

In what follows, information from the apocryphal books of early Christianity are examined to assess the Qur'anic statement that Jesus Christ was not crucified. This examination is necessarily incomplete, as the apocryphal literature is simply too vast and voluminous for someone to review it all. However, the following discussion and presentation do illustrate that at least some of the apocryphal books clearly state that Jesus was not crucified. In each presentation, the format utilized is to identify the apocryphal book being referenced, comment on the provenance of that book, and then present the relevant evidence from the same source. However, as most readers, whether Muslim or Christian, have very little understanding of the *New Testament* apocrypha, a brief digression is in order.

There is a prevalent myth among both Christians and Muslims that the early Christian church was monolithic. This myth is far from the historical truth. In fact, each church (e.g., at Alexandria, Antioch, Damascus, Jerusalem, Rome, Lyons, etc.) was fairly independent from every other church. Each and every church had its own bishop or leader, its own doctrinal and theological preferences, and its own set of recognized scripture. In that sense, there was no "orthodox" set of Christian beliefs in the first few centuries of Christianity. Likewise, several centuries would pass before there was a universally accepted canon of scripture within Christianity. Early on, each church determined its own dogma and recognized its own scripture, independently from what any other church had decided. However, beginning in the fourth century CE, this state of affairs began to change quite radically, with such change being ushered in by the Council of Nicaea in 325 CE.[10]

At Nicaea, orthodox doctrine and creeds began to be established, and steps were taken to begin an authorized canon of scripture, which later became known as the *New Testament*. The process of arriving at a set and universally accepted canon of scripture was filled with rancor and dispute, and consumed the early Christian churches for the next couple of centuries. At the end of this process, the canon of *New Testament* scriptures that finally emerged represented only a very small selection of the voluminous Christian writings that were regarded as scriptural by this or that early Christian church. As presently constituted, the *New Testament* consists of 27 books, of which four are classified as gospels. Those books, which were not included within the *New Testament* canon, but which were once part and parcel of early Christianity, were dubbed apocryphal. To give the reader an indication of just how much early Christian writing came to be regarded as apocryphal, the author has included in Table 1 below, a partial listing of apocryphal gospels, not all of which continue to exist.[11] The list, obviously does not include apocryphal epistles, acts, apocalypses, etc., but only apocryphal gospels. Table 1 would have been greatly enlarged if these other types of apocryphal writings were to be included.

Table 1: A list of *Apocryphal Gospels*[12]

The Dialogue of the Savior
The Gospel of Andrew
The Gospel of Apelles

The Gospel of Bardesanes
The Gospel of Barnabas
The Gospel of Bartholomew
The Gospel of Basilides
The Gospel of the Birth of Mary
The Gospel of Cerinthus
The Gospel of Eve
The Gospel of the Ebionites
The Gospel of the Egyptians
The Gospel of the Encratites
Gospel of the Four Heavenly Regions
The Gospel of the Hebrews
The Gospel of Hesychius
The Gospel of the Infancy of Jesus Christ
The Gospel of Judas Iscariot
The Gospel of Jude
The Gospel of Marcion
The Gospel of Mani
The Gospel of Mary
The Gospel of Matthias
The Gospel of Merinthus
The Gospel According to the Nazarenes
The Gospel of Nicodemus
The Gospel of Perfection
The Gospel of Peter
The Gospel of Philip
The Gospel of Pseudo-Matthew
The Gospel of Scythianus
The Gospel of the Seventy
The Gospel of Thaddaeus
The Gospel of Thomas
The Gospel of Titan
The Gospel of Truth
The Gospel of the Twelve Apostles
The Gospel of Valentinus
The Protevangelion of James
The Secret Gospel of Mark
Thomas's Gospel of the Infancy of Jesus Christ

As noted earlier, Table 1 (above) lists 41 books, and is still not a complete listing of even the apocryphal gospels, much less of other types of apocryphal books. In marked contrast, the *New Testament* canon includes only four gospels, i.e., *Matthew, Mark, Luke,* and *John.* The contrast is quite dramatic, and illustrates the wealth of early Christian scripture, which the early Christian church found convenient to ignore, ban, or destroy, once it began its campaign to construct a unified dogma, theology, and set of beliefs. In short, only four of over 45 gospels found their way into the *New Testament,* a meagre 9% of what was possible.

With this introductory background to the apocrypha of the early Christian churches, one can now move to consider the evidence from five different apocryphal sources: *Gospel of Barnabas; Two Books of Jeu; Apocalypse of Peter; The Second Treatise of the Great Seth*; and the *Acts of John.*

Gospel of Barnabas

Provenance

Muslim authors have occasionally made extravagant and highly unsupported claims regarding the *Gospel of Barnabas.*[13] Wishing to spare embarrassment to these authors, whose intentions and motivations were presumably quite good, the present author refrains from referencing these claims. However, among the claims made for the *Gospel of Barnabas* are that it: was considered canonical by the Alexandrian church until 325 CE; was quoted extensively by Irenaeus, the second century CE bishop of Lyon; and served as the basis for Jerome's *Vulgate,* the Latin translation of the *Bible,* as authorized by the Roman Catholic Church. In fact, none of these claims is accurate.

The first claim appears to be based on a simple confusion, in which the claimant is merging the identities of two separate books, i.e., the *Gospel of Barnabas* and the *Epistle of Barnabas.* It was the latter book, which was considered canonical by the Alexandrian church, or at least which was read in their services, and it was the latter book, which was mentioned by a variety of early church fathers[14], including Clement of Alexandria[15], Origen[16], Eusebius[17], and Jerome[18]. In fact, the *Epistle of Barnabas* is even found in the *Sinaitic Syriac,* a fourth century version of the *Bible.*

As to the second claim, there is no mention of the *Gospel of Barnabas* in any existing writings of Irenaeus. How did this erroneous claim come to be so frequently made? There are two possible answers. First, Irenaeus did refer to the *Epistle of Barnabas*. The second possible answer is more complicated and complex, and begins by noting that the claim, is that Irenaeus quoted extensively from the *Gospel of Barnabas*. A simple procedure of checking quotes should have shown the fallacy of this claim, if the relevant portions of the writings of Irenaeus existed. The problem is, however, that this claim is reportedly based on the statements of a 16th century Father Marino, the person who allegedly stole the manuscript of the *Gospel of Barnabas* from the library of Pope Sixtus V.

In an attempt to reconstruct the genesis of the claim, it is hypothesized that Father Marino alleged that he had access to "hidden" or "suppressed" writings of Irenaeus, wherein Irenaeus quoted from the *Gospel of Barnabas*. Thus, the whole claim can be seen to be based on the word of a reportedly self-confessed thief who claimed that he had access to a secret manuscript of Irenaeus. This manuscript, which no one else can attest to,in turn attests to the provenance of the *Gospel of Barnabas,* for which the only source is Father Marino. Clearly, this claim for the provenance of the *Gospel of Barnabas* is little short of being laughable.

As to the third claim, this author is absolutely perplexed as to how anyone with any familiarity with the Latin *Vulgate* could possibly associate it with the *Gospel of Barnabas*. The only association perhaps, is that Jerome was responsible for the *Vulgate*, and he referenced the *Epistle of Barnabas* in some of his writings. After all, the *Vulgate* was one of the sources for the King James translation of the *Bible*, and bears much more in common with the modern *Bible* than it does with the *Gospel of Barnabas.*

So, what is the provenance of the *Gospel of Barnabas*? The earliest reference to it that this author can identify, is in the *Decretum Gelasianum de Libris Recipiendis et non Recipiendis (Decree of Gelasius of Accepted and non-Accepted Books)*, where it is listed as an apocryphal and rejected book.[19] The Decree of Gelasius is a precursor of the Roman Catholic Church's *Index Librorum Prohibitorum* (Index of Prohibited Books), and is often attributed to Pope Gelasius I, who died in 496 CE, but the actual provenance of the Decree of Gelasius cannot be traced back beyond the sixth century CE. Be that as it may, the fact that the *Gospel of Barnabas* was banned in the Decree of Gelasius establishes that there was a *Gospel of Barnabas* by at least the sixth century.

However, it remains an open question as to whether or not the book that is presently identified as being the *Gospel of Barnabas* is the same *Gospel of Barnabas* identified in the *Decree of Gelasius*. The reported provenance of the book currently identified as the *Gospel of Barnabas* is as follows: 1) in 383 CE, Pope Damasus I secured a copy of the *Gospel of Barnabas,* and kept it in his private library; 2) apparently, it was then passed down within the private libraries of the various popes; 3) in the late 16th century, a Father Marino stole the manuscript from the personal library of Pope Sixtus V; 4) the manuscript then passed through the possession of a variety of unnamed persons; 5) around the start of the 18th century, the manuscript came into the possession of a J.E. Cramer, reportedly a counselor to the King of Prussia; 6) in 1713, Cramer reportedly gave the manuscript to Prince Eugene of Savoy; and 7) in 1738, the manuscript passed from the prince to the Hofbibliothek in Vienna, where it reportedly remains to date.[20]

What of the above information can be confirmed from independent sources? (1) Damasus I was pope from 366-384 CE.[21] (2) Sixtus V was pope from 1585-1590 CE.[22] (3) Prince Eugene of Savoy lived from 1663-1736 CE.[23] (4) The prince's library of over 10,000 books was given to the Hofbibliothek in Vienna.[24] However, even with such confirmation, intellectual honesty compels the admission that the *Gospel of Barnabas,* as currently received, cannot be traced in unbroken provenance prior to around the start of the 18th century. Quite simply, it may or may not be the same book referred to in the *Decree of Gelasius*. The reader is urged to keep this caution in mind when considering material from the *Gospel of Barnabas*.

Evidence

The basic tenet of the *Gospel of Barnabas* is that when Judas Iscariot led the soldiers into the Garden of Gethsemane to arrest Jesus and bring him to trial, the appearance of Judas was miraculously changed, and Jesus ascended into heaven. With Jesus safe in heaven, Judas took on the appearance of Jesus Christ. According to this source, Jesus was never arrested, was never tried, and was never crucified. Instead, it was Judas, the traitorous disciple, who was arrested, tried, whipped, mocked, and crucified. The relevant portions of the *Gospel of Barnabas* are quoted below.

When the soldiers with Judas drew near to the place where Jesus

was...God, seeing the danger of His servant, commanded Gabriel,
Michael, Rafael, and Uriel, His ministers, to take Jesus out of the
world. The holy angels came and took Jesus...and placed him in the
third heaven in the company of angels blessing God for ever-
more...Judas was so changed in speech and in face to be like
Jesus...the soldiery entered, and laid their hands upon Judas,
because he was in every way like to Jesus...The soldiers took Judas
and bound him, not without derision...Then the soldiers lost their
patience, and with blows and kicks they began to flout Judas, and
they led him with fury into Jerusalem...[25]

In Jerusalem, Judas was variously questioned by the Jewish high
priests and Sanhedrin, by Pontius Pilate, (who is identified as being a
secret follower of Jesus), and by Herod the tetrarch. Judas kept arguing
in vain that he was not Jesus, but Judas. Arriving back before Pilate for
the second time, Judas was whipped, clad in an old purple garment,
crowned with thorns, and mocked. Finally, Pilate condemned Judas to
death by crucifixion, assigning him to be crucified with two robbers.[26]

So they led him to Mount Calvary, where they used to hang male-
factors, and there they crucified him naked, for the greater ignominy.
Judas truly did nothing else but cry out: "God, why hast thou
forsaken me, seeing the malefactor hath escaped and I die unjustly?"
Verily I say that the voice, the face, and the person of Judas were so
like to Jesus, that his disciples and believers entirely believed that he
was Jesus; wherefore some departed from the doctrine of Jesus...for
Jesus had said that he should not die till near the end of the world;
for that at that time he should be taken away from the world. But
they that stood firm in the doctrine of Jesus were so encompassed
with sorrow, seeing him die who was entirely like to Jesus, that they
remembered not what Jesus had said...Those disciples who did
not fear God went by night (and) stole the body of Judas and hid it,
spreading a report that Jesus was risen again; whence great
confusion arose.[27]

Post crucifixion, the angels transported Jesus back to earth
from the third level of heaven, in order that Jesus might
make an appearance to his mother and her two sisters, to
Martha, Mary Magdalene, and Lazarus, and to John, James,
Peter, and Barnabas. A later appearance was then made to
the seven (of the 12?) "faithful disciples", Nicodemus and

Joseph (of Arimathea?). Finally, Jesus again ascended into heaven, with this ascension being witnessed by 47 of the greater 72 disciples.[28]

Conclusion

While the shakiness of the provenance of the *Gospel of Barnabas* must be noted, this book does clearly state that Judas Iscariot was the one crucified in place of Jesus Christ. As such, the *Gospel of Barnabas* supports the Qur'anic account of the crucifixion, while refuting the orthodox Christian position.

Two Books of Jeu

Provenance

The *Two Books of Jeu* are found in the Codex Brucianus, which has been dated to anywhere between the third and the tenth centuries CE. The *Two Books of Jeu* were mentioned in the *Pistis Sophia* (Faith-Wisdom), a third century CE Coptic and Gnostic text[29], and were probably composed in Egypt around the third century CE.[30]

Evidence

The statement from this apocryphal source is probably the weakest of any in supporting the Qur'anic account, in that the relevant statement from this manuscript is somewhat ambiguous. However, the reader may judge for him or herself, by reviewing the following quotation.

> Jesus, the living one, answered and said to his apostles: "Blessed is he who has crucified the world, and has not allowed the world to crucify him."[31]

Conclusion

According to the *Two Books of Jeu*, the blessed one is he who has not allowed the world to crucify him. The clear implication is either that Jesus Christ was not blessed, or that he was not crucified. As the former option is unthinkable to both Christians and Muslims, the latter option is the only one remaining.

Apocalypse of Peter

Provenance

The *Apocalypse of Peter* was one of the many exciting books of early Christianity, which were brought to light in 1945 by the immeasurably important archaeological discoveries at Naga Hammadi, Egypt. These discoveries unearthed a library of fourth century CE papyrus manuscripts, many of which were in the Coptic language. Given this provenance, the latest possible creation for the *Apocalypse of Peter* would be the fourth century CE. However, extensive literary analysis of the manuscript indicates that the Apocalypse of Peter was originally authored at some point probably in the third century CE.[32]

Evidence

In the following quotation from the Apocalypse of Peter, italics have been added by the present author, in order to highlight crucial words and phrases, which illustrate that this apocryphal work maintains that Jesus Christ was only crucified in appearance, not in reality. Jesus was only seemingly seized by the soldiers, while in reality he remained by the side of Peter, where he guided Peter to a true understanding of the crucifixion event. (However, later in the passage, it is stated that Jesus was initially seized, and then released, a point that will be explored more fully when examining the canonical gospels.) The crucified victim is a substitute or simulacrum of Jesus, a substitute who came into being in the likeness of Jesus, and who appears to be identified as a demon.

> When he had said those things, I saw him seemingly being seized by them. And I said, "What do I see, O Lord, that it is you yourself whom they take, and that you are grasping me? Or who is this one, glad and laughing on the tree? And is it another one whose feet and hands they are striking?" The Savior said to me, "He whom you saw on the tree, glad and laughing, this is the living Jesus. But this one into whose hands and feet they drive the nails is his fleshly part, which is the *substitute* being put to shame, *the one who came into being in his likeness.* But look at him and me." But I, when I had looked, said, "Lord, no one is looking at you. Let us flee this place." But he said to me, "I have told you, leave the blind alone! And you, see how they do not know what they are saying. For the son of their glory instead of my servant they have put to shame."...And he said to me, "Be strong, for you are the one to whom these mysteries have been given, to know them through revelation, that *he whom they crucified is the first-born, and the home of demons...*But he who stands near him is *the living Savior, the first in him, whom they seized and released,* who stands joyfully looking at those who did him violence, while they are divided among themselves."[33]

Conclusion

While the above quoted text is somewhat difficult to follow and to interpret in places, the *Apocalypse of Peter* can be seen as clearly rejecting the notion that Jesus Christ was crucified, even though it appeared that way to most onlookers. In that regard, the *Apocalypse of Peter* supports the Qur'anic presentation of the crucifixion event, and differs radically from traditional Christian orthodoxy.

The Second Treatise of the Great Seth

Provenance

Like the *Apocalypse of Peter*, this book was discovered in 1945 at Naga Hammadi, Egypt. As such, its provenance remains unquestioned between its burial in the fourth century CE, and its discovery in 1945. However, the origins of this work can probably be pushed back further in time than the fourth century CE. A theological analysis of its account of the crucifixion indicates a core taken from Basilides[34], who was a second century, Egyptian Christian of the Gnostic persuasion.[35] (In order not to reveal prematurely some of the surprises to be found within the accounts of the crucifixion found in the canonical gospels, this point will be elaborated later.) At this juncture it would suffice to say that the provenance of *The Second Treatise of the Great Seth* traces to anytime between the second and fourth centuries CE., with the earlier date being most probable.

Evidence

The presentation of the crucifixion in *Seth* is reported in the reputed words of Jesus, who is the speaker in the passage quoted below. The passage clearly states that Jesus died only in appearance, and that it was someone other than Jesus who was nailed to the cross, who drank the gall and vinegar, and who wore the crown of thorns. Throughout this whole procedure, Jesus was miraculously altering his form or physical appearance at will, and was witnessing the entire series of events. (In the following passage from *Seth*, italics have been added by the present author to highlight relevant issues.)

> And the plan which they devised about me to release their error and
> their senselessness—I did not succumb to them as they had planned.
> But I was not afflicted at all. Those who were there punished me.
> And *I did not die in reality but in appearance*, lest I be put to shame

by them because these are my kinsfolk...For my death which they think happened, (happened) to them in their error and blindness, *since they nailed their man unto their death*...for they were deaf and blind...Yes, they saw me; they punished me. *It was another, their father, who drank the gall and the vinegar; it was not I.* They struck me with the reed; *it was another, Simon, who bore the cross on his shoulder. It was another upon whom they placed the crown of thorns*...And I was laughing at their ignorance...For *I was altering my shapes, changing from form to form.* [36]

Comclusion

Once again, the message is clear. While Jesus Christ appeared to be crucified, this was mere illusory appearance. In reality, Jesus was not crucified. Rather, it was Simon who was crucified in substitution for Jesus Details of this appear later on in the chapter.) In short, *Seth* clearly rejects the concept of the crucifixion of Jesus Christ, being thus consistent with the Qur'anic presentation of the crucifixion. Once again, the traditional Christian orthodoxy is outrightly rejected by an early Christian text.

Acts of John

Provenance

The *Acts of John* is found in a solitary Greek manuscript from Vienna unearthed in 1897 CE, but there is a notation which states that the manuscript may have been the work of a scribe who lived in 1324 CE. However, its provenance does not stop there. The *Acts of John* was condemned as heretical at the Second Nicene Council of 787 CE, indicating its existence in the eighth century CE. Moreover, Augustine [37] quoted a fragment from it in a letter written in the fifth century CE. The quotation from Augustine matches the manuscript of 1897 CE, establishing that the *Acts of John* found in 1897 is the same book that was in circulation in the fifth century CE. However, literary analysis suggests a composition date in the first half of the second century CE.[38]

Evidence

The passage quoted below from the *Acts of John* takes place after the supposed arrest of Jesus. The author of the manuscript claims to be a disciple of Jesus Christ, i.e. John, the son of Zebedee.

(Since the account is written in the first person, the reader is to assume that the first person pronoun refers to John, unless it is part of a statement enclosed in quotation marks, in which case it refers to Jesus, who is talking to John.)

John narrates in the quotation that follows, how he and the rest of the disciples scattered and fled near the time of crucifixion, and how he had sought refuge by hiding in a cave on the Mount of Olives. While hiding in the cave, Jesus appeared to him during the time of the crucifixion, and explained to John that the crucifixion was illusory, and that Jesus was not the one being crucified. While explaining this to John, Jesus reminds him of a symbolic dance, which Jesus allegedly had performed with his disciples earlier, to predict and depict the illusory crucifixion event that was to take place later. Jesus categorically states to John that he is suffering none of the things that will later be said about him, e.g. that he was pierced with a lance and wounded, that he was hung on the cross, that blood flowed from him, etc., *(In the passage quoted below, italics have been added by the present author to highlight relevant statements.*

And we were like men amazed or fast asleep, and we fled this way and that. And so I saw him suffer, and did not wait by his suffering, but fled to the Mount of Olives, and wept at what had come to pass. And when he was hung (upon the Cross) on Friday, at the sixth hour of the day there came a darkness over the whole earth. And my Lord stood in the middle of the cave and gave light to it and said, "John, for the people below in Jerusalem I am being crucified and pierced with lances and reeds, and given vinegar and gall to drink. But to you I am speaking and listen to what I speak…" And when he had said this he showed me a Cross of Light firmly fixed, and around the Cross a great crowd, which had no single form; and in it (the Cross) was one form and the same likeness. And I saw the Lord himself above the Cross…"this is not that wooden Cross which you shall see when you go down from here; *nor am I the (man) who is on the Cross.* (I) whom now you do not see but only hear (my) voice. I was taken to be what I am not, I who am not what for many others I was; but what they will say of me is mean and unworthy of me…So then *I suffered none of those things which they will say of me;* even that suffering which I showed to you and to the rest in my dance, I will that it be called a mystery…*You hear that I suffered, yet I suffered not;* and that I suffered not, yet I did suffer; and that *I was pierced, yet I was not wounded; that I was hanged, yet I was not hanged; that blood flowed from me, yet it did not flow; and, in a word, that what they say of me, I did not endure, but what they do not say, those things I did suffer...*"[39]

Conclusion

The Gnostic flavor of this passage from the *Acts of John* may be confusing for some readers who are not well versed in Gnostic doctrine and philosophy. However, the relevant verses leave no doubt that the crucifixion of Jesus was only an illusion. Once again, an apocryphal writing of early Christianity totally refutes traditional Christian orthodoxy about the crucifixion event, and is consistent with the Qur'anic position on that issue.

Summary and Conclusions

Whether or not one accepts the *Gospel of Barnabas* as predating the beginning of the preaching of Prophet Muhammad, there is no denying that much of the apocryphal literature within the early Christian churches maintained that Jesus was not really crucified. Quite simply, the early Christian churches did not unanimously hold that Jesus died on the cross. There were many divisions within the early Christian churches, and some sections of early Christianity clearly believed that Jesus' crucifixion was illusory and/or that someone else was crucified in his place. By examining the provenance of these apocryphal books, one can demonstrate that this belief in the illusory and/or substitute nature of the crucifixion was quite prevalent in the early Christian churches during the second and third centuries CE. Further, by reference to the polemics against this position by the so-called apostolic fathers, one can trace this position back to the first decade of the second century CE. Allowing reasonable time for such a belief system to have spread to the point that the apostolic fathers felt the need to attack it, it becomes clear that the belief that Jesus was not really crucified was well represented in the early Christian churches during the last half of the first century CE. In short, this belief was common at a time prior to, or concomitant with, the authorship of the canonical gospels of the *New Testament*!

Canonical Gospels

Provenance

Having digressed to examine the provenance of the apocryphal books, it is only fair to present a brief statement about the provenance of *Matthew, Mark, Luke,* and *John.* Without getting into a detailed and lengthy discussion of source and text criticism, it is worth noting that: *Matthew, Mark,* and *Luke* frequently present a united front that is at variance with *John,* which is why the earlier three are referred to as the *Synoptic Gospels.* Further, all four gospels are based, at least in part, on prior written sources, such as *Q, proto-Mark, M, L,* and other hypothesized documents and none of these four *canonical gospels* were actually written by a disciple of Jesus. Morevover, the order of composition of these gospels is usually held to be *Mark,* followed by *Matthew,* followed by *Luke,* and finally followed by *John.* It should be further noted that both *Matthew* and *Luke* based part of their accounts on *Mark.* In their initially completed form, none of the four gospels can be dated earlier than about the last quarter of the first century CE, with *John* being dated to the first quarter of the second century CE. Editing of the four *canonical gospels* continued throughout the first few centuries CE. The sum total of the above proves that none of the authors of the four canonical gospels was an actual eye-witness to the events of the crucifixion, although their respective books may seem to include such first-hand accounts, which in reality were only stories of news happenings as told to them, either directly or though intermediaries.[40]

In what follows, different crucifixion stories in the *canonical gospels* are examined. In each case, a careful reading would clearly suggest that the person who was crucified may not have been Jesus at all.

Evidence: The denial of Peter

The Heroic Peter

All four of the *canonical gospels* are in unison on various issues concerning the arrest of Jesus. All four agree that Jesus and his disciples ate a common meal together in Jerusalem on the night of the arrest (although *Matthew, Mark,* and *Luke* portray this meal as being the *Passover* meal, while *John* portrays it as being the day prior to the *Passover*[41]). Further, all see eye-to-eye on the fact that Jesus was arrested the night before the crucifixion, and that his arrest took place outside the walls of the city of Jerusalem (which was consistently, but variously, identified as the Garden of Gethsemane, a place on the Mount of Olives, and a garden on the far side of the Kidron Valley from Jerusalem). They are also of a common opinion, that in the course of the arrest, one of Jesus' disciples drew his sword and attacked, in order to attempt to defend Jesus. While John identifies this disciple to be Peter (Simon bar Jonah)[42], *Matthew, Mark,* and *Luke* are silent about this name

> After Jesus had spoken these words, he went out with his disciples across the Kidron valley to a place where there was a garden, which he and his disciples entered. Now Judas, who betrayed him, also knew the place, because Jesus often met there with his disciples. So Judas brought a detachment of soldiers together with police from the chief priests and the Pharisees, and they came there with lanterns and torches and weapons. Then Jesus, knowing all that was to happen to him, came forward and asked them, "Whom are you looking for?" They answered, "Jesus of Nazareth." Jesus replied, "I am he." Judas, who betrayed him, was standing with them. When Jesus said to them, "I am he," they stepped back and fell to the ground. Again he asked them, "Whom are you looking for?" And they said, "Jesus of Nazareth." Jesus answered, "I told you that I am he. So if you are looking for me, let these men go." This was to fulfill the word that he had spoken, "I did not lose a single one of those whom you gave me." Then Simon Peter, who had a sword, drew it, struck the high priest's slave, and cut off his right ear. The slave's name was Malchus. Jesus said to Peter, "Put your sword back into its sheath. Am I not to drink the cup that the Father has given me?" So the soldiers, their officer, and the Jewish police arrested Jesus and bound him.[43]

In the above account from *John*, Judas Iscariot, the disciple who reportedly betrayed Jesus, leads a group of armed men to arrest Jesus. *John* identifies these armed men as being "a detachment of soldiers" and "police from the chief priests and the Pharisees."[44] The former identification implies that Roman legionnaires were put under the direction of the Jewish officials, in order to assist in the arrest of Jesus. The latter identification clearly refers to the Temple police force. In the face of this numerically superior and armed authority, one disciple stood his ground. Peter bravely drew his sword, and single-handedly attacked the armed multitude of professional soldiers and police arrayed against him. He had to have known that his act of heroism would lead to his immediate death, yet he was more than willing to sacrifice his life in his desperate attempt to save Jesus. However, Peter was able to get in only one thrust of his sword, thus cutting off the ear of Malchus, the slave of the high priest, before Jesus intervened. Stopping the fight before it could really begin, Jesus surrendered himself to the arresting force, and his disciples then fled into the night. (*Luke* adds that Jesus healed the ear of Malchus.[46])

The Cowardly Peter

Following his arrest, Jesus was taken either: to Annas, the father-in-law of Caiaphas, the Jewish high priest, and then to Caiaphas [47]; or directly to Caiaphas[48]. Unlike all of the other disciples, the ever-faithful and heroic Peter followed at a distance, and gained entrance to the outer courtyard[49]. There the intrepid Peter waited for word on the fate of Jesus. However, while Peter was standing in the courtyard, the authors of the four *canonical gospels* would have the reader believe that Peter did a complete about-face. They would have the reader believe that the heroic Peter, who had single-handedly attacked the Roman legionnaires and Temple police, and who had risked his life in even following Jesus into the outer courtyard, had suddenly become a coward, because he three times denied any association with Jesus before the cock crowed that morning. Because the exact wording of Peter's denials is so important, all four gospel accounts are presented immediately below.

Matthew's account of Peter's denials:

Now Peter was sitting outside in the courtyard. A servant-girl came to him and said, "You also were with Jesus the Galilean." But he denied it before all of them, saying, "I do not know what you are talking about." When he went out to the porch, another servant-girl saw him, and she said to the bystanders, "This man was with Jesus of Nazareth." Again he denied it with an oath, "I do not know the man." After a little while the bystanders came up and said to Peter, "Certainly you are also one of them, for your accent betrays you." Then he began to curse, and he swore an oath, "I do not know the man!" At that moment the cock crowed. Then Peter remembered what Jesus had said: "Before the cock crows, you will deny me three times." And he went out and wept bitterly.[50]

Luke's account:

When they had kindled a fire in the middle of the courtyard and sat down together, Peter sat among them. Then a servant-girl, seeing him in the firelight, stared at him and said, "This man also was with him." But he denied it, saying, "Woman, I do not know him." A little later someone else, on seeing him, said, "You also are one of them." But Peter said, "Man, I am not!" Then about an hour later still another kept insisting, "Surely this man also was with him; for he is a Galilean." But Peter said, "Man, I do not know what you are talking about!" At that moment, while he was still speaking, the cock crowed. The Lord turned and looked at Peter. Then Peter remembered the word of the Lord, how he had said to him, "Before the cock crows today you will deny me three times." And he went out and wept bitterly.[51]

Mark's narration:

While Peter was below in the courtyard, one of the servant-girls of the high priest came by. When she saw Peter warming himself, she stared at him and said, "You also were with Jesus, the man from Nazareth." But he denied it, saying, "I do not know or understand what you are talking about." And he went out into the fore-court. Then the cock crowed. And the servant-girl, on seeing him, began again to say to the bystanders, "This man is one of them." But again he denied it. Then after a little while the bystanders again said to Peter, "Certainly you are one of them; for you are a Galilean." But he began to curse, and he swore an oath, "I do not know this man you are talking about." At that moment the cock crowed for the second time. Then Peter remembered that Jesus had said to him, "Before the cock crows twice, you will deny me three times." And he broke down and wept.[52]

Finally, the account of *John*:

The woman said to Peter, "You are not also one of this man's disciples, are you?" He said, "I am not." Now the slaves and the police had made a charcoal fire because it was cold, and they were standing around it and warming themselves. Peter also was standing with them and warming himself...Now Simon Peter was standing and warming himself. They asked him, "You are not also one of his disciples, are you?" He denied it and said, "I am not." One of the slaves of the high priest, a relative of the man whose ear Peter had cut off, asked, "Did I not see you in the garden with him?" Again Peter denied it, and at the moment the cock crowed.[53]

What Peter denied

In considering these four versions of what is reportedly the same event, one needs to begin by carefully considering what is it that Peter is denying. In that regard, Table 2 is presented below.

Table 2: The Accusations (A) that Peter denied (D)

Mt1 A: You were with Jesus the Galilean.
D: I do not know what you are talking about.

Mt2 A: This man was with Jesus of Nazareth.
D: I do not know the man.

Mt3 A: You are one of them, for your accent betrays you.
D: I do not know the man.

L1 A: This man also was with him.
D: I do not know him.

L2 A: You also are one of them.
D: Man, I am not.

L3 A: This man also was with him.
D: I do not know what you are talking about.

M1 A: You were with Jesus from Nazareth.
D: I do not know what you are talking about.

M2 A: This man is one of them.
D: But again he denied it.
M3 A: You are one of them; for you are a Galilean.
D: I do not know this man.

J1 A: You are one of this man's disciples.
D: I am not.

J2 A: You are one of his disciples.
D: I am not.

J3 A: Did I not see you in the garden with him.
D: Peter denied it.
Mt1, Mt2, & Mt3 = 1st, 2nd, and 3rd accusations
and denials reported by *Matthew.*
L1, L2, & L3 = 1st, 2nd, and 3rd accusations
and denials reported by *Luke.*
M1, M2, & M3 = 1st 2nd and 3rd accusations
and denials reported by *Mark.*
J1, J2, & J3 = 1st, 2nd, and 3rd accusations
and denials reported by *John.*

As a brief digression, it should be noted that the four *canonical gospels* agree that Peter made three denials, and they agree in reporting three accusations. However, the *canonical gospels* do not agree as to what those accusations were. Be that as it may, the data presented in Table 2 can be summarized into the following accusations: (1) Peter was with Jesus, the Galilean (Mt1); (2) Peter was with Jesus of Nazareth (Mt2,M1); (3) Peter was with "them", where the context indicates that them "refers" to Galileans and/or to the disciples of Jesus of Nazareth (Mt3,M2,M3); (4) Peter was with the disciples of the man being tried (L2,J1,J2); (5) Peter was with the man being tried (L1,L3); and (6) Peter was in the garden with the man being tried (J3). In making the summary list of six accusations, care has been taken not to pre-judge the outcome, i.e. one cannot assume that Jesus of Nazareth is the one being tried, but one must look directly at the statements involved.

As can be seen *Luke* and *John* present a united front, in which Peter's denials are specifically directed towards the man being tried or interrogated. Quite simply, Peter is denying any association with the man being tried or interrogated. What if that man were not Jesus Christ? What if Judas were seized instead of Jesus Christ (*Gospel of Barnabas*), or what if some other substitute for or simulacrum of Jesus Christ were seized in place of Jesus Christ (*Apocalypse of Peter, The Second Treatise of the Great Seth,* and *Acts of John*)? In that case, Peter's denials are totally truthful. In that case, there exists no bewildering contradiction, reportedly occurring within a matter of mere hours, between: Peter's willingness to fight single-handedly Roman soldiers and Temple police, which implies his heroic bravery and unwavering faith; and Peter's denials, which imply cowardice and lack of faith. In short, the hypothesis exists that a superficial reading of the *canonical gospels* misrepresents Peter's denials into being a denial of Jesus Christ, when, in fact, Peter is simply stating "I do not know this man", where "this man" may not be Jesus Christ. Read in the light of maintaining the consistency of Peter's portrayal within the *canonical gospels,* Peter's denials reflect a denial that the man being tried and/or interrogated was Jesus Christ.

However, what about the accounts of *Matthew* and *Mark*? Here one encounters the denials within the context of such phrases as "Jesus the Galilean", "Jesus of Nazareth", and "Jesus, the man from Nazareth". One option is to dismiss these phrases as later and erroneous elaboration of an earlier account, as preserved in *Luke* and in *John.* Certainly, this option has much to recommend it, and is not to be dismissed out of hand. However, a second option also exists, which is based upon examination of the key words "Galilean" and "Nazareth". In that regard, it is noted that most superficial readers of the *Bible* equate "Galilean" with "a man from the geographical area of Galilee", which the *Bible* indicates Jesus Christ was. Likewise, most such readers equate "Nazareth" with a town in Galilee, which the *Bible* indicates was the town, in which Jesus Christ was raised. However, both of these terms had radically alternative meanings during the first half of the first century CE.

Judaism in the First Century CE

During the first half of the first century CE, Judaism was divided into numerous religious and political sects. A partial listing of such sects and their various divisions included:Sadducees (Zadokites); Hasidim (the root group for both the Pharisees and the Essenes); Pharisees (Perishaiya); Zealots; Hasmoneans; Sicarii; Essenes; Herodians; Nazoreans (Nazarites or Nazirites); and Galileans.[54] It is only within this context that terms such as "Jesus the Galilean", "Jesus of Nazareth", and "Jesus, the man from Nazareth" can be properly and fully understood.

Galileans

If one were to rank these different Jewish sects and sub-sects along a cultural-political dimension, the left-right axis would be anchored as follows. The far left would indicate acceptance of and accommodation with Hellenistic culture and with Roman rule, and the far right the complete rejection of Hellenistic culture and Roman rule, coupled with extreme nationalistic aspirations. Given this axis and definition, the Sadducees would occupy the far left, the Pharisees would occupy the middle ground position to the right side of the fulcrum, and the Zealots and Hasmoneans would occupy the far right.[55] It was the far right, which consistently gave birth to revolutionary movements against Roman authority. Typically, the groups of the far right are referred to as Zealots, where Zealot becomes an umbrella word, covering various groups and sub-groups, including the Sicarii (from the Greek word "sikarioi", meaning "dagger men", and indicating a sub-group of Zealots, who were assassins[56]) and the Galileans. The *Bible* indicates that at least two of Jesus' disciples were from the far right of the cultural-political spectrum: Simon, the Zealot[57] ; and Judas Iscariot (the Sicarii).[58]

As noted above, the Zealot movement represented the far right of the cultural-political axis within first century CE Judaism. However, identification of a person as a Zealot said very little about that person's actual religious orientation. Some Zealots were quasi-secular, and others were deeply committed to the Jewish religious tradition. Among the latter group of Zealots, there is a sub-group known as the Galileans.[59] The origin and history of the Galileans are as follows:

In six CE, Quirinius, a Roman senator of consular rank, was appointed governor of Syria by Caesar Augustus.[60] One of his first tasks was to administer a census in Palestine for the sake of registering property for the construction of a proper tax roll.[61] While most Jews in Palestine acquiesced to this census, a dissident faction of Jews, led by Judas of Gamala (a.k.a. Judas, the Galilean) entered into open revolt against the authority of Rome, claiming that: the end purpose of the census would amount to slavery for the Jewish people; adherence to the census was an agreement by Jews that pagans had the right to rule Palestine; and that it was time for the Jews to establish their own theocratic state.[62] The revolt of Judas, the Galilean, was short-lived, Judas was killed, and his followers were scattered for a while.[63] However, the uprising of Judas, the Galilean, was the birth of the Zealot movement, and particularly of that part of the Zealot movement known as the Galileans.[64]

Following the aborted uprising of Judas the Galilean, the Galileans continued to engage in isolated acts of guerrilla warfare against Rome, which steadily increased in intensity across the decades between 6 and 70

CE. In 44 CE, such revolutionary and paramilitary activities on the part of the Galileans led to the crucifixions of James and Simon, the sons of Judas, the Galilean, by order of Tiberius Alexander, procurator of Judaea. Finally, in 66 CE, Menahem, another son of Judas, the Galilean, led the Galileans and Zealots in open revolt against Rome. Menahem and his followers seized the armory at Masada, and then marched on Jerusalem. Taking most of Jerusalem, Menahem, who had pretensions of being king, established a despotic rule, and assassinated Ananias, the Jewish high priest. However, Menahem was then assassinated by Eleazar, the son of Ananias, in the Temple of Jerusalem. Menahem's followers then fled back to Masada, under the command of another Eleazar, who was a descendant of Judas, the Galilean. At Masada, the Jewish revolt continued until 73 CE, when the besieged inhabitants of Masada committed mass suicide, in order not to be captured by the Roman army, which surrounded them.[65]

Given the above account, one can readily see that the identification of "Jesus the Galilean" cannot automatically be equated with "Jesus from the geographical region of Galilee". Given the context of the times, the more likely identification would be "Jesus, a member of the Galilean party of paramilitary insurrectionists". Such a Jesus would obviously not be Jesus Christ, and Peter's denial of such a Jesus would be truthful.

The Nazorean

Among the accusations leveled against Peter, one refers to "Jesus of Nazareth"[66], and one refers to "Jesus, the man from Nazareth".[67] The former statement is, in fact, a misleading translation of the Greek word "Nazorean"[68], and the latter statement a misleading translation of the Greek "Nazarene".[69] The Greek word "Nazorean" or "Nazarene" is a transliteration (Nazarenoi or Nazoraioi) of the Aramaic word "Nasren" or "Nasraya", which means "the preservers".[70] In turn, the Aramaic word can be traced to the Hebrew "Nazir", meaning "consecrated", "holy", or "abstainer".[71] If the Jewish sects and sub-sects of the first century CE were aligned on an religious axis, in which the left pole represented Jewish liberalism, and in which the right pole represented religious conservatism, then the Pharisees would fall in the middle, and the Essenes and Nazoreans would fall on the far right.

So, who were, and what were, the Nazoreans? Quite simply, they were the same group referred to in the *Old Testament* as Nazarites or as Nazirites. A Nazarite or Nazorean was a person, who took a vow of abstinence and of severe adherence to the Mosaic Law, where such vow could be for life or for a specified amount of time.[72] The specific rules governing the period of being a Nazarite or Nazorean are enumerated in *Numbers* 6:1-21 in the *Bible*, and are not repeated in this chapter. However, it is noted that the Nazarites or Nazoreans were characterized by refusal to cut their hair, by absolute abstinence from alcohol and from any derivative of the grape, by absolute refusal to be anywhere near a corpse, etc. Prominent Biblical figures who have been identified as being Nazarites or Nazoreans include: Samson[73]; Samuel[74]; probably John (Yahya), the Baptist [75], possibly James, the first head of the Christian church at Jerusalem[76]; and temporarily Paul.[77] However, the Biblical portrayal of Jesus Christ is mutually exclusive with that of a Nazorean, as a Nazorean could never have taken from the fruit of the grape, and could never have come anywhere close to the departed Lazarus, whom Jesus, through the power of Allah, reportedly raised from the dead.[78]

Given the above discussion, Peter's denial of being associated with Jesus, the Nazorean, appears to have been a truthful statement, although Jesus, the Nazorean, was not Jesus Christ. Of note, a Nazorean might also have been a Galilean, but would not have to have been. (As an aside, it is noted that in the passage quoted earlier from John 18:1-12, the phrase "Jesus of Nazareth" should read "Jesus, the Nazorean", thus raising the possibility that Jesus Christ may never have been arrested in the first place.)

The Name 'Jesus'

During the first century CE, Jesus (the Greek rendition of Joshua) was a very popular name in Palestine. For example, of the 28 high priests of Judaism from the time of Herod the Great to the destruction of the Temple, four were named Jesus (Jesus son of Phabet or Phiabi, Jesus son of Sec or Sei, Jesus son of Damneus, Jesus son of Gamaliel).[79] Using this list of Jewish high priests as a representative sample of male names in Palestine in the first century CE, one can expect about 14% of the male population to have been named Jesus. Clearly, it is not too much to imagine that a second Jesus was being interrogated the night before the crucifixion, that it was this man that Peter denied, and that it was this man who would be crucified the next day.

Summary

The denial of Peter presents the *canonical gospels* with two mutually exclusive options. 1) Within a matter of just a few hours, Peter went from being a heroic figure of unlimited bravery to being a coward, who verbally denied his affiliation with Jesus Christ at three separate times in rapid succession. Quite frankly, this portrayal of Peter tends to strain the imagination. 2) Peter was straightforward and honest in denying his affiliation, either with an unknown man, or with a paramilitary insurrectionist and extreme right-wing adherent of Judaism, who happened to be named Jesus. Assuming that the man was unknown, Peter's denial was quite consistent with the evidence from the apocryphal books presented previously. Assuming that the man was a paramilitary insurrectionist named Jesus, Peter's denial is in keeping with the story of the release of Barabbas, recounted below.

Evidence: The Release of Barabbas

From the Arreest to Barabbas

Before moving directly to the story of the release of Barabbas, it is instructive to chart the supposed movements of Jesus Christ from the time of his alleged arrest until the time of the release of Barabbas. Using the four *canonical gospels* as the source for this information, a quick comparison of these four gospels reveals significant disagreement among them. This information is presented in Table 3, and the reader is free to draw his own conclusions about the reliability of the gospel accounts of the various movements of Jesus Christ, during these events.

Table 3: Sequence of the reported movements of
Jesus Christ between his arrest and the release of Barabbas

Matthew	*Mark*	*Luke*	*John*
			To Ann
To Caiaphas	*To Caiaphas*	*To Caiaphas*	*To Caiaphas*
To Sanhedrin?	*To Sanhedrin*	*To Sanhedrin*	
		To Pilate	
		To Herod	
To Pilate *To Pilate* *To Pilate*		*To Pilate*	*To Pilate*

The Matthean sequence is dependent on
Mahew 26:57; 27:1; 27:1-2.
The Markan sequence is dependent on
Mark 14:53, 15:1, 15:1.
The Lukan sequence is dependent on
Luke 22:54; 22:66; 23:1; 23:6-8; 23:11.
The Johanine sequence is dependent on John 18:12-13; 18:24; 18:28.

The Release of Barabbas

The release of Barabbas is reported by all four *canonical gospels*[80], and
many of the details are the same across the four narratives. In each
account, Pontius Pilate, the Roman governor of Judaea, gives the Jewish
crowd a choice between the release of two prisoners, one of whom has
been traditionally presented as Jesus Christ, and the other of whom has
been presented as a notorious outlaw, who is known only as Barabbas.
The agitated crowd selects Barabbas to be released. Pilate thus releases
Barabbas, and Jesus Christ is supposedly crucified. However, as will soon
be seen, this Sunday School interpretation of the gospel portrayal is less
than accurate, primarily because the most ancient and accurate texts of
the gospels have been kept away from the laity until very recent times.
Of the four accounts, that of *Matthew* is by far the most illuminating and
detailed, and it is this narrative that is reported below:

> Now Jesus stood before the governor; and the governor asked him,
> "Are you the King of the Jews?" Jesus said, "You say so."...Now at
> the festival the governor was accustomed to release a prisoner for
> the crowd, anyone whom they wanted. At that time they had a noto-
> rious prisoner, called Jesus Barabbas. So after they had gathered,
> Pilate said to them, "Whom do you want me to release for you, Jesus
> Barabbas or Jesus who is called the Messiah? For he realized that it
> was out of jealousy that they had handed him over. While he was sit-
> ting on the judgment seat, his wife sent word to him, "Have nothing
> to do with that innocent man, for today I have suffered a great deal
> because of a dream about him." Now the chief priests and the elders
> persuaded the crowds to ask for Barabbas and to have Jesus killed.
> The governor again said to them, "Which of the two do you want me
> to release for you?" And they said, "Barabbas." Pilate said to them,
> "Then what should I do with Jesus who is called the Messiah?" All
> of them said, "Let him be crucified!" Then he asked, "Why, what

evil has he done?" But they shouted all the more, "Let him be crucified!" So when Pilate saw that he could do nothing, but rather that a riot was beginning, he took some water and washed his hands before the crowd, saying, "I am innocent of this man's blood; see to it yourselves." Then the people as a whole answered, "His blood be on us and on our children!" So he released Barabbas for them; and after flogging Jesus, he handed him over to be crucified.[81]

As a slight digression, it is noted that apocryphal writings consistently identify Pilate's wife's name as Procla.[82](More about her perceived status by the early Christian churches will be presented later on in the chapter.)

The Identity of Barabbas

The text quoted above from *Matthew*, as found in *The Holy Bible: New Revised Standard Version (NRSV)*, clearly identifies Barabbas as having the given name of Jesus. In making this identification, the NRSV utilizes the most ancient texts[83], in order to correct the deletion of Barabbas' given name, i.e., Jesus, which happened in earlier versions of the *Bible*. As a point of fact, Biblical scholars have long known from these ancient texts of *Matthew* that Barabbas' name was Jesus. However, this information was typically not presented to the laity. In the *King James Version* of the *Bible* of 1611, there is absolutely no mention of Barabbas' name as being Jesus. In the *Revised Standard Version (RSV)* of 1946, this information finally makes it into the text as an obscure footnote. Finally, in the *New Revised Standard Version (NRSV)* of 1989, the earliest and most complete information regarding Barabbas is presented directly in the text, where it originally was supposed to be, and the previously unknown Barabbas has once again become Jesus Barabbas.

However, the Biblical translators are still holding out on the laity. They have still not completed their job of educating the Christian laity, and of making the Biblical text accessible to the average Christian. They have now presented Barabbas as Jesus Barabbas, but they are still not pointing out that "Barabbas" is not a given name, but is a patronymic.[84] A patronymic is an identifier, whereby the person is stated to be the son of X. Thus, in the *New Testament*, one finds the disciple Simon Peter also called Simon bar Jonah, i.e., Simon the son of Jonah.[85] However, Biblical translators have consistently run together the Aramaic words "bar" and "Abbas", thus rendering "Jesus **bar** Abbas" as "Jesus Barabbas", or, worse yet, only as "Barabbas". With this in mind, and realizing that "bar" merely means "son of", one can now identify Barabbas as "Jesus the son of Abbas". However, even taking the translation to this point, it would still be somewhat misleading, because "Abbas" is not a given name. The word "Abbas" still needs to be translated from the Aramaic. "Abbas" means "father", and Barabbas is directly and unambiguously identified in Matthew as being "Jesus, the son of the Father"[86]! Now, if one were to ask 100 randomly selected Christians the identity of "Jesus, the son of the Father", one would get 100 positive identifications of Jesus Christ.

Barabbas was none other than Jesus, the son of the Father[87]! This is not an identification based upon some apocryphal book, which may or may not have a provenance back to the early Christian churches, such as the case with the *Gospel of Barnabas*. This is not even an identification based upon apocryphal books, which can be directly traced to the early Christian churches, such as the case with the *Two Books of Jeu, the Apocalypse of Peter, The Second Treatise of the Great Seth,* or the *Acts of John.* This is an identification that is directly made by the *canonical gospel of Matthew.* However, it is an identification that can only be made once: the earliest texts of *Matthew* are finally the acknowledged ones, as in the case of the *NSRV*; and the reader has completed the translation of two words, which the Biblical translators are still refraining from translating, thus keeping the laity in the dark as to the actual statement of *Matthew.* Understanding this passage of *Matthew* is similar to peeling an onion. There is layer after layer that needs to be removed, before one gets to the actual core. While one can see that the Biblical translators have begun peeling that onion for the laity, the peeling process has been awfully slow, and is still incomplete. These various layers are presented in Table 4 below:

Table 4: The Layers of Identity of Barabbas

Layer	Identity Revealed	Version of the *Bible*
1	Barabbas	King James Version, 1611
2	Jesus Barabbas as footnote	Revised Standard Version, 1946
3	Jesus Barabbas	New Revised Standard Version, 1989
4	Jesus bar Abbas	――
5	Jesus, son of Abbas	――
6	Jesus, son of the Father	――

Based on the above discussion, we can see that as per *Matthew* Pilate offered to release one of the two captives that day viz., "Jesus, the son of the Father" or "Jesus who is called the Messiah."[88] According to the *Matthean* narration, the crowd selected "Jesus, the son of the Father" for release. Pilate met their request, releasing "Jesus, the son of the Father", and condemning "Jesus called the Messiah."[89] At the very least, the *Matthean* account indicates that there was marked confusion regarding who was released and who was crucified. Oscillating between the two, "Jesus, the son of the Father" and "Jesus who is called the Messiah", how is one to decide who is who?

The answer is available, but takes a bit of sleuthing. Prior to Pilate asking the crowd whom they want released, *Matthew* has Pilate asking a single, pointed question to Jesus, i.e., "Are you the King of the Jews?".[90] This was the only thing in which Pilate appeared to be interested. Was Jesus laying claim to being the King of the Jews, and thus leading an insurrection against Rome? Pilate had no concern about internal bickering among the Jewish religious establishment. Whether or not someone claimed to be a religious figure such as the Messiah was not his concern. He wanted to affirm the claim of kingship, since this encompassed temporal and secular authority, posing a challenge to the imperial rule of Rome. Hence, he did not ask Jesus if Jesus were the theological Messiah, because Pilate didn't care about this issue. However, Pilate did care if Jesus were claiming to be King of the Jews. Claiming to be the theological Messiah was not a crime under Roman law, while claiming to be the King of the Jews certainly was.

Here, one needs to examine what is meant by "Jesus who is called the Messiah". Generations of Sunday School-attending Christians have been indoctrinated with a theological concept of the Messiah, which dates from the time of the early Christian churches. However, the Hebrew word "Mashiah", which is rendered "Messiah" in the *Bible*, simply means "anointed". Likewise, the Greek word "Christos", which is rendered Christ in the *Bible*, is simply a Greek translation of the Hebrew word "Mashiah". Thus, even if Pilate's words were "Jesus who is called the Messiah", all he was saying was "Jesus who is called the anointed." Who were the anointed of Israel? The answer is the kings and high priests of Israel. In that regard, any insurrectionist who was laying claim to being the king of Israel, and there were many such people in the first century CE, would have had himself anointed as king of Israel, and could have been referred to as "Messiah".[91]

Having established Pilate's concern, and thus having established the actual charge against Jesus, i.e. claiming to be King of the Jews, and having established the actual meaning of the word "Messiah", one now turns to the parallel passage of the release of "Jesus, the son of the Father" in *Mark*.

> So the crowd came and began to ask Pilate to do for them according to his custom. Then he answered them, "Do you want me to release for you the King of the Jews?" ...But the chief priests stirred up the crowd to have him release Barabbas for them instead.[92]

Note the subtle, but all-important change. The choice is between "Jesus, the King of the Jews" and "Jesus, the son of the Father"! Given this version, there is no ambiguity or confusion as to identity. Jesus, who claimed to be the King of the Jews, and had thus been anointed as such, i.e. had become a Messiah, was turned over for crucifixion, while Jesus, the son of the Father, was released. What could be simpler or more straightforward than that? Now, who was this Jesus, who claimed to be King of the Jews? He was probably a person already encountered in this chapter, i.e., "Jesus, the Galilean", i.e., the paramilitary insurrectionist, whom Peter denied knowing.[93] It was this Jesus, who was the actual murderer and insurrectionist, whose charges were falsely being attributed to Jesus, the son of the Father, simply through the confusion, deliberate or otherwise, created by the writers of the gospels or their renderers, redactors, or editors.[94]

Summary

The story of the release of Jesus, the son of the Father, is of enormous significance. Even if the reader rejects the reconstruction of the *Matthean* passage suggested by this author, which was based upon Pilate's question to Jesus and upon the parallel *Markan* narrative, the reader of the *canonical gospels* is still left with confusion and ambiguity. The respective identities of who was released (Jesus, the son of the Father) and of who was crucified (Jesus who is called the Messiah) are confusing and unanswered questions. That confusion and ambiguity is sufficient, in and of itself, to serve notice that at least one viable answer to the above questions from the *canonical gospels* supports the Qur'anic account of the crucifixion. Further, if one accepts the reconstruction of the *Matthean* account as proposed by this author, then it is clear that Jesus, the King of the Jews (a.k.a. Jesus, the Galilean), was crucified, while Jesus, the son of the Father, was released. Here, one has total vindication of the Qur'anic account of the crucifixion, as though one were needed, based solely on the *canonical gospels.*

By this point, the Christian reader, indoctrinated by a childhood of Sunday School lessons, may be thinking that this whole line of argument is preposterous. Never mind what *Matthew* actually said about Jesus, the son of the Father, it's easier just to ignore the whole thing. However, before taking that step, one more piece of information should be considered. If Pilate did, indeed, sentence Jesus Christ to death by crucifixion, how should the early churches have viewed Pilate and his associates? Would not Pilate have been vilified to the ends of the earth by the early Christian churches? Might not Pilate have been formally condemned by the early churches to eternity in hell? One would certainly think so. However, the facts are radically different. On October 28th, the Eastern Orthodox Church calendar lists the feast day of Saint Procla, the wife of Pontius Pilate.[95] On June 25th, the Coptic Christian Church lists the feast day of Saint Procla and of Saint Pontius Pilate[96]! Procla was canonized as a saint by both the Eastern Orthodox Church and by the Coptic Christian Church, while Pontius Pilate was canonized as a saint by the Coptic Christian Church. How did the early Coptic Christian Church ever justify canonizing as a saint the man, who condemned Jesus Christ to death by crucifixion? This just defies all reason and all logic. What did these early Christians know that modern Christians don't know? Perhaps, they knew that Pontius Pilate, their beloved saint, was the man who released Jesus Christ. Perhaps, they had a better understanding of *Matthew*, than do most modern Christians.

At this point, it is very tempting to say "case closed, court adjourned." However, there is one more piece of evidence from the *canonical gospels,* which needs to be examined.

Evidence: The Recruitment of Simon of Cyrene

The traditional Christian interpretation of the crucifixion has Jesus Christ moving from the sentencing before Pontius Pilate to the site of crucifixion, i.e. Golgotha (Calvary in the Latin). This journey is ritualized by the Roman Catholic Church as part of its 14 Stations of the Cross, of which the fifth station is of special interest. The fifth Station of the Cross refers to an event that is narrated in the three synoptic gospels, but not in *John*. It is at the fifth Station that Simon of Cyrene was reportedly enlisted to carry the cross of Jesus: [97]

> As they went out, they came upon a man from Cyrene named Simon; they compelled this man to carry his cross. And when they came to a place called Golgotha (which means Place of a Skull), they offered him wine to drink, mixed with gall; but when he tasted it, he would not drink it. And when they had crucified him, they divided his clothes among themselves by casting lots; then they sat down there and kept watch over him.[98]

> They compelled a passer-by, who was coming in from the country, to carry his cross; it was Simon of Cyrene, the father of Alexander and Rufus. Then they brought *Jesus* to the place called Golgotha (which means the place of a skull). And they offered him wine mixed with myrrh; but he did not take it. And they crucified him, and divided his clothes among them, casting lots to decide what each should take.[99]

> As they led him away, they seized a man, Simon of Cyrene, who was coming from the country, and they laid the cross on him, and made him carry it behind Jesus…Two others also, who were criminals, were led away to be put to death with him. When they came to the place that is called The Skull, they crucified *Jesus* there with the criminals, one on his right and one on his left.[100]

Now, two points need to be made with regard to the above narratives. First, the gospels never have the cross being transferred back to Jesus from Simon. Second, in the passage from *Mark* and in the passage from *Luke*, the present author has italicized the word "Jesus" in one place. In each such place, the *NRSV* footnote to the text clearly states that the Greek reads "him", not "Jesus". In other words, the translators were concerned that the average reader would read "him" as referring to Simon of Cyrene, if it weren't for their insertion of "Jesus" for "him". In that regard, the translators are absolutely correct. The average reader would read "him" as referring to Simon of Cyrene, indicating that it was Simon of Cyrene, who was crucified. In the above passages, *Matthew*, *Mark*, and *Luke* all seem to be saying that Simon of Cyrene was crucified in the place of Jesus.

It should be emphasized that the above interpretation of the synoptic tradition is not limited to the present author. In fact, that very interpretation was widely held by segments of the early Christian churches. Readers of of this chapter have already encountered that interpretation in *The Second Treatise of the Great Seth,* the apocryphal book of the early Christian churches, where it stated, "it was another, Simon, who bore the cross on his shoulder." As a point of fact, the substitution, of Simon of Cyrene (as the crucifixion victim), for Jesus was a cardinal tenet of belief among those early Christians known as Basilidians[101], who were prominent in the middle of the second century CE. They congregated in Egypt and continued in existence through the fourth century CE. Their lineage can be traced back to people who were the followers of Basilides, claimed to be the receiver of certain secret traditions from Glaucias (an interpreter of Peter, the disciple of Jesus).[102]

Summary and Conclusions

It is not the author's intent to prove any one tradition, as opposed to any other, in which it was not Jesus Christ who was crucified. However, the foregoing reviews of Christian scripture, both apocryphal and canonical, dramatically illustrate that the early Christian churches had no unanimous acceptance of the doctrine of Christ's crucifixion. Clearly, they were confused as to what actually took place. Different theories on this subject floated within the early churches. Among the various candidates for the dubious honor of having been the crucified victim, one can list: Judas Iscariot; Simon of Cyrene; simulacrums of Jesus Christ; unidentified others; and a paramilitary insurrectionist known as Jesus, the Galilean, who claimed to be the King of the Jews, and who is to be distinguished from Jesus, the son of the Father, i.e., Jesus Christ.

The *Qur'an* clearly states that Jesus Christ was not crucified. Large segments of the early Christian churches, and of the early Christian scriptures, agree with that statement.

For Muslims, the lesson may be that many of the early Christian churches were much closer to Islam than previously thought. For Christians, the lesson may be that the doctrine of the crucifixion was very much questioned and debated by the early churches. With that in mind, perhaps they might be willing to take a second look at the teachings of Islam, and to consider the similarities between the teachings of Islam and the foundations of early Christianity.

Chapter 6

The Mission and Ministry of Jesus

The mission and ministry of Jesus, peace be upon him[1], may be analyzed in several different ways. One would be to examine the content of his message to his listeners/followers. Another way would be to analyze the source and precedents of Jesus' message. For example, how often are the alleged words of Jesus actually a quotation or paraphrase of earlier canonical, apocryphal, or pseudepigraphical scripture. A third way would be to determine the scope of his mission, i.e. to what range of people did Jesus deliver his message. In this brief chapter, the third approach has been attempted.

The modern Christian churches, with their theology primarily influenced by and based on the post-Jesus writings of Paul and on the Pauline tradition, maintain that the message of Jesus was addressed to the whole world, both to Jews and to gentiles. As such, Jesus is seen as a universal messenger of Allah.[2] In marked contrast, Islam reserves the concept of the universal messenger to Prophet Muhammad, peace be upon him, and sees Jesus as being a prophet and messenger whose prophetic mission and ministry were limited to the Jews alone. (From the Islamic perspective, these Jews were Israelites who were backsliders and deviaters from the true religion of Allah, i.e. Islam, and who adopted a specific, formalistic, and ritualistic code of conduct termed Judaism.[3])

> Behold! the angels said: "O Mary! Allah giveth thee glad tidings of a word from Him: his name will be Christ Jesus...And Allah will teach him the book and wisdom, the law and the gospel, and (appoint him) a messenger to the children of Israel..."[4]

> When (Jesus) the son of Mary is held up as an example, behold thy people raise a clamor threat (in ridicule)! And

they say, "Are our gods best, or he? This they set forth to
thee, only by way of disputation: yea, they are a contentious
people. He was no more than a servant: We granted Our
favor to him, and We made him an example to the children
of Israel.[5]

As will be seen in what follows, the preponderance of evidence from
that part of the Christian scriptures, specifically attributed to the words of
Jesus, as opposed to those of his alleged disciples or to Paul (Saul of
Tarsus), clearly refute the concept that the mission and ministry of Jesus
were universal in nature. Rather, the alleged words of Jesus in Christian,
as opposed to Islamic, scripture delineate a mission and ministry that are
defined by stringent, nationalistic and ethnic boundaries.

Jesus limits the mission field

There are several places within the canonical gospels in which Jesus
allegedly discusses his mission field. Here, only those statements
in which Jesus restricts his mission according to national and ethnic
limitations are presented. The clearest statements in this regard are to be
found in *Matthew*.

The first example is the Matthean account of Jesus commissioning
his 12 disciples to go into the land of Palestine, and to preach his message
to the people there. This passage, quoted below, specifically refutes the
Sunday school interpretation of a universal ministry for Jesus and his
disciples.

These twelve Jesus sent out with the following instructions:
"Go nowhere among the Gentiles, and enter no town of the
Samaritans, but go rather to the lost sheep of the house of
Israel..."[6]

As can be judged from the above citation, Jesus specifically instructed his disciples not to preach his gospel to the gentiles, i.e. non-Jews, but
restricted the teaching to "the lost sheep of the house of Israel". Further,
Jesus also commanded the disciples not to enter the towns of the
Samaritans, i.e., individuals of mixed Assyrian and Israelite descent, who
practiced their own brand of Judaism, complete with their own version of
the Torah. With this restriction, Jesus reportedly limited his mission, and
that of his disciples, not only to "the lost sheep of the house of Israel", but
also to just one segment of those "lost sheep", i.e., those, whose ancestry

was not "polluted" with Assyrian blood.

However, only five chapters later, *Matthew* offers an even more dramatic account of Jesus limiting his mission and ministry to "the lost sheep of the house of Israel". In this account, Jesus refuses to heal an afflicted sufferer, only because the victim's mother is a Canaanite, i.e. a member of the ethnic group of people, who inhabited Palestine before, and then along side of, the Israelites.

> Jesus left that place and went away to the district of Tyre and Sidon. Just then a Canaanite woman from that region came out and started shouting, "Have mercy on me, Lord, Son of David; my daughter is tormented by a demon." But he did not answer her at all. And his disciples came and urged him, saying, "Send her away, for she keeps shouting after us." He answered, "I was sent only to the lost sheep of the house of Israel." But she came and knelt before him, saying, "Lord, help me." He answered, "It is not fair to take the children's food and throw it to the dogs." She said, "Yes, Lord, yet even the dogs eat the crumbs that fall from their master's table." Then Jesus answered her, "Woman, great is your faith! Let it be done for you as you wish." And her daughter was healed instantly.[7]

Once again, the quoted passage runs counter to the image of the universal ministry, which is typically portrayed for young Christians attending Sunday school. However, it is the Sunday school lesson, which indoctrinates the Christian youth, and which later guides the Christian adult in his understanding of the Christian scriptures, regardless of what those scriptures may actually state. If one is taught long enough, often enough, and early enough what something "really" means, then that is what he or she will understand, even when the actual words convey something far different.

In the above case, the alleged words of Jesus convey something far different than a universal ministry. Furthermore, Jesus reportedly refers to non-Jews, i.e. those with descent other than that from the Israelite tribe of Judah[8], with the metaphor of being "dogs". It is only after the extreme statement of faith attributed to the grieving mother that Jesus reportedly condescended and deigned to make a specific exception, and to heal the woman's daughter. However, the use of the metaphor of "dogs" allows

one to interpret a third passage from *Matthew* as being a restriction on the
mission and ministry of Jesus. Again, the words reported in this passage,
quoted below, are attributed by *Matthew* to Jesus.

> Do not give what is holy to dogs; and do not throw your
> pearls before swine, or they will trample them under foot
> and turn and maul you.[9]

It may be noted that the above Matthean passage is corroborated by
an almost identical one found in the 93rd saying recorded in the *Gospel
of Thomas,* discovered in 1945 among the Coptic manuscripts at Nag
Hammadi, Egypt. This passage is quoted below:

> (Jesus said,) "Do not give what is holy to dogs, lest they
> throw them on the dung heap. Do not throw the pearls (to)
> swine, lest they...it (...)"[10]

The presence of this saying in both *Matthew* and *Thomas*, despite its
absence from Luke, clearly demonstrates that this saying was initially
found in *Q*, a book of alleged sayings of Jesus. This book preceded even
the gospel of *Mark*, i.e., the earliest of the four canonical gospels, and
was probably in existence during the middle part of the first century CE.
Q had a probable origin within 20 years of Jesus' actual ministry and at
least 20 years before *Mark*; though this book no longer exists.

Read together, the three passages from Matthew and the one from
Thomas clearly demarcate and limit the mission field of Jesus to "the lost
sheep of the house of Israel". This is in total contrast to the belief of
Christians that the message of Jesus was universal. Further, each of these
passages is attributed to Jesus' ministry prior to his alleged crucifixion.[11]
This point will become increasingly important in what follows, when
apparently contrary evidence surfaces from the Christian scriptures.

Contrary Evidence to the limited Ministry of Jesus

Notwithstanding the convincing nature of the above quoted statements
from the early gospel writers of the Christian tradition, it must be
acknowledged that there are verses within the Christian scriptures
where Jesus is alleged to have confirmed a universal ministry. In what
follows, these passages are presented, and their grave defects regarding
authenticity are illustrated.

The alleged behavior of Jesus

One example, which is frequently cited by Christians in support of the so-called universality of the ministry of Jesus, is the healing of the slave of a Roman centurion in Capernaum, a town at the northern end of the Sea of Galilee (Lake Tiberias). Because this example is so frequently cited, a single exception will be made to the usual format of restricting evidence to the alleged sayings of Jesus as recorded in the Christian scripture. This instance appears both in *Luke* and *Matthew*. However, as the former passage provides the most revealing details surrounding the circumstances of this healing, it is the Lukan account, which is reproduced below.

> After Jesus had finished all his sayings in the hearing of the people, he entered Capernaum. A centurion there had a slave whom he valued highly, and who was ill and close to death. When he heard about Jesus, he sent some Jewish elders to him, asking him to come and heal his slave. When they came to Jesus, they appealed to him earnestly, saying, "He is worthy of having you do this for him, for he loves our people, and it is he who built our synagogue for us." And Jesus went with them, but when he was not far from the house, the centurion sent friends to say to him, "Lord, do not trouble yourself, for I am not worthy to have you come under my roof; therefore I did not presume to come to you. But only speak the word, and let my servant be healed...When Jesus heard this he was amazed at him, and turning to the crowd that followed him, he said, "I tell you, not even in Israel have I found such faith." When those who had been sent returned to the house, they found the slave in good health.[12]

Granted that Jesus healed the slave of a Roman centurion (a minor Roman army officer in command of a contingent of 100 Roman soldiers), the specific text actually tends to confirm that the mission and ministry of Jesus were limited to "the lost sheep of the house of Israel". In that regard, one must note the highly unusual circumstances involved in this example of healing. First, the Roman centurion did not, himself, entreat Jesus to heal the slave. Rather, the centurion sent a delegation of Jewish elders to appeal to Jesus. Second, these Jewish elders were able to make a direct and convincing case for special circumstances, stating that the centurion: loved the Jewish people; and had actually gone to the extremely unusual step of building a synagogue for the Jewish people of Capernaum, no doubt the same synagogue in which Jesus occasionally taught. Third, like the example of the Canaanite woman cited earlier, the Roman centurion completely abases himself before Jesus, by saying, "I am not worthy to have you come under my roof". Fourth, the faith of the Roman centurion, like that of the Canaanite woman, was immense and impressive. For the centurion, it was sufficient that Jesus merely say a word from a distance, to heal the slave.

Given these highly unusual considerations, it must be seen that the example cited is actually the exception that proves the rule. Only in the most exceptional of circumstances, e.g., that of the Canaanite woman of Tyre and Sidon and the Roman centurion of Capernaum, did Jesus reach out beyond "the lost sheep of the house of Israel". However, even then, the outreach of Jesus was in the form of a miraculous healing, not in the form of preaching the message with which he had been entrusted. Nowhere do the Christian scriptures indicate that Jesus taught or preached to either this Canaanite woman or that Roman centurion. The example merely confirms that Jesus did, under very exceptional circumstances, heal outside of the "the house of Israel", but he still did not preach to other than "the lost sheep of the house of Israel".

The alleged Sayings of Jesus

The various books of the *New Testament* record three alleged sayings of Jesus, each of which appears to suggest an international or universal ministry for Jesus and his followers. In what follows, after a brief presentation of the purported setting to which the alleged saying is affixed, each of these three passages is quoted verbatim, and the Biblical passage in question is critiqued.

THE FIRST EXAMPLE. The first passage to be considered is from the gospel according to *Matthew*. The setting is in Galilee, which is in the north of Palestine. The time is some days after the alleged crucifixion and resurrection of Jesus[13], as it would have taken the eleven disciples[14] at least a few days to walk from Jerusalem, where they supposedly were on Easter Sunday, to Galilee.

> Now the eleven disciples went to Galilee, to the mountain
> to which Jesus had directed them. When they saw him, they

worshiped him; but some doubted. And Jesus came and said to them, "All authority in heaven and on earth has been given to me. Go therefore and make disciples of all nations, baptizing them in the name of the Father and of the Son and of the Holy Spirit, and teaching them to obey everything that I have commanded you. And remember, I am with you always, to the end of the age."[15]

On the face of it, the above passage appears to be a pretty strong piece of evidence that Jesus was proclaiming a universal ministry. However, there are grave and serious defects in the above passage. Let us examine these.

First and foremost, it must be noted that *Matthew* portrays the above statement as being from the mouth of the "risen" Jesus, not from the time of Jesus' "earthly ministry". Within the *New Testament* scriptures, the use of the concept of the "risen" Jesus is often a code, which indicates that the so-called "witness" has had a "vision". In that regard, one need only consider the case of the "vision" of Paul (Saul of Tarsus), as he journeyed from Jerusalem to Damascus, in order to persecute the early followers of Jesus.[16] Clearly, a "vision" cannot on its own authority claim the same sort of historical credence as a saying made by Jesus during his earthy life and ministry. As such, some considerable doubt regarding historical accuracy becomes immediately apparent.

Second, the reported wording of Jesus' alleged command to his disciples is in the literary form of a liturgical baptismal formula, which indicates an origin in the nascent Christian churches. With later editing and redacting of *Matthew*, this liturgical baptismal formula appears to have been retrofitted into the mouth of the "risen" Jesus. Thus, a form critical analysis (Formgeshichte) of the purported saying leads to its attribution to early Christian churches, probably at some point not earlier than the second century CE. That this baptismal formula dates to a time much later than Jesus can be seen by the fact that the disciples continued to baptize only in the name of Jesus, eschewing any mention of a so-called trinity in their liturgical baptismal formula.

Peter said to them, "Repent, and be baptized every one of you in the name of Jesus Christ so that your sins may be forgiven; and you will receive the gift of the Holy Spirit."[17]

Third, text criticism indicates that the above passage from Matthew has suffered from various later interpolations. For example, in his fourth century CE quoting of the above passage, Eusebius[18] has it as "baptizing them in my name", instead of "baptizing them in the name of the Father and of the Son and of the Holy Spirit".[19] Thus, as late as the fourth century CE, the above passage from *Matthew* was still undergoing editorial redaction and interpolations by those within the Christian churches! This fact alone is sufficient to render the historical value of the Matthean passage totally without merit.

Fourth, if Jesus actually gave the disciples the command to carry the ministry to "all nations", the historical record clearly indicates that they greatly hesitated in obeying this command, and often flatly disobeyed it. Such disobedience and/or hesitance in obeying the alleged command of the "risen" Jesus to take the message to "all nations" is quickly and easily verified and corroborated by numerous *New Testament* passages, including *Acts* 11:1-18, in which Peter was chastised by members of the early Jerusalem "church"[20] for even eating with gentile Christians. How could these elders of the Jerusalem "church" have confronted Peter about his eating with gentile Christians, if Jesus had actually given the command to go out into "all nations"? In addition, *Galatians* 2:1-9 documents the difficulty Paul had in convincing the early Jerusalem "church" to allow him to take the gospel message to the gentiles. How could Paul have had any such difficulty, if Jesus had actually given a universal commission to his disciples? Remember, Paul was not and had never been a disciple of Jesus, and had never even met Jesus during Jesus' earthly life. Further, *Acts*, which is basically a book of propaganda, allegedly reporting the history of the early churches, but really proselytizing for the deviant Pauline tradition in early Christianity, even goes to the extent to record that Jesus' actual disciples explicitly rejected Paul as being a fellow disciple.

> When he had come to Jerusalem, he attempted to join the disciples; and they were all afraid of him, for they did not believe that he was a disciple.[21]

As such, Paul's argument for taking the gospel message to the gentiles is not in any way the action of a disciple, and this action of his met with frequent reproof from the original "church", which was in Jerusalem.[22] One additional example is worth quoting verbatim.

> Now those who were scattered because of the persecu-
> tion that took place over Stephen traveled as far as
> Phoenicia, Cyprus, and Antioch, and they spoke the word
> to no one except Jews.[23]

In regard to the purported commissioning of the disciples to "(g)o
therefore and make disciples of all nations", just this fourth defect is
sufficient to indicate that "(i)t is improbable that Jesus said this..."[24]

Taken together, the four defects noted above provide convincing
proof that the words narrated in Matthew 28:18-20 cannot be said to
be coming from Jesus, if any semblance of historical accuracy is to be
maintained. As noted by one Christian theologian and Biblical commentator: "(t)hese verses probably reflect the early church's interpretation
more than Jesus' actual words..."[25]

THE SECOND EXAMPLE. The second passage to be considered is
from the gospel of *Luke*. The setting of this passage is Jerusalem, where
Jesus allegedly confronts many of his remaining 11 disciples, as well as
a few other believers. At this time, he reportedly instructs them in the real
meaning, interpretation, or understanding of his earthly sayings and
ministry. The date of this meeting is assumed to have been on Easter
Sunday. With the above context and background in mind, the relevant
passage from *Luke* is quoted here.

> Then he opened their minds to understand the scriptures,
> and he said to them, "Thus is it written, that the Messiah is
> to suffer and to rise from the dead on the third day, and that
> repentance and forgiveness of sins is to be proclaimed in his
> name to all nations, beginning from Jerusalem. You are
> witnesses of these things. And see, I am sending upon you
> what my Father promised; so stay here in the city until you
> have been clothed with power from on high."[26]

Once again, there are grave defects in the passage under consideration. Yet again, the defects undermine any claim for the alleged historical accuracy of the passage. Four of these defects are presented immediately below.

The first defect is that the words attributed to Jesus in the above
passage are attributed to the allegedly "risen" Jesus. The alleged words
and actions of the "risen" Jesus are frequently to be understood as
words heard and actions seen in a "vision". The historical authenticity,

credibility, and reliability of such "vision" testimony have to be approached with a healthy dose of skepticism.

The second flaw is that the actual disciples of Jesus had great hesitations in approaching gentiles, and tended to avoid proselytizing to those who were not of "the house of Israel".[27] In that regard, it is worthwhile to note once again the following passage from *Acts*, which clearly states the position of the early "church" at Jerusalem, whose "membership" included the original disciples of Jesus.

> Now those who were scattered because of the persecution
> that took place over Stephen traveled as far as Phoenicia,
> Cyprus, and Antioch, and they spoke the word to no one
> except Jews.[28]

In addition to the above demerits, the Lukan account is tied to a statement regarding the alleged crucifixion and resurrection of Jesus, which both the apocryphal and canonical gospels suggest may never have happened.[29] This raises some additional concern about the historical veracity of the Lukan passage under consideration.

The fourth defect is that the Lukan narrative is not an absolute endorsement of a universal ministry. Rather, if taken at face value, the Lukan account is at most a conditional endorsement of a universal ministry. Christians, who attempt to use this passage as a commissioning to a universal ministry, too frequently overlook this conditional nature of the statement in *Luke*. However, the passage clearly states that: A) the ministry was to begin in Jerusalem; B) the ministry was to stay centered in Jerusalem until Jesus had sent "upon you what my Father promised" and until "you have been clothed with power from on high"; and C) only after the conditions in "B" were met, was the ministry to expand out from Jerusalem into "all nations".

Quite simply, the mission and ministry were to be restricted to "the lost sheep of the house of Israel", until such time as: "what my Father has promised" has been fulfilled; and "you have been clothed with power from on high". What had Allah promised to send? What was this "power from on high"? Traditional Christian interpretation has been that it was the descent of the Holy Spirit at Pentecost. If that interpretation were accepted, then the condition was met on Pentecost, just 50 days after the events described in the above passage from *Luke*. However, there are good and sufficient reasons to doubt that interpretation, and recorded statements made elsewhere in the *New Testament* scriptures dramatically refute that interpretation.

THE THIRD EXAMPLE. The third example, in which it is alleged that Jesus authorized a universal mission and ministry, is found in the book of *Acts*. The setting is the Mount of Olives, which is east of Jerusalem, and just across the Kidron Valley from the walls of Jerusalem. The time is 40 days after Easter Sunday.

> "While staying with them, he ordered them not to leave Jerusalem, but to wait there for the promise of the Father. "This," he said, "is what you have heard from me; for John baptized with water, but you will be baptized with the Holy Spirit not many days from now...But you will receive power when the Holy Spirit has come upon you; and you will be my witnesses in Jerusalem, in all Judea and Samaria, and to the ends of the earth." When he had said this, as they were watching, he was lifted up, and a cloud took him out of their sight.[30]

The first two defects in this passage have been previously encountered in analyzing the previous Matthean and Lukan narratives. First, the alleged commissioning to a universal mission and ministry is purported to be given by the "risen" Jesus, not by the earthly Jesus. As previously noted, the "risen" Jesus is frequently a metaphor for having received a "vision", in which Jesus was allegedly seen and heard. Second, the early disciples of Jesus continually exercised great hesitation in preaching, if not actual refusal to preach, the gospel message of Jesus to other than those of "the house of Israel."[31]

The third defect in utilizing the above passage from Acts to support a universal ministry for Jesus is the same as that previously noted as the fourth defect undermining the Lukan narrative, i.e. the commissioning to a universal ministry is conditional, not absolute. Jesus specifically ordered his disciples to wait in Jerusalem, i.e. to confine their ministry to the "house of Israel", until "the promise of the Father" had been fulfilled. Only after Allah had fulfilled this promise, which is never specifically identified in the above passage, were the followers of Jesus to take the gospel message to "the ends of the earth". Until Allah's promise had been fulfilled, the followers of Jesus were to restrict their mission and ministry to Jerusalem, i.e. to "the house of Israel". As was the case with the Lukan narrative previously quoted, the traditional Christian interpretation of this "promise of the Father" is that it refers to the coming of the Holy Spirit. This traditional Christian interpretation finds some superficial support in the above passage from Acts, in that the conditional clause concerning the "promise of the Father" is immediately followed by a discussion of the Holy Spirit and a prediction of the Pentecost (the day the disciples were supposedly filled with the Holy Spirit, who allegedly descended on them), which reportedly followed 10 days later. However, as will be seen below, this interpretation of the conditional nature of the universal commissioning represents a serious distortion of the actual Biblical message.

The Conditional Commissioning:
The Advocate and the Holy Spirit

It is an unfortunate fact that people of understanding often restrict their thinking only to what they have been taught to understand, rather than comprehending the real meaning of the words in front of them. This is evident among Christians when one considers their understanding of many key Biblical passages. They understand only what they have been taught to understand in Sunday school, decade after decade, with additional Sunday morning sermons further setting limits on the subject. In other words, their understanding of the *Bible* is not so much based upon what the *Bible* actually says, but upon what they have been taught that the *Bible* says. This is especially the case when considering the Biblical portrayal of the Advocate, Holy Spirit, and Spirit of Truth. The average Christian's understanding of the Holy Spirit is vague and fuzzy, often consisting of no more than a rote recital that the Holy Spirit is the third person of the trinity. However, the average Christian is quite clear, because he/she has been indoctrinated and programmed by the church to believe, that the Holy Spirit first entered the world of man at Pentecost, i.e., 50 days after Easter Sunday. Given this understanding, it is easy to see how the average Christian can maintain that the conditional clause in the alleged commissioning to a universal ministry (as reported both in *Luke* and in *Acts*) was fulfilled at Pentecost by the descent of the Holy Spirit. In support of that position, Christians often refer to the reported words of Jesus, as recorded in a passage from the gospel of *John*, consisting of only two verses, which need to be understood in the context provided by the five verses that follow them. The above referenced verses are given below for ready reckoning, with the five additional verses being placed in italics. This gives a clear picture as to what is typically quoted and what is left out.

> I have said these things to you while I am still with you. But the Advocate, the Holy Spirit, whom the Father will send in my name, will teach you everything, and remind you of all that I have said to you. Peace I leave with you; my peace I give to you. I do not give to you as the world gives. Do not let your hearts be troubled, and do not let them be afraid. You heard me say to you, "I am going away, and I am coming to you." If you loved me, you would rejoice that I am going to the Father, because the Father is greater than I. And now I have told you this before it occurs, so that when it does occur, you may believe. I will no longer talk much with you, for the ruler of this world is coming. He has no power over me; but I do as the Father has commanded me, so that the world may know that I love the Father. Rise, let us be on our way.[32]

In a second passage, i.e., *John* 16:7, it is definitively stated that the Advocate cannot come into the world, until Jesus has left the world. This establishes a clear temporal sequence in which Jesus precedes the Advocate, and in which the roles of Jesus and the Advocate are not allowed to overlap chronologically.

> Nevertheless I tell you the truth: it is to your advantage that I go away, for if I do not go away, the Advocate will not come to you; but if I go, I will send him to you.[33]

Did the Holy Spirit enter the world of man only after the ascension of Jesus? Was it necessary that Jesus should leave, in order that the Holy Spirit would first come? Was Jesus speaking of the Holy Spirit when he reportedly uttered, according to the Lukan narrative quoted previously, "I am sending upon you what my Father promised"? Was it the Holy Spirit who would, according to the same Lukan narrative, clothe mankind "with power from on high?" Was the Holy Spirit "the promise of the Father" noted in the quoted passage from *Acts*? The Biblically based answer to all of the above questions is "no". The *Bible* records numerous examples of the Holy Spirit working within the world of man far before the reported ascension of Jesus.

More than one Biblical passage refers to the Holy Spirit being present in the world during the time of King David, peace be upon him, during the 11th and 10th centuries BCE, and as being the source of David's inspiration and revelation.[34] Likewise, it was the Holy Spirit, who reportedly was the source of revelation to Isaiah.[35] It was the Holy Spirit, who allegedly enlightened the entire nation of Israel prior to Isaiah's prophecies in *Old Testament* times.[36] It was the Holy Spirit, who reportedly imparted revelation to Simeon of Jerusalem during the first centuries BCE and CE.[37] It was the Holy Spirit, who gave revelation to John the Baptist, peace be upon him.[38] It was the Holy Spirit, who gave revelation to Elizabeth, the mother of John the Baptist.[39] It was the Holy Spirit, who gave revelation to Zechariah, the father of John the Baptist.[40] It was the Holy Spirit, who descended upon Mary, the mother of Jesus.[41] It was the Holy Spirit, who infused Jesus with inspiration and revelation.[42] Clearly, the Holy Spirit was already at work in the world of mankind, fulfilling its role of giving revelation and inspiration, far before and many times before the ascension of Jesus!

So how could it be the Holy Spirit upon whom the disciples must wait before undertaking a universal ministry? The Holy Spirit was already present. In fact, Jesus, had already given the gift of the Holy Spirit as a source of inspiration and revelation to the disciples via the power given to him by Allah, prior to the ascension of Jesus.[43] Perhaps the clearest Biblical statements that the disciples had already received the Holy Spirit are to be found in *John* and in *Acts*, with both passages quoted below.

> When he had said this, he breathed on them and said to them, "Receive the Holy Spirit..."[44]

> In the first book, Theophilus, I wrote about all that Jesus did and taught from the beginning until the day when he was taken up to heaven, after giving instructions through the Holy Spirit to the apostles whom he had chosen.[45]

Quite obviously, the disciples could not be waiting for the gift of something that they had already been given!

(A brief digression is in order at this point. In the above referenced and quoted verses of the *Bible*, the consistent presentation of the Holy Spirit is as the one who brings inspiration and revelation from Allah to the chosen one of Allah, whether that be David, Isaiah, the children of Israel, Simeon of Jerusalem, Elizabeth, Zechariah, John the Baptist, Mary, Jesus, or the disciples of Jesus. In that regard, it is worth noting that the traditional Islamic understanding of the term "Holy Spirit" is that it refers to the angel Gabriel, who is the intermediary between Allah and His prophets and messengers, the one who conveys the revelation of Allah to those men who declare that revelation to others.[46])

As noted above, the *Bible* gives numerous statements that the Holy Spirit was present and operating in the world as a source of inspiration and revelation far before the ascension of Jesus. Further, the disciples of Jesus had already received the gift of the Holy Spirit prior to the ascension of Jesus. So, what was it, for which the disciples must wait, before expanding the ministry of Jesus outside the confines of "the house of Israel"? *Luke* 24:49 indicates that it was "what my father promised" and that which was promised would result in Jesus' followers being "clothed with power from on high". *Acts* 1:4 refers to the "promise of the Father", and *Acts* 1:8 refers to the receipt of "power when the Holy Spirit has come upon you". Both passages refer to something coming, which has been promised by Allah. Clearly, that is not the Holy Spirit, because the Holy Spirit was already present and had already been received by the disciples. Both passages link that promised "something" with the receipt of power, one of which links that power with something to do with the Holy Spirit, i.e., with the receipt of revelation.

Having arrived at this point in the analysis, one needs now to turn to the passages previously quoted from *John* 14:25-31 and 16:7.

> But the Advocate, the Holy Spirit, whom the Father will send in my name, will teach you everything, and remind you of all that I have said to you...if I do not go away, the Advocate will not come to you; but if I go, I will send him to you.[47]

Since it has already been shown that the Holy Spirit was already present and active in the world, i.e. had already been sent by Allah, prior to the time Jesus reportedly spoke the above quoted words, the only way the above verses make conceptual sense is to interpret the "Advocate" and the "Holy Spirit" are two different entities.

So, who is the "Advocate"? The clues to the identity of the Advocate are presented in the passage of *John* 14:25-31, in the verses originally italicized when quoted previously. "And now I have told you this before it occurs, so that when it does occur, you may believe." This simply cannot be a reference to Pentecost. Why would Jesus need to say this for the disciples to believe post Pentecost in the Holy Spirit, when they had just reportedly been filled with the Holy Spirit at Pentecost? The infusion of the Holy Spirit should be an event beyond the recipient being in any doubt about it! The recipient of the Holy Spirit would not need to reflect back on the words of Jesus in order to believe. The reported words of Jesus cannot refer to the Holy Spirit, whom the disciples have already received, and in whom they already believe. Therefore, the words must be applied to the Advocate. The followers of Jesus may not readily believe the Advocate, so Jesus specifically reports his coming, in order that when the appearance of the Advocate "does occur, you may believe". Does the passage from *John* provide any other clues as to the identity of the Advocate? Yes, it does. "I will no longer talk much with you, for the ruler of this world is coming." The Advocate is a coming, temporal "ruler of this world".

To summarize, the "promise of the Father" is the Advocate. The Advocate will be inspired by and receive revelation from the Holy Spirit, and that revelation will clothe those who accept it with "power from on high". Unfortunately, the followers of Jesus may have trouble in recognizing the Advocate, and in believing in the revelation received by the Advocate. Therefore, Jesus must warn his followers about the coming of this Advocate, who will also be "the ruler of this world". While Muslim readers will probably be quick to identify the only person who can possibly fit this identification, it is now gently suggested to Christian readers that the only person after Jesus who can even vaguely fit this identification is Prophet Muhammad. In that regard, for the benefit of Christian readers, it may be noted that: the passage in *John* 14 states that the Advocate is the one "whom the Father will send in my name"; and the *Qur'an* (the revelation received by Muhammad) repeatedly refers to Jesus and to the revelation sent to him.[48]

> Say ye: "We believe in Allah, and the revelation given to us,
> and to Abraham, Isma'il, Isaac, Jacob, and the tribes, and
> that given to Moses and Jesus, and that given to (all)
> prophets from their Lord: we make no difference between
> one and another of them: and we bow to Allah (in Islam)"[49]

> Those messengers We endowed with gifts, some above others: to one of them Allah spoke; others He raised to degrees (of honor); to Jesus, the son of Mary, We gave clear (signs), and strengthened him with the Holy Spirit. If Allah had so willed, succeeding generations would not have fought among each other, after clear (signs) had come to them, but they (chose) to wrangle, some believing and others rejecting. If Allah had so willed, they would not have fought each other; but Allah fulfilleth His plans.[50]

Given the above understanding, one can readily see that the revelation, mission, and ministry of Jesus were to stay confined to "the house of Israel", until the coming of Prophet Muhammad, i.e., the Advocate, and his undoubted international and universal ministry!

A Problem of Chronology

There is yet one other defect relating to the assumption of the universal ministry of Jesus. *Luke* 24:50 indicates that the ascension of Jesus was on Easter Sunday, which would indicate that Jesus was not present to have made the speeches recorded in *Matthew* 28:16-20 (the first example above) and *Acts* 1:7-8 (the third example above) both of which were previously quoted verbatim. However, as the author of *Luke* is held to have also been the author of *Acts*, one is immediately struck by a major discrepancy and inconsistency. In *Luke*, the ascension is said to have been on Easter Sunday.[51] However, in *Acts*, the very same writer maintains that the ascension was 40 days after Easter Sunday.[52] Thus, if the Lukan narrative were accepted, the passages from *Matthew* and from *Acts* must be considered baseless and faulty. However, if the passages from *Matthew* and *Acts* were accepted, the Lukan narrative would have to be rejected.

Conclusions

An in depth analysis of the relevant Biblical passages has revealed that the traditional Christian interpretation of the mission and ministry of Jesus is erroneous. Rather than having had a ministry to both Jews and gentiles, Jesus' ministry was limited to "the house of Israel". Further, Jesus appears to have given his disciples explicit instructions that the ministry and revelation of Jesus and his followers were to remain limited

and circumscribed until the arrival of the international and universal
ministry of Prophet Muhammad, i.e., the Advocate. In short, the actual
Biblical portrayal of the scope of the ministry of Jesus is highly
consistent with the traditional Islamic interpretation found in the *Qur'an*.

> Behold! the angels said: "O Mary! Allah giveth thee glad
> tidings of a word from Him: his name will be Christ
> Jesus...And Allah will teach him the book and wisdom, the
> law and the gospel, and (appoint him) a messenger to the
> children of Israel...[53]

Chapter 7

One Size Fits All
– The Matthean Use of Prophecy

One who has done any shopping in America would certainly have come across articles of apparel bearing the tag "one size fits all". The purchaser would have learned the hard way that "one size fits all" translates into either: that the article in question is so baggy and voluminous that it could serve as a tent, and can hardly be said to "fit" the shorter and/or leaner members of the populace; or that the clothing has to be stretched beyond the endurance of the fabric, in order to cover the taller and/or more corpulent participants of society. Quite simply, one size doesn't and cannot fit all, and this simile leads us to the topic of this chapter viz., the use of so-called prophecy in the canonical gospel of *Matthew*.

(However, at this point in the discussion, a brief digression is needed. The etymology of the word "prophecy" is from the Greek "prophetes", which originates from the Greek "phemi", which means "to say" and "in place of".[1] Likewise, the Hebrew word "Nabi", which is typically translated as "prophet", is derived from the Akkadian language, an ancient Semitic language related to both Hebrew and Arabic, and which means "to call" or "to announce".[2] As such, the etymology of the word "prophecy" leads to an understanding that "prophecy" means "to speak for". Within a religious context, "prophecy" is thus understood to mean "to speak for Allah".[3] Of note, "prophecy" does not necessarily mean to foretell the future, although that might occur in the process of "speaking for Allah". However, within the confines of the present narration, the author's use of the word "prophecy" in no way implies that the author necessarily believes "prophecy" to be a statement "spoken for Allah". Rather, the author's use of the term "prophecy" should be understood to mean that the author of *Matthew* maintained or implied that the statement in question was a prophecy, and that it was prophecy that foretold the events surrounding the life and ministry of Jesus, peace be upon him.[4] Bearing this view in mind, we can now proceed with the narration.)

More than any other book of the *New Testament,* the gospel of *Matthew* attempts to demonstrate that the life and ministry of Jesus were the fulfillment of *Old Testament* prophecy. The reader of *Matthew* is barraged by phrases such as: "(a)ll this took place to fulfill what had been spoken"[5]; "for so it had been written by the prophet"[6]; "(t)his was to fulfill what had been spoken by the Lord through the prophet"[7]; "(t)hen was fulfilled what had been spoken through the prophet Jeremiah"[8]; "so that what had been spoken through the prophets might be fulfilled"[9]; "(t)his is the one of whom the prophet Isaiah spoke when he said"[10]; etc. Given a superficial / cursory reading, this looks pretty convincing. Time and again, the life and ministry of Jesus, at least as they are presented by *Matthew,* conform to *Old Testament* prophecy, and it appears that *Matthew* builds a pretty strong case for its portrayal of Jesus. However, as will be seen in what follows, the use of prophecy in *Matthew* is much like the clothing label/tag, which announces/proclaims that "one size fits all".

An introduction to the Gospel of *Matthew*

The gospel of *Matthew* was probably the second of the four canonical gospels to be compiled, with Biblical scholars typically placing the origin of Matthew sometime between 80 and 90 CE.[11] It appears to have been compiled in Syria[12], probably in the vicinity of Antioch, and was written in Greek[13] by a person whose *Old Testament* was the Greek *Septuagint,* as opposed to a Hebrew text of the *Old Testament.*[14] This latter consideration, which is squarely based on an analysis of the *Old Testament* passages quoted in *Matthew,* as well as on the obvious reliance of *Matthew* on the Greek gospel of *Mark*[15], contraindicates that the gospel was written by a Palestinian[16] disciple of Jesus, whether or not he was called *Matthew*[17], because he would then not ·be using the Greek *Septuagint.* Rather, such a person would have used the Hebrew manuscripts and texts of Jewish scripture.

As stated earlier, the gospel of *Matthew* was compiled in a cut-and-paste manner and not written as a fresh literary work. In that regard, the sources used by the compiler of *Matthew* included at least two earlier, written sources: 1) the gospel of *Mark* or an earlier proto-Mark; and 2) a collection of reported sayings of Jesus, which can be termed *Q,* which stands for the German word "*Quelle*", meaning "source".

In addition, to these two written sources, the compiler of *Matthew* utilized material, which was not included in the other canonical gospels. This could have been written or oral, may or may not have been confined to a single source, and may or may not have originated with the compiler of *Matthew*. For the sake of convenience, this material can be referred to as *M*.[18]

Among the *M* material of *Matthew*, one finds a frequent use of *Old Testament* prophecy, which purportedly establishes that the *Old Testament* accurately foretold the life and ministry of Jesus as they are represented in *Matthew*. This material is typically presented in such a way as to offer "authoritative" proof that Jesus was exactly what the early Christian church, or at least that portion of it represented by *Matthew*, was saying Jesus was. It has been argued that this type of literary endeavor, i.e. constructing collections of *Old Testament* prophecy, which supposedly applied to Jesus, was among the earliest types of religious writing engaged in by the early Christians. Such collections would then have been used as the basis of preaching and evangelizing by the early Christian missionaries and ministers. At this time, it cannot be determined if the compiler of *Matthew* utilized such a hypothetical collection as part of his *M* source, or if he simply constructed his own list of *Old Testament* prophecies.[19]

The Matthean use of Prophecy

At least 19 times, *Matthew* directly and unequivocally purports to show the fulfillment of *Old Testament* prophecy. Typically, these instances refer specifically to alleged events in the life of Jesus, and are presented as editorial comments. However, occasionally these instances are seen in words, which the compiler of *Matthew* has placed into the mouth of Jesus, and occasionally these instances refer to John the Baptist, peace be upon him, or to some other collateral aspect of the life of Jesus. In addition, there is at least one "hidden" statement of fulfilled prophecy to be found in Matthew. In what follows, each one of these acts of "prophetic fulfillment" is examined individually. The end result of that examination will show that the compiler of *Matthew*: frequently did not understand *Old Testament* prophecy, often because he was dependent upon the Greek *Septuagint;* has on a number of occasions misquoted prophecy; and frequently quoted prophecy out of context. Further, he probably even altered at least one event in Jesus' life, with rather disastrous and humorous consequences, to achieve a "prophetic fulfillment". It can therefore be assumed that he may have fabricated other events in the life of Jesus, to get a "fit" with some particular prophecy. However, these are total assumptions and one should not take the author's word as proof of these allegations. In lieu of this, each "prophetic fulfillment" should be examined, and compared with the original *Old Testament* prophecy.

Case 1: The Son of David

The gospel of *Matthew* begins with an alleged genealogy of Jesus, which is supposed to emphasize the Davidic descent of Jesus. In that regard, the author traces Jesus through Joseph, the husband of Mary, back to King David, peace be upon him. The problem is that *Matthew* acknowledges the fact that Jesus was the result of a virgin birth, thus negating the lineage through Joseph. So, how does this genealogy demonstrate prophetic fulfillment that Jesus, as the Messiah, was of the lineage of David? The answer is that the prophetic fulfillment is hidden in a numerological code, which would have been quite easy to break for anyone who knew Hebrew in the first century CE, but which eludes most modern readers.

> So all the generations from Abraham to David are fourteen generations; and from David to the deportation to Babylon, fourteen generations; and from the deportation to Babylon to the Messiah, fourteen generations.[20]

Why waste time and space by repetitiously emphasizing three sets, each of which is comprised of 14 generations? The answer lies in ancient Hebrew numerology, which maintained that each letter in the Hebrew alphabet had a certain numerical weight. By converting the letters of a word into the sum of their associated numbers, and then finding a different word whose letters added up to the same sum, one could supposedly find the "real", the "hidden", or the numerological meaning, which rested behind the original cover word. As noted previously, this entire system of numerology relied on the numerical weight assigned to each letter in the Hebrew alphabet. Numbers could mean words, and words could mean numbers, which had to be deciphered into new words. *Matthew* is using the first option in the passage quoted above, and is using a number to "reveal" the hidden truth of Jesus' Davidic descent. In this case the number is 14.

Bearing in mind that Hebrew did not have vowels, and using English letters in place of the original Hebrew letters, David can be written as "DVD". The Hebrew letter corresponding to "D", i.e. Daleth, had a numerical weight of four, because it was the fourth letter in the Hebrew alphabet. The Hebrew letter corresponding to "V", i.e. Waw, had a numerical weight of six, because it was the sixth letter in the Hebrew alphabet. In short, "DVD" equals 14, i.e. 14 = 4 + 6 + 4, and 4 + 6 + 4 = David. Therefore, since we have the "magic" number 14 emphasized three times in the reported genealogy, Jesus is of Davidic descent, regardless of the fact that the genealogy lists Joseph as being the father of someone born of a virgin. This is *Matthew*'s hidden example of prophetic fulfillment.

However, one size doesn't fit all! To get one size to fit all, one either has to cut the fabric so voluminously that it becomes totally shapeless and formless, or one has to stretch the fabric past the point of endurance. In the above example, *Matthew* has *stretched the fabric to the point of tearing*. This is easily illustrated by counting the generations listed in *Matthew*'s three sets. The first set consisted of the generations from Abraham to David, the second from David to the deportation to Babylon, and the third from the deportation to Jesus. Table 1, which is presented immediately below, provides a numerical count of the generations in each of these three sets.

Table 1: Generations in the three sets of *Matthew* 1:2-16

	Set 1	Set 2	Set 3
01	Abraham	Solomon	Salathiel
02	Isaac	Rehoboam	Zerubbabel
03	Jacob	Abijah	Abiud
04	Judah	Asaph	Eliakim
05	Perez	Jehoshaphat	Azor
06	Hezron	Joram	Zadok
07	Aram	Uzziah	Achim
08	Aminadab	Jotham	Eliud
09	Nahshon	Ahaz	Eleazar
10	Salmon	Hezekiah	Matthan
11	Boaz	Manasseh	Jacob
12	Obed	Amos	Joseph
13	Jesse	Josiah	Jesus
14	David	Jechoniah (deportation)	

In this case, the fabric has been stretched to the point where it has torn, leaving a gaping hole. That hole is the missing 14th generation in the third set. Now some might want to argue that *Matthew* said 14 generations from "the deportation to Babylon to the Messiah", and so Jechoniah should be counted as the 14th generation in the second set, and as the first generation in the third set, resulting then in 14 generations in the third set. However, if that were the case, then David should be counted as both the 14th generation in the first set and as the first generation in the second set, resulting in 15 generations in the second set.

There is yet another problem in the above genealogy, namely in the second set of 14 names. The listing of this part of the genealogy appears to have been taken from *I Chronicles,* which is one of the books of the *Old Testament.* However, *Matthew* has left out four generations reported in the account of *I Chronicles.* The genealogy should read Joram, then Ahaziah (Uzziah), then Joash, then Amaziah, then Azariah, and then Jotham.[21] This adds three more generations. In addition, the name of Jehoiakim should be added between that of Josiah and Jechoniah.[22] This adds yet a fourth generation. As such, the second set should add up to 18 generations, not 14. However, Matthew conveniently left out four generations to make the numerology work. In short, no matter how one tries to sew the fabric back together, the hole only rips a little farther. In the words of one Biblical commentator:

> (The compiler of Matthew) seems to have been more interested in ideas than in facts; and sometimes to have been prepared to arrange the facts so as to fit the ideas.[23]

The above example has been listed as much for fun as for any other reason, in that the statement of prophetic fulfillment is "hidden" in the practice of Jewish numerology, and not explicitly stated in the text of *Matthew.* (The whole issue of what the compiler of *Matthew* is doing in practicing numerology, which is a most questionable practice for an evangelist, is outside the scope of the present article.) However, explicit statements of alleged prophetic fulfillment are made by *Matthew* in the following examples.

Case 2: Emmanuel, Son of the "Virgin"

Following the presentation of the alleged genealogy of Jesus, the compiler of Matthew immediately presents the story of Jesus' birth from the Virgin Mary. This begins with a swift report of Mary's pregnancy, and is then followed by a brief narrative of a dream given to Joseph, in which he is told not to divorce Mary for supposed infidelity, and in which Joseph is given an explanation of the true nature of Mary's pregnancy. *Matthew* then claims that all of the above was direct prophetic fulfillment.

> All this took place to fulfill what had been spoken by the Lord through the prophet: "Look, the virgin shall conceive and bear a son, and they shall name him Emmanuel," which means, "God is with us." [24]

In claiming prophetic fulfillment, *Matthew* quotes from the *Old Testament* book of Isaiah. In doing so, the compiler used the Greek *Septuagint* translation of the original Hebrew text of *Isaiah*, and never checked his quotation against the original Hebrew. Clearly, this was not the action of an Aramaic-speaking, Palestinian disciple of Jesus. Rather, this was the action of someone who was fully Hellenized, and for whom Greek was the language of religious discourse, not Hebrew. If the compiler of *Matthew* had only bothered to check the Hebrew original of Isaiah, he would have instantly seen that his prophecy did not fit. Following is the relevant passage from *Isaiah*.

> Therefore the Lord himself will give you a sign. Look, the young woman is with child and shall bear a son, and shall name him Emmanuel.[25]

The difference in the spelling of the name "Emmanuel" is of no consequence, as this is merely a matter of transliteration. However, there is a world of difference between "the virgin shall conceive and bear a son" and "the young woman is with child and shall bear a son". The former directly posits a virgin birth, while the latter makes absolutely no mention of a virgin birth. This discrepancy is directly attributable to the compiler of *Matthew* using the Greek *Septuagint*, instead of using the Hebrew scriptures. In the Hebrew, the relevant word is "almah", which can be translated into English as "young woman" or "woman of ill repute". Typically, when the *Old Testament* scriptures use the word "almah", it is clear by context, that the word signifies "woman of ill repute", e.g., a harlot or prostitute. When the Hebrew scriptures were translated into Greek, the translators of the *Septuagint* translated "almah" into the Greek "parthenos", which means either "young woman" or "virgin". The compiler of *Matthew*, in his haste to find a prophetic fulfillment in the virgin birth, poured through the Greek translation of the *Old Testament* scriptures, found a "parthenos" with child, and immediately assumed that "parthenos" meant "virgin", and that the passage from Isaiah was a prophecy of Jesus' virgin birth. If he had only checked the Hebrew original, he would have immediately seen that such an interpretation of *Isaiah* was impossible.

However, the lack of any mention of a virgin in the original of *Isaiah* 7:14 is only one of two problems encountered in attempting to show that Jesus' virgin birth was prophetic fulfillment. The other problem is obvious. Jesus' name was "Jesus". ("Jesus" is actually the Greek form of the Hebrew "Yeshua" or Joshua, which means "God will save", where "God" is translated from the Hebrew "Yahweh".) His name was not "Emmanuel" ("God is with us", where "God" is translated from the Hebrew word "El"), which is what his name would have had to have been if Jesus' birth were to be seen as the prophetic fulfillment of *Isaiah* 7:14. Ironically, immediately after quoting the *Septuagint* version of *Isaiah* 7:14, *Matthew* 1:25 explicitly states that the infant was called Jesus.

It may be noted that the only use of the word "Emmanuel" in the entire *Bible* is in the passage from *Matthew* 1:23 quoted above, and "Immanuel" appears only twice in the entire *Bible*, i.e., *Isaiah* 7:14 and 8:8.[26] Attempts to resurrect the prophetic fulfillment of *Isaiah* 7:14 in the virgin birth of Jesus by claiming that Jesus was "God with us" continue to distort *Isaiah* 7:14, where it clearly states that the person's name is Immanuel, not that the person was Immanuel, but that his name was Immanuel. So, what has the compiler of *Matthew* done here? It is as though he took a prophecy that said "Jim will catch the ball", saw Bob catching a ball, and claimed that Bob's catch was prophetic fulfillment, even though the two individuals had different names. Once again, the fabric has been stretched to the point of tearing, and a gaping hole has been left in its wake.

Case 3: The Bethlehem Birth Site

Matthew states that Jesus was born in Bethlehem[27], and sees this as prophetic fulfillment.

> ...so it has been written by the prophet: "And you, Bethlehem, in the land of Judah, are by no means least among the rulers of Judah; for from you shall come a ruler who is to shepherd my people Israel."[28]

The prophecy in question is a loose paraphrase from the Old Testament book of Micah, which is quoted in full below.

> But you, O Bethlehem of Ephrathah, who are one of the little clans of Judah, from you shall come forth for me one who is to rule in Israel, whose origin is from of old, from ancient days. Therefore he shall give them up until the time when she who is in labor has brought forth; then the rest of his kindred shall return to the people of Israel. And he shall stand and feed his flock in the strength of the Lord, in the majesty of the name of the Lord his God. And they shall live secure, for now he shall be great to the ends of the earth; and he shall be the one of peace.[29]

Apart from the fact that Jesus never established his "rule in Israel", the prophecy is not a bad fit. However, the fabric has been cut so large, that it covers practically anyone who was ever born in Bethlehem. There is nothing in the prophecy to distinguish this person from Bethlehem from that person from Bethlehem, except that the person in question is "to rule in Israel", that his "origin is from of old", that he will "feed his flock in the strength of the Lord", that those living under him will "live secure", that he will be "great to the ends of the earth", and that he will be the "one of peace". As noted before, Jesus never established any rule in Israel. The other points can be debated regarding their meaning, and will not be addressed here.

However, there is a prior question. Was Jesus actually born in Bethlehem? Both *Matthew* and *Luke* record that Jesus was born in Bethlehem.[30] *Mark* makes no mention of the birth of Jesus, and *John* appears to deny that Jesus came from Bethlehem.[31] Except for the second chapters of *Matthew* and *Luke*, in which the birth of Jesus is recounted, and besides its one-time mention in *John*, which appears to deny that Jesus came from Bethlehem, nowhere else in the entire *New Testament*[32] is there a mention of Bethlehem.. If it weren't for the apparently independent confirmation from *Luke*, one would be tempted to posit that the compiler of *Matthew* fabricated a Bethlehem birth site in order to meet his own understanding of prophetic fulfillment.

Case 4: Out of Egypt

Following the birth of Jesus in Bethlehem, *Matthew* maintains that astrologers came from the East looking for Jesus. In their quest, they inquired at the court of King Herod, who was quite jealous of his throne. Having determined that a Messiah would be born in Bethlehem (see case 3), Herod reportedly had every two-year-old and younger child in Bethlehem slaughtered/put to death. However, Jesus escaped this fate, because Joseph had been warned of this in a dream, and so he took Mary and Jesus to Egypt, where they reportedly remained until the death of Herod. Soon thereafter, they returned to Palestine.[33]

Matthew maintains that the return of Jesus to Palestine, as a young child, was a fulfillment of a prophecy.

> This was to fulfill what had been spoken by the Lord through the prophet, "Out of Egypt I have called my son."[34]

Matthew is here quoting from *Hosea*, and apparently from the Hebrew text.[35] However, he appears to be quoting out of context, and thus distorting the prophecy beyond semblance/all recognition. The relevant passage from Hosea is presented below.

> When Israel was a child, I loved him, and out of Egypt I called my son. The more I called them, the more they went from me; they kept sacrificing to the Baals, and offering incense to idols. Yet it was I who taught Ephraim to walk, I took them up in my arms; but they did not know that I healed them. I led them with cords of human kindness, with bands of love. I was to them like those who lift infants to their cheeks. I bent down to them and fed them. They shall return to the land of Egypt, and Assyria shall be their king, because they have refused to return to me...They shall go after the Lord who roars like a lion; when he roars, his children shall come trembling from the west. They shall come trembling like birds from Egypt, and like doves from the land of Assyria; and I will return them to their homes, says the Lord.[36]

Its clear from the above passage of the *Old Testament* book of *Hosea* that it has nothing to do with Messianic prophecy. The "son" is clearly identified as being the Israelite people, when they were led out of captivity in Egypt. The passage then goes on to talk about the backsliding and idolatry of Ephraim, one of the Israelite sub-tribes, which is often identified with the whole of the 10 tribes of the northern Kingdom of

Israel. The passage further notes the deportation of the ten northern tribes to Assyria, at the time of the fall of the northern Kingdom of Israel[37], and goes on to conclude that the 10 northern tribes will return to Palestine some day, and will again be the "children" of Allah – a prophecy that was never fulfilled.[38]

Quite obviously, the few words quoted by *Matthew* from *Hosea* were ruthlessly ripped out of context, in order to fabricate a Messianic prophecy, which could then be fulfilled in the life of Jesus. However, it is possible that even this analysis of the Matthean use of prophecy in this instance is being overly generous. Nowhere else in the entire *New Testament* is there any confirmation that Jesus spent any time in Egypt.[39] It almost appears that *Matthew* first fabricated a Messianic prophecy by ripping words from *Hosea* out of context, and then fabricated an event in the life of Jesus to conform to that fabricated prophecy.

Why would *Matthew* fabricate a prophecy, and then fabricate a life event to meet that prophecy? The answer is to create a parallel between the life of Jesus and the life of Moses, peace be upon him. Just as Moses led the Israelites out of Egypt, so the infant Jesus came out of Egypt. In this manner, Jesus could be seen as the prophet like Moses, as predicted in *Deuteronomy*, a book erroneously attributed to the authorship of Moses.

> The Lord your God will raise up for you a prophet like me from among your own people; you shall heed such a prophet. This is what you requested of the Lord your God at Horeb on the day of the assembly when you said: "If I hear the voice of the Lord my God any more, or ever again see this great fire, I will die." Then the Lord replied to me: "They are right in what they have said. I will raise up for them a prophet like you from among their own people. I will put my words in the mouth of the prophet, who shall speak to them everything that I command. Any-one who does not heed the words that the prophet shall speak in my name, I myself will hold accountable.[40]

It would appear that here is another "hidden prophetic fulfillment", to which *Matthew* is alluding, but which is never directly mentioned.

Be that as it may, what is clear is that the "prophetic fulfillment" of "(o)ut of Egypt I have called my son" is totally incorrect and is only based on a past event in Israelite history, which had nothing to do with Messianic prophecy. Further, there is no independent confirmation that Jesus was ever in Egypt.

Case 5: Rachel's Weeping

While presenting the background to case #4, Matthew maintains that King Herod had all the children in the age group of two or younger killed in Bethlehem, and Matthew presents this act as being a prophetic fulfillment.

> When Herod saw that he had been tricked by the wise men, he was infuriated, and he sent and killed all the children in and around Bethlehem who were two years old or under, according to the time that he had learned from the wise men. Then was fulfilled what had been spoken through the prophet Jeremiah: "A voice was heard in Ramah, wailing and loud lamentation, Rachel weeping for her children; she refused to be consoled, because they are no more."[41]

Once again, *Matthew* has ripped a statement completely out of context. The relevant *Old Testament* passage from the book of *Jeremiah* is quoted immediately below.

> Thus says the Lord: a voice is heard in Ramah, lamentation and bitter weeping. Rachel is weeping for her children; she refuses to be comforted for her children, because they are no more. Thus says the Lord: keep your voice from weeping, and your eyes from tears; for there is a reward for your work, says the Lord: they shall come back from the land of the enemy; there is hope for your future, says the Lord: your children shall come back to their own country. Indeed I heard Ephraim pleading: "You disciplined me, and I took the discipline; I was like a calf untrained. Bring me back, let me come back, for you are the Lord my God..."[42]

As can be clearly seen when the passage from *Jeremiah* is examined at close quarters that the statement paraphrased by *Matthew* has whatsoever nothing to do with Messianic prophecy. Once again, the actual *Old Testament* passage talks about the deportation of the 10 tribes of the northern Kingdom of Israel to Assyria, in the eighth century BCE.

This is the only possible interpretation of the passage from Jeremiah. This is clearly understood when one notes that: Rachel was the mother of Joseph[43], whereas Leah was the mother of Judah[44]; and the son of Joseph[45] was Ephraim. It must also be borne in mind that the name of the Isrelite sub-tribe was often used to refer to all of the 10 lost tribes of the northern Kingdom of Israel.[46] From this one can conclude that Judah and his descendants, not Ephraim, were associated with Bethlehem.[47] Thus, the descendants of Judah, living in Bethlehem, were the "children" of Leah, and not of Rachel. The passage from *Jeremiah* specifically says that the "children" are in "the land of the enemy", i.e., Assyria, which makes it clear that the children are not dead. Thus, the passage from *Jeremiah* predicts, incorrectly, that the children would return to Palestine from Assyria. Futher, it's interesting and convincing to note that while Ramah was about six miles north of Jerusalem, Bethlehem was about six miles south of Jerusalem, which goes to prove that even the geography doesn't fit with the Matthean account of the reported slaughter of the children of Bethlehem.[48]

Clearly, *Matthew* has misrepresented *Jeremiah*, and has paraphrased a passage from *Jeremiah* well out of its context. Once again, *Matthew* has stretched the fabric of an *Old Testament* passage until it has torn. Moreover, there is no other passage in the entire *New Testament* or in any secular writing that mentions King Herod's slaughtering of the children in Bethlehem. Even the first century CE, Jewish historian, Flavius Josephus (who takes such evident pain to detail King Herod's abuses) fails to make any reference to this alleged, barbaric act of Herod. It is. therefore difficult to accept as historical reality the mass killing of children in Bethlehem, a supposed event that totally escapes attention from everyone except from *Matthew*.

One solution to this dilemma is to posit that *Matthew* fabricated the entire story of the slaughter of the children in Bethlehem. In that regard, the motive would have, once again, been to create a parallel between the lives of Jesus and Moses. *Exodus* states that: the pharaoh of Egypt had all male children of the Hebrews in Egypt put to death; Moses, however, escaped this fate, by being placed in a basket on the river; and he was then found and nurtured by none other than the pharaoh's daughter.[49] *Matthew* appears to be reaching once again for a "hidden prophetic fulfillment" of *Deuteronomy* 18:15-19, i.e. the prophet like Moses. In brief, the compiler of *Matthew* appears to have fabricated the story of the slaughter of the children, in order to create a parallel between Jesus and Moses. He then attempts to camouflage his fabrication by misrepresenting a passage from Jeremiah, and by using it as a claim of fulfillment of Messianic prophecy.

Case 6: The Nazorean

When Joseph, Mary, and Jesus allegedly return to Palestine from Egypt, *Matthew* claims that Joseph was warned in a dream to relocate to the city of Nazareth in the district of Galilee. *Matthew* presents this relocation as another example of prophetic fulfillment.

> There he made his home in a town called Nazareth, so that what had been spoken through the prophets might be fulfilled. "He will be called a Nazorean."[50]

In presenting this example of prophetic fulfillment, *Matthew* opts for something entirely new. This time, the quotation is not taken ought of context, nor is it a quotation that obviously applies to someone or something else. This time, the fact is that the alleged quotation simply doesn't exist! No where in the entire *Old Testament*, including the apocryphal books of the *Old Testament*, can one find the words "(h)e will be called a Nazorean", or even the word "Nazorean".[51]

The word Nazorean relates back to the Nazarites (Nazirites), a group of Jews who were supposedly especially dedicated to Allah, and who maintained a rigorously ascetic lifestyle.[52] The lifestyle portrayed by the four canonical gospels for Jesus was a far cry from that of a Nazarite, although it would fit with that of John (Yahya) the Baptist.[53] However, even if one substitutes "Nazirite" for "Nazorean", there is still no Old Testament passage stating "(h)e will be called a Nazirite".[54] Moreover, the word "Nazorean" does not relate to the town of Nazareth at all.

Some Biblical commentators[55] have tried to save *Matthew* at this point by claiming that *Matthew* mistakenly related the word "Nazorean" to the Hebrew "netzer", meaning "sprout" or "shoot", and thus may have seen an allusion to *Isaiah* 11:1, where there is mention of "a shoot shall come out from the stump of Jesse" (Jesse being the father of King David). However, "netzer" has a different consonantal root structure than does "Nazorean".[56] Even the Biblical commentators who make the suggestion that *Matthew* is reaching for "netzer" acknowledge that this would have been a "far-fetched"[57] interpretation. Further, the passage from *Isaiah*

11:1 does not say "he will be called a shoot (netzer)", which is what it would need to say if it were to satisfy any of the requirements of *Matthew*'s alleged quotation.

Matthew has "quoted" prophecy, which simply doesn't exist!

Case 7: John the Baptist

Having finished with the nativity and infancy of Jesus, *Matthew* abruptly pushes almost 30 years farther along in time, and introduces the figure of John the Baptist, whom *Matthew* wishes to portray as the fulfillment of yet another Messianic prophecy. In this case, it is not that John the Baptist is the Messiah, but that John the Baptist was the prophetic fulfillment of the figure, who was supposed to precede the Messiah.

> In those days John the Baptist appeared in the wilderness of Judea, proclaiming, "Repent, for the kingdom of heaven has come near." This is the one of whom the prophet Isaiah spoke when he said, "The voice of one crying out in the wilderness: prepare the way of the Lord, make his paths straight."[58]

This time, *Matthew* is actually referring to an *Old Testament* passage that really exists, but has again resorted to quoting from the Greek *Septuagint* version of the *Old Testament*.[59] In what follows, the English translation of the Hebrew text of the relevant passage from Isaiah is quoted.

> A voice cries out: "In the wilderness prepare the way of the Lord, make straight in the desert a highway for our God..."[60]

The rendition from *Matthew* of the Greek *Septuagint* looks like a pretty good fit with John the Baptist. Certainly, this prophet of Allah appeared and preached his message in the wilderness areas surrounding the Jordan River, and the message of *John* was not inconsistent with that reported in the *Isaiah* quotation. However, as soon as one moves to the English translation of the actual Hebrew, as opposed to the Greek, text of *Isaiah*, one sees the glaring problem. It wasn't the "voice of one crying out in the wilderness", it was the voice who cried out that one should prepare the way of the Lord "(i)n the wilderness". The voice wasn't in the wilderness; the "way of the Lord" was in the wilderness. What a crucial change this is! *Matthew*, by using the Greek Septuagint, renders the passage is such a way as to fit John the Baptist. However, that isn't what *Isaiah* said. The actual words of Isaiah from the Hebrew text have no obvious link to John the Baptist.

Case 8: The Land of Zebulun and Naphtali

Following the arrest of John the Baptist, Matthew reports that Jesus left the wilderness of Judea, returned to Galilee, and then relocated his home from Nazareth to Capernaum, a city located on the northern edge of the Sea of Galilee (Lake Tiberias). At this point, Jesus reportedly begins his own ministry. Once again, Matthew alleges that this event fulfilled Messianic prophecy.

> He left Nazareth and made his home in Capernaum by the sea, in the territory of Zebulun and Naphtali, so that what had been spoken through the prophet Isaiah might be fulfilled: "Land of Zebulun, land of Naphtali, on the road by the sea, across the Jordan, Galilee of the Gentiles—the people who sat in darkness have seen a great light, and for those who sat in the region and shadow of death light has dawned."[61]

Interestingly, the passage from *Isaiah*, to which *Matthew* is alluding, is presented in a form that corresponds neither to the Greek *Septuagint* nor to the Hebrew text. For an immediate reference, the actual text from *Isaiah* is reproduced below.

> But there will be no gloom for those who were in anguish. In the former time he brought into contempt the land of Zebulun and the land of Naphtali, but in the latter time he will make glorious the way of the sea, the land beyond the Jordan, Galilee of the nations. The people who walked in darkness have seen a great light; those who lived in a land of deep darkness—on them light has shined.[62]

Matthew does not take the quotation from Isaiah out of context, but *Matthew* does provide a rather free and easy paraphrase of the actual passage. In that regard, it is interesting to note the change from "nations" in *Isaiah* to "gentiles" in *Matthew*. This change is not attributable to *Matthew*, but to the respective translators of Isaiah and *Matthew* into

English. Nonetheless, "nations" in Isaiah is the Hebrew "goyim", while "gentiles" in *Matthew* is the Greek "ethnikio".[63] From a Jewish perspective, either word could be translated as "nations" or as "gentiles". However, Jesus himself specifically contradicted the concept that his ministry was to the gentiles[64], which would tend to negate the idea that this prophecy could apply to him. It must, however, be noted that the land of Zebulun refers to that geographical territory that was assigned to the Israelite tribe of Zebulun, conforming to the area west of the Sea of Galilee.[65] The land of Naphtali denotes the territory assigned to the Israelite tribe of Naphtali, an area to the west and north of the Sea of Galilee[66], which would appear to include Capernaum.

All in all, despite the free and easy paraphrase of *Isaiah* rendered by *Matthew*, this use of *Old Testament* prophecy by *Matthew* is about as accurate a representation of an *Old Testament* passage as *Matthew* has made so far. The only significant problem is that *Matthew* appears to be representing a ministry by Jesus to the gentiles to the east of the Jordan River, while Jesus himself specifically denied having any ministry outside of the "house of Israel"[67], thus, making the issue a debatable one.

Case 9: He bore our diseases

As Jesus' ministry progressed, Matthew reports that Jesus performed many miracles, including healing those afflicted with a variety of physical conditions, and exorcising demons. For Matthew, this is again prophetic fulfillment.

> This was to fulfill what had been spoken through the prophet Isaiah, "He took our infirmities and bore our diseases."[68]

Here, *Matthew* quotes from that part of Isaiah known as the "suffering servant".

> He was despised and rejected by others; a man of suffering and acquainted with infirmity; and as one from whom others hide their faces he was despised, and we held him of no account. Surely he has borne our infirmities and carried our diseases; yet we accounted him stricken, struck down by God, and afflicted.[69]

As can be seen *Matthew* rather accurately reports the passage from

Isaiah, and there is no blatant taking of a passage out of context. In short, the only real issue is whether or not the individual reader believes the passage from *Isaiah* applies to Jesus. Biblical scholars have long argued this point, with most believing that the entire "suffering servant" motif of *Isaiah* is better applied to the people of Israel as a whole.

Case 10: The prior Messenger

Matthew maintains that Jesus' miraculous healings came to the attention of John the Baptist, while the latter was in prison. In response, *John* reportedly sent some of his disciples to Jesus to inquire as to whether or not Jesus was the Messiah. According to *Matthew*, Jesus did not directly answer that question, but urged *John*'s disciples to observe what Jesus was doing and what he had done. After *John*'s disciples left, Jesus reportedly addressed the crowd around him about John the Baptist. In this address, *Matthew* has Jesus saying that *John*'s ministry was prophetic fulfillment.

> As they went away, Jesus began to speak to the crowds about John: "What did you go out into the wilderness to look at?...A prophet? Yes, I tell you and more than a prophet. This is the one about whom it is written, 'See, I am sending my messenger ahead of you, who will prepare your way before you.'"[70]

The *Old Testament* passage, which *Matthew* has placed into the mouth of Jesus, is to be found in *Malachi*. This passage is quoted below, and the reader is urged to note the all-important change in pronouns, which *Matthew* has introduced into the passage.[71] It is not that the messenger will prepare the way before "you", but before "Me", i.e. the messenger will prepare the way of Allah. Even within a trinitarian concept of the deity, this change in pronouns presents problems. Assuming a trinitarian posture for the sake of argument, the passage from *Malachi* would suggest that the messenger is preparing the way of "God the Father", not of "God the Son". No matter how you stretch the fabric, it just doesn't fit.

> See, I am sending my messenger to prepare the way before me, and the Lord whom you seek will suddenly come to his temple. The messenger of the covenant in whom you delight—indeed, he is coming, says the Lord of

hosts...Then I will draw near to you for judgment...For I the Lord do not change...[72]

Case 11: The Servant

Reportedly in reaction to the Pharisees plotting against him, Jesus left one area, and moved to another. Large crowds reportedly followed him, and he reportedly performed many miraculous healings, while ordering the crowds "not to make him known". In all of this, *Matthew* again posits prophetic fulfillment.

> This was to fulfill what had been spoken through the prophet Isaiah: "Here is my servant, whom I have chosen, my beloved, with whom my soul is well pleased. I will put my Spirit upon him, and he will proclaim justice to the Gentiles. He will not wrangle or cry aloud, nor will anyone hear his voice in the streets. He will not break a bruised reed or quench a smoldering wick until he brings justice to victory. And in his name the Gentiles will hope."[73]

The passage in question is from *Isaiah*. Interestingly, in presenting this passage, *Matthew* appears to be jumping back and forth between the Hebrew text and the Greek *Septuagint*, utilizing whichever meaning best suits his theological purposes at the moment.[74] And so one finds the final rendition given by *Matthew* is somewhat of a distortion of the actual words of *Isaiah*, quoted below.

> Here is my servant, whom I uphold, my chosen, in whom my soul delights; I have put my spirit upon him; he will bring forth justice to the nations. He will not cry or lift up his voice, or make it heard in the street; a bruised reed he will not break, and a dimly burning wick he will not quench; he will faithfully bring forth justice, he will not grow faint or be crushed until he has established justice in the earth; and the coastlands wait for his teaching.[75]

A comparison of *Matthew*'s rendition of *Isaiah* with the actual passage from *Isaiah* illustrates *Matthew*'s concern with stressing and justifying a supposed ministry to the gentiles by Jesus. This is especially apparent in *Matthew*'s fabrication of the statement "(a)nd in his name the Gentiles will hope", which appears nowhere in the actual passage from Isaiah. This is the second time that *Matthew*'s bias towards a ministry to the gentiles has come to the surface, with the earlier instance being in case 8. As this is the second such occurrence, it needs to be stressed again that Jesus specifically contradicted that he had any ministry to anyone outside of the house of Israel.[76]

In its original form, the passage from *Isaiah* might well apply to Jesus, but it might equally well apply to many other prophets of Allah. In short, the fabric of the garment is so baggy and voluminous that it could cover many different individuals, and there is nothing specific enough in the passage to pinpoint an identification with Jesus.

Case 12: The sign on Jonah

Matthew has the scribes and Pharisees approach Jesus, and ask for a sign from him, which confirms that he is the Messiah. *Matthew* then places into the mouth of Jesus words to the effect that the only sign to be given is the sign of Jonah, peace be upon him, which will be revealed later in the alleged crucifixion and resurrection of Jesus. While *Matthew* does not directly quote from *Jonah*, the allusion is obvious.

> But he answered them, "An evil and adulterous generation
> asks for a sign, but no sign will be given to it except the sign
> of the prophet Jonah. For just as Jonah was three days and
> three nights in the belly of the sea monster, so for three days
> and three nights the Son of Man will be in the heart of the
> earth..."[77]

There is no distortion involved in *Matthew*'s reference to *Jonah*, as can be seen by examining the following passage from *Jonah*.

> But the Lord provided a large fish to swallow up Jonah; and
> Jonah was in the belly of the fish three days and three
> nights.[78]

However, there is absolutely no way that this situation from the life of the prophet Jonah can be accurately applied to the alleged crucifixion and resurrection of Jesus. Assuming for the moment that the alleged crucifixion and resurrection of Jesus actually did happen[79], then it appears that *Matthew* has problems counting (something that was demonstrated during case 1)

The traditional Christian account of the crucifixion and resurrection of Jesus is outlined here. Christian tradition holds that Jesus was crucified on a Friday, and that his body was removed from the cross right before sunset. It was then immediately buried in a tomb. By Sunday morning, the resurrection was completed. Given this account, Jesus was dead for one complete day (Saturday), part of one day (Friday), and possibly part of another day (Sunday). This would result in parts of two or three days, depending upon when one wanted to begin counting the start of a day.[80] However, no matter how one begins counting the start of the nights, Jesus would have been dead and in the tomb only on Friday and Saturday nights[81], i.e., for two nights only. This is a direct contradiction of Matthew's statement that "for three days and three nights the Son of Man will be in the heart of the earth". In short, *Matthew*'s equation of the sign of Jonah with the alleged crucifixion and resurrection of Jesus has no more validity than the equation of three equals two, which is exactly what *Matthew* is maintaining. This is dramatically illustrated in Table 2 below, in which the Jewish calendar of the time of Jesus is utilized in construct-ing the start of days and nights[82], and which demonstrates that the gospels maintain that Jesus was allegedly in the tomb for only two days (Friday and Saturday) and for two nights (Saturday and Sunday).

Table 2
The alleged status of Jesus from Good Friday through Easter

SOLAR EVENT	JEWISH TIME	ALLEGED STATUS
Prior to sunset on Friday	Friday daytime, i.e. day 1	Dead and in tomb
Post sunset on Friday	Saturday night, i.e. night 1	Dead and in tomb
Post sunrise on Saturday	Saturday daytime, i.e. day 2	Dead and in tomb
Post sunset on Saturday	Sunday night, i.e. night 2	Dead and in tomb
Post sunrise on Sunday	Sunday daytime, i.e. day 3	Arisen and out of tomb

Interestingly, *Luke* also refers to Jesus talking about the sign of Jonah. However, in *Luke*, there is no reference to Jonah being in the belly of the fish, and there is no reference to any alleged crucifixion or resurrec-tion. Rather, *Luke* appears to be maintaining that the sign of Jonah has to do simply with Jonah's preaching to the inhabitants of Ninevah. As Jonah preached to the populace of Ninevah, so Jesus preached to his generation.[85]

> When the crowds were increasing, he began to say, "This
> generation is an evil generation; it asks for a sign, but no
> sign will be given to it except the sign of Jonah. For just as
> Jonah became a sign to the people of Nineveh, so the Son
> of Man will be to this generation..." [86]

The occurrence of this "sign of Jonah" story in both Matthew and
Luke, and its absence in *Mark*, confirms that the original source for this
story was *Q*. One assumes that *Luke* reported the *Q* source material rather
faithfully, while *Matthew* simply couldn't leave it alone. *Matthew* simply
had to construe a Messianic prophecy in this reference to Jonah, and then
had to maintain that that prophecy was fulfilled, even if it meant
maintaining that three equals two.

Case 13: The Parables

Matthew alleges that Jesus often spoke in parables, in order to keep the
truth hidden from those, who did not deserve to know it. Such people
could hear Jesus speak, but they would never understand his message. In
contrast, Jesus' disciples were able to grasp these "secrets", which were
embedded in the parables of Jesus. In this, Matthew sees prophetic fulfillment.[87]

> With them indeed is fulfilled the prophecy of Isaiah that
> says: "You will indeed listen, but never understand, and you
> will indeed look, but never perceive. For this people's heart
> has grown dull, and their ears are hard of hearing, and they
> have shut their eyes; so that they might not look with their
> eyes, and listen with their ears, and understand with their
> heart and turn—and I would heal them." But blessed are
> your eyes, for they see, and your ears, for they hear.[88]

Matthew is here utilizing the Greek *Septuagint* translation of *Isaiah*.[89]
The actual statement of *Isaiah* is as follows.

> Then I heard the voice of the Lord saying, "Whom shall I
> send, and who will go for us?" And I said, "Here am I: send
> me!" And he said, "Go and say to this people: 'Keep lis-
> tening, but do not comprehend; keep looking, but do not
> understand.' Make the mind of this people dull, and stop
> their ears, and shut their eyes, so that they may not look

with their eyes, and listen with their ears, and compre-
hend with their minds, and turn and be healed."[90]

Many of the differences between the above quotation from *Isaiah* and
Matthew's rendition of this statement can be attributed to *Matthew*'s use
of the Greek *Septuagint* version of *Isaiah*, instead of the Hebrew text of
Isaiah. As noted previously, *Matthew*'s reliance on the Greek *Septuagint*
is strong evidence that the compiler of *Matthew* was not one of the
disciples of Jesus, nor even a Jew from Palestine. Instead, the compiler of
Matthew would have to be seen as a Hellenized Jewish or gentile
Christian, living somewhere in the Diaspora (probably in Syria).

However, the use of the Greek Septuagint is not the real issue in
Matthew's rendition of Isaiah. The real issue is that *Matthew* has tried to
twist the words of *Isaiah* into a Messianic prophecy, by once again lifting
a passage out of context. By deleting the initial section of the passage
from Isaiah, in which Isaiah reportedly volunteers to deliver a message
from Allah, *Matthew* hides the fact that the passage from *Isaiah* is
actually talking about the commissioning of *Isaiah* as a reported prophet
of Allah.[91] The passage clearly identifies *Isaiah* as having been the
messenger in question, and clearly identifies the events as having been
completed during the lifetime of *Isaiah*. Once again, *Matthew*'s boast
of prophetic fulfillment falls far short of the mark. Once again, an
examination of the relevant *Old Testament* passage reveals that *Matthew*
has torn the fabric of the *Old Testament* passage by trying to stretch it to
fit the life and ministry of Jesus.

Case 14: Parables again

There is yet a second time, in which *Matthew* maintains that Jesus'
speaking in parables was a fulfillment of *Old Testament* prophecy.

> Jesus told the crowds all these things in parables; without a
> parable he told them nothing. This was to fulfill what had
> been spoken through the prophet: "I will open my mouth to
> speak in parables; I will proclaim what has been hidden
> from the foundation of the world."[92]

The quotation is from the *Old Testament* book of *Psalms*, demonstrates reliance on both the Hebrew and Greek texts[93], and is quoted
immediately below.

Give ear, O my people, to my teaching; incline your ears to
the words of my mouth. I will open my mouth in a parable;
I will utter dark sayings from of old, things that we have
heard and known, that our ancestors have told us. We will
not hide them from their children; we will tell to the
coming generation the glorious deeds of the Lord, and his
might, and the wonders that he has done.[94]

One might wish to quibble with *Matthew*'s rendition of this passage
from the *Psalms*, but that would be to miss the point. The point is that the
passage from the *Psalms* is so general as to be true of any prophet or religious instructor, who spoke in parables. Here again, the fabric has been
cut large so as to cover anyone in shapeless anonymity. There is nothing
specific enough in the passage from the *Psalms* to point singularly to
Jesus.

Case 15: Lip Service

In the 15th chapter of *Matthew*, the compiler of this gospel reports a
situation, in which the scribes and Pharisees of Judaism question Jesus
about his disciples' apparent laxness in practicing certain aspects of the
"tradition of the elders". Reportedly, Jesus then uses this opportunity
to confront the religious hypocrisy of his questioners, and ends his
confrontation by reportedly citing the behavior of his questioners as being
prophetic fulfillment of a passage from *Isaiah*.

You hypocrites! Isaiah prophesied rightly about you when
he said: "This people honors me with their lips, but
their hearts are far from me; in vain do they worship me,
teaching human precepts as doctrines."[95]

In reporting the above, the compiler of *Matthew* is simply following
the report of the gospel of *Mark*[96], although *Matthew* has added the
phrase "you hypocrites" to the reported words of Jesus. The passage from
Isaiah, as it appears in *Matthew* and in *Mark*, appears to have been taken
from the Greek *Septuagint*[97]. The actual statement of *Isaiah* is stated
below.

The Lord said: because these people draw near with their
mouths and honor me with their lips, while their hearts
are far from me, and their worship of me is a human
commandment learned by rote; so I will again do amazing

things with this people, shocking and amazing. The wisdom
of their wise shall perish, and the discernment of the
discerning shall be hidden.[98]

Some alteration in the text of *Isaiah* can be discerned between the
Hebrew text, quoted immediately above, and the Greek *Septuagint*.
However, by and large, the passage has not been distorted, nor has it been
quoted out of context. The problem is that the passage is applicable to the
hypocrites encountered by all of the prophets of Allah, not just those
encountered by Jesus. One could just as easily imagine these words
coming from John the Baptist, Elijah, peace be upon him, or Muhammad,
peace be upon him. Once again, the fabric has been cut so large and so
shapelessly that one size really does fit all.

As a brief digression, one has a great deal of difficulty imagining that
Jesus would quote from the Greek Septuagint version of *Isaiah*, instead
of from the Hebrew text.

Case 16: The Trick Rider

In the traditional Christian narrative, the life and ministry of Jesus end
in an alleged crucifixion and resurrection in Jerusalem. This last week
of Jesus' earthly life reportedly begins with a triumphant entry into
Jerusalem, which marks the beginning of the so-called "Passion Week".
This triumphant entry finds expression in all four canonical gospels[99],
although each has its own unique twists and turns. However, it is only
in *Matthew* and *John* that one aspect of this event is seen as direct
prophetic fulfillment. *Matthew*'s version is given below.

According to *Matthew*, when Jesus and his disciples were approaching Jerusalem from the east, they arrived near the village of Bethphage,
which was located on the eastern slope of the Mount of Olives. Jesus then
summoned two of his disciples, and directed them to enter the village,
where they would find a donkey tied, with a colt at her side. The disciples were to bring the two donkeys to Jesus. If anyone tried to stop the
disciples, they were merely to say that the "Lord needs them". Following
the completion of this task, the disciples placed their cloaks on the
donkeys, and Jesus rode them into Jerusalem. In this event, *Matthew*
claims prophetic fulfillment.

This took place to fulfill what had been spoken through the
prophet, saying, "Tell the daughter of Zion, look your king
is coming to you, humble, and mounted on a donkey, and on
a colt, the foal of a donkey."[100]

It is important to note that *Matthew* is alleging that there were two donkeys[101], and that Jesus "sat on *them*"[102] (italics added by present author). In short, taking *Matthew* at its literal word, Jesus simultaneously rode two donkeys into Jerusalem, thus performing something akin to a circus trick-riding act. Where on earth could *Matthew* have come up with something this bizarre? The answer lies in: the inability of the compiler of Matthew to understand Hebrew literary style, which is another indication that the compiler of *Matthew* was not a Palestinian disciple of Jesus, but was someone from the Hellenized world; and the apparent willingness of the compiler to alter events in the life of Jesus, in order to meet his understanding of prophecy. However, before proceeding to unravel this mystery, the actual *Old Testament* text from *Zechariah*, to which *Matthew* refers, needs to be presented.

> Rejoice greatly, O daughter Zion! Shout aloud, O daughter Jerusalem! Lo, your king comes to you; triumphant and victorious is he, humble and riding on a donkey, on a colt, the foal of a donkey. He will cut off the chariot from Ephraim and the war horse from Jerusalem; and the battle bow shall be cut off, and he shall command peace to the nations; his dominion shall be from sea to sea, and from the River to the ends of the earth.[103]

The passage from *Zechariah* refers to "a donkey, on a colt, the foal of a donkey". This represents a basic and formal literary technique in Hebrew poetry, i.e. parallelism. Hebrew parallelism can be understood as repetition of the same idea in different words, and as a balance of ideas, in which the thought in one line of poetry is enhanced, compared, or emphasized by a parallel thought in the next line. In short, the passage from *Zechariah* is only talking about one donkey, not two. The phrase "on a colt, the foal of a donkey" is merely Hebrew parallelism for the original mention of "donkey". The same concept can be seen earlier in the passage from *Zechariah*, where "O daughter Jerusalem" is used as a parallel for "O daughter Zion".[104]

The compiler of *Matthew* once again demonstrates that he is not a Palestinian Jew or an immediate disciple of Jesus, by failing to recognize the Hebrew parallelism in *Zechariah*. Instead, he takes the passage from *Zechariah* literally, and assumes that two donkeys are required to constitute prophetic fulfillment. If two donkeys are required to fulfill the prophecy of *Zechariah*, then two donkeys are introduced into the text of *Matthew*. Without any apparent qualms, the compiler of *Matthew* simply alters the events in the reported life of Jesus. While *Mark*, *Luke*, and *John* are unanimous in saying there was only one donkey[105], the compiler of *Matthew* introduces a second donkey, because he did not understand the Hebrew parallelism of *Zechariah*. It may be noted that while neither *Mark* nor *Luke* refer to the passage from *Zechariah*, *John* does. However, the compiler of *John* apparently understood the nature of Hebrew parallelism, and felt no need to create a second donkey.

In previous examples of Matthean use of alleged prophecy, it has been shown that, in order to create a prophetic fulfillment, the compiler of *Matthew* misquoted and fabricated at least one prophecy, which does not exist, and lifted passages out of context. In addition, it has been suggested that *Matthew* may have fabricated some events in the life of Jesus, in order to fulfill a prophecy. In the current case, there is no reason to speculate about possible fabrication of an event in the life of Jesus, by comparing *Matthew* with *Mark*, *Luke*, and *John*, since one can clearly demonstrate the willingness of the compiler of *Matthew* to alter events, in order to claim prophetic fulfillment. This goes far beyond stretching the fabric of prophecy to make the clothing fit, even if that means tearing the cloth. Likewise, it goes far beyond using a tent-like cloth, which can drape over anyone and anything. Here, in order to make the prophetic clothing fit, the solution is to perform radical plastic surgery on the body.

What if one doesn't add the second donkey? What if one merely takes the passage from *Zechariah*, and applies it to Jesus' entry into Jerusalem? One imagines that literally thousands of individuals have ridden into Jerusalem on a donkey, and there is no reason to apply the passage from *Zechariah* specifically to Jesus alone.

Case 17: The Mouths of Infants

Following the reported driving of the moneychangers from the Temple, *Matthew* reports that Jesus healed the blind and the lame who came to him in the Temple. Observing these miracles, children allegedly began to cry out, "Hosanna to the Son of David". Apparently indignant at what Jesus had done and at what the children were shouting, the priests and scribes reportedly confronted Jesus. *Matthew* has Jesus responding by quoting a passage from the *Old Testament,* which supposedly illustrates yet another fulfillment of Messianic prophecy.[106]

> Jesus said to them, "Yes; have you never read. 'Out of the
> mouths of infants and nursing babies you have prepared
> praise for yourself.?'" [107]

The *Old Testament* passage is taken from the *Psalms*, and *Matthew* is once again using the Greek *Septuagint* text[108]. Even when one takes the passage as *Matthew* uses it from the Greek *Septuagint*, the relationship to Jesus appears to be weak. However, when one looks at the original Hebrew text, the text that Jesus would undoubtedly have used if he had actually quoted this passage, the relationship to Jesus becomes far weaker, if not non-existent.

> Out of the mouths of babes and infants you have founded a
> bulwark because of your foes, to silence the enemy and the
> avenger.[109]

Quite obviously, the Hebrew text has no relationship to what *Matthew* reports Jesus was doing in the Temple. Yet, the Hebrew text of *Psalms* would have been the text quoted by Jesus, not the Greek text. Given these two considerations, the conclusion appears to be that *Matthew* arbitrarily and falsely inserted these words from the *Septuagint* into the mouth of Jesus in order to create another example of prophetic fulfillment.

Case 18: The Rejected Stone

Sometime later, *Matthew* has Jesus make a self-statement regarding prophetic fulfillment. The only context *Matthew* supplies for this self-statement is that it follows the parable of the wicked tenants.

> Jesus said to them, "Have you never read in the scriptures:
> 'The stone that the builders rejected has become the corner-
> stone; this was the Lord's doing, and it is amazing in our
> eyes'? Therefore I tell you, the kingdom of God will be
> takenaway from you and given to a people that produces the
> fruits of the kingdom. The one who falls on this stone will
> be broken to pieces; and it will crush anyone on whom it
> falls."[110]

The passage in question is taken from the *Old Testament* book of *Psalms*, and is quoted below.

> The stone that the builders rejected has become the chief
> cornerstone. This is the Lord's doing; it is marvelous in our
> eyes.[111]

Matthew is accurate enough in the quoting of the passage from *Psalms,* which does appear to apply to Jesus. It is interesting to note that *Mark* and *Luke* also report this statement from *Psalms* at the same point in the life of Jesus.[112] However, the passage is perfectly general enough to apply not only to Jesus, but to almost all the prophets of Allah, each of whom was rejected at times by the people to whom he was sent. For example, the passage appears to apply equally well to Prophet Muhammad's rejection by the Quraish, before he left Makka for Madina. In effect, what one has here is what is known in psychology as the Barnum Effect, which was named after the great showman and circus promoter, P.T. Barnum.

The Barnum Effect is a staple of fortunetellers, palm readers, Tarot card readers, and the like. It consists of a statement, which on a superficial level, appears to be specific to a given individual. However, upon a little thought, it can be seen that the statement would be true of almost anyone. An example might be the palm reader, who peers studiously at one's hand, and then pronounces that, "I see you are troubled by something." The uninitiated thinks, "Wow, how did he know that about me?" However, the reality is that almost everyone is troubled by something. In short, the statement is so vague and general that the palm reader is almost assured that the individual will accept the statement as being accurate.

The passage from *Psalms* is a good example of a Barnum Effect statement. How many people have been initially rejected, only to find acceptance and vindication in the end? Certainly, Jesus was one such person. However, so were King David, Muhammad, Job, Moses, Abraham, etc., peace be upon them. In short, the fabric of the "one size fits all" garment is so voluminous and shapeless that it does, in fact, fit almost all.

Case 19: The scattering of the Flock

As *Matthew* leads up to the alleged arrest of Jesus in the Garden of Gethsemane, he has Jesus prophesy that once he is arrested, all his disciples will scatter and desert him. In making this prophecy, *Matthew* has Jesus quote a passage from the *Old Testament,* thus linking the scattering of the disciples not only with prophetic fulfillment of Jesus' words, but also with prophetic fulfillment of the words of the *Old Testament.*

> Then Jesus said to them, "You will all become deserters
> because of me this night; for it is written, 'I will strike the
> shepherd, and the sheep of the flock will be scattered.' But
> after I am raised up, I will go ahead of you to Galilee."[113]

The passage in question is taken from *Zechariah*, and *Matthew* is merely following the lead of *Mark* in using this passage at this point.[114] The actual passage from *Zechariah* is quoted below.

> "Awake, O sword, against my shepherd, against the man
> who is my associate," says the Lord of hosts. Strike the
> shepherd, that the sheep may be scattered; I will turn my
> hand against the little ones.[115]

Matthew's quotation from *Zechariah* is accurate enough. However, is the quotation actually applicable to the events being discussed? *Matthew* has Jesus saying, "You will all become deserters because of me this night." Is that what actually happened? All four of the canonical gospels state that Peter followed the arrested Jesus, i.e., Peter did not scatter.[116] Further, *John* indicates that a second disciple also followed Jesus.[117] Be that as it may, the author concedes that the actual passage from *Zechariah* does not state that "all" of the sheep will be scattered. However, if the statement in Zechariah is to be applied to Jesus, Christians should note that in that passage Allah is reported to have specifically referred to his shepherd as being a mere "man".

Case 20: The Potter's Field

Matthew reports that Judas Iscariot, one of the 12 disciples, betrayed Jesus to the Jewish authorities for 30 pieces of silver. Later, Judas reportedly repented, returned to the Jewish authorities, threw down the 30 pieces of silver in the Temple, and then went and hung himself. Because the 30 pieces of silver were "blood money", the money could not be put into the general Temple treasury.[118]

The following quotation from *Matthew* picks up the story at this point, and includes another example of alleged prophetic fulfillment.

> After conferring together, they used them to buy the potter's
> field as a place to bury foreigners. For this reason that field
> has been called the Field of Blood to this day. Then was
> fulfilled what had been spoken through the prophet
> Jeremiah. "And they took the thirty pieces of silver, the

> price of the one on whom a price had been set, on whom some of the people of Israel had set a price, and they gave them for the potter's field, as the Lord commanded me." [119]

This is by far the most detailed and specific prophecy utilized by *Matthew*. Included in the specifics are: the 30 pieces of silver; the 30 pieces of silver being blood money or a bounty price, i.e. "the price of the one on whom a price had been set"; the purchase of the field; and the name of the field. What more detail could a person want? How better could a person want that detail to fit the events being described? Surprisingly, however, as strange as it may sound, this prophecy exists nowhere in the entire Old Testament![120]

It is even impossible to figure out for what *Old Testament* passage *Matthew* is reaching. The most common texts of *Matthew* specifically associate the alleged prophecy with *Jeremiah*. However, the closest one can come to such a text from *Jeremiah* is to piece together the following widely scattered verses.

> "Come, go down to the potter's house, and there I will let you hear my words." So I went down to the potter's house, and there he was working at his wheel...Thus said the Lord: Go and buy a potter's earthenware jug...Jeremiah said, The word of the Lord came to me: Hanamel son of your uncle Shallum is going to come to you and say, "Buy my field that is at Anathoth, for the right of redemption by purchase is yours."[121]

As one can see, even with a massive cut-and-paste job, one cannot come close to approximating the alleged *Old Testament* passage referred to by *Matthew*. But, in all fairness, it is noted that some versions of *Matthew* attribute the *Old Testament* passage to *Isaiah*, and some to *Zechariah*. There is nothing in Isaiah that can be associated with Matthew's reference[122], and the closest one can find in *Zechariah* to *Matthew*'s alleged quotation is the following.

> I then said to them, "If it seems right to you, give me my wages; but if not, keep them." So they weighed out as my wages thirty shekels of silver. Then the Lord said to me, "Throw it into the treasury"—this lordly price at which I was valued by them. So I took the thirty shekels of silver and threw them into the treasury in the house of the Lord.

> Then I broke my second staff Unity, annulling the family
> ties between Judah and Israel.[123]

Here, one has mention of 30 pieces of silver, and of throwing the silver. Further, the Hebrew phrase that has been translated "into the treasury" is very similar to the Hebrew phrase that would be translated "to the potter"[124]. However, there is no mention in this passage of the 30 pieces of silver being blood money, instead the money is simply the worker's wages for tending a flock of sheep[125]. Likewise, there is no mention of the purchase of a field. In short, no matter how hard one tries to find *Matthew*'s *Old Testament* passage, the inescapable conclusion is that it just doesn't exist. *Matthew* has fabricated an *Old Testament* prophecy to explain its presentation of events in Jesus' life.

Summary and Conclusions

In the preceding discussion, 20 different examples of so-called prophetic fulfillment have been analyzed from the book of *Matthew*. The analysis has been simple and straightforward, typically consisting of merely bothering to look at the *Old Testament* passage that Matthew is alleging finds prophetic fulfillment in the life and ministry of Jesus. The results of that analysis have been damaging and overwhelming! One finds that *Matthew* has systematically:relied on passages so general that they can be seen as prime examples of the Barnum Effect; has often misquoted other passages; has ripped passages out of context, where they clearly were referring to some other, already completed event; and has fabricated *Old Testament* passages out of whole cloth, to the extent that events in the life of Jesus have been inaccurately twisted and presented, with the sole objective being to create a so-called prophetic fulfillment. All in all, it is a devastating indictment against the trustworthiness of *Matthew*'s presentation.

This analysis of alleged prophetic fulfillment in the book of *Matthew* provides one specific example of the accuracy of the Islamic position, which maintains that the original gospel of Jesus was subsequently altered and distorted by some of the early Christians.

> From those, too, who call themselves Christians, We did
> take a covenant, but they forgot a good part of the message
> that was sent them: so We estranged them, with enmity
> and hatred between the one and the other, to the day of
> judgement. And soon will Allah show them what it is
> they have done.[126]

Chapter 8

The Prophet Job (Ayyoub)

The Biblical book of Job is an enduring masterpiece of literature, in which the trials and tribulations inflicted upon a steadfast and enduring believer in Allah[1] fail to diminish that believer's faith in Allah. The hero of the book is *Job*, peace be upon him[2], after whom the book is named. A rich and prosperous man, Job is reportedly tried by Allah with loss of his material possessions, with loss of his children and family, and with loss of his health. After Job's faith is shown to be steadfast and unaffected by all that he has endured, Allah rewards Job with greater riches and blessings than he had previously owned. This story of Job is also referred to in the *Qur'an*, where Job is known as Ayyoub.

The Biblical Book of *Job*

Despite its well-deserved reputation as a literary milestone, the book of *Job* is not a unitary literary product. Rather, it is a cut-and-paste compilation. Within its 42 chapters, there are disparate sections of material, whose literary creation span many different centuries. These different sections of material were then sewn together with very heavy and easily recognized seams. In this regard, the easiest division to see is between the prose and poetry sections of the narrative. The prose section includes the prologue (chapters 1:1 through 2:13) and epilogue (chapter 42:7-17), while the poetry section includes everything in between (chapters 3:1 through 42:6). Further, there are definite divisions within the poetry section, with such divisions being partially demarcated by the word (Yahweh, El, Eloah, Shaddai, or Elyon) used to name Allah. As such, the poetry section of *Job* is often demarcated into the "Dialogue" (chapters 3:1-27:23; 29:1-31:40), the "Elihu section" (chapters 32:1-37:24), the "Yahweh section" (chapters 38:1-42:6), and chapter 28, which is a later insertion into the text. Most of the poetry section is attributable to writings from the sixth to fourth centuries BCE, while the Elihu section (chapters 32:1-37:24) and chapter 28 are even later in construction, and probably arose only by the third century BCE or later. In contrast, the prologue and epilogue sections appear to be quite ancient, possibly dating in written form to the eighth to 10 centuries BCE, and being based on even more ancient oral legends and traditions.[3]

From a purely linguistic viewpoint, the book of *Job* is rather unique in Judaeo-Christian scripture. This uniqueness is illustrated in the "Arabized" nature of the Hebrew language employed in many places in the text[4], in the presence of many "Egyptian" loan words[5], in the presence of several Aramaic idioms[6], and in the presence of many "Arabic" names.[7] These linguistic findings have led some scholars to suggest that there is a heavy Arabic influence on the book of *Job*, or even to suggest that the original version of *Job* was written in Arabic or in proto-Arabic, and later appropriated by the Israelites and paraphrased or translated into Hebrew.[8]

Viewed from the standpoint of the Jewish system of classification of scripture, the book of *Job* falls within that group of scripture known as the *Ketuvim* (writings), as opposed to the *Torah* (law) and the *Nevi'im* (prophets). In regard to the Christian system of classification, *Job* is part of the *Old Testament*.

Who, When, and Where

Neither the book of *Job* in the *Bible*, nor the *Qur'an*, provides explicit information allowing for easy identification of Job relative to other people, to chronology, or to location. However, there are scattered clues, some of which are located in *Job*, and some of which are located in other Biblical books, such as *Genesis, Exodus, I Kings, I Chronicles, Jeremiah,* and *Lamentations*, which allow some answers to be generated. Sifting through those clues, one can first address the question of Job's location, then the question of who he was, and then, finally, the question of when he lived.

Where

The Biblical book of *Job* opens with the statement that Job lived "in the land of Uz" , and that *Job* was "the greatest of all the people of the east."[10] Tackling these two clues in reverse order of presentation, and assuming that the geographical references that are used in *Job* reflect a Palestinian orientation, one is first left with a vague association to the land of Job being somewhere east of Palestine. However, this still leaves a rather large area of land as being the potential home of Job. Moving from southeast of Palestine to northeast of Palestine, and using contemporary national terms, one could place Job anywhere from the Arabian Peninsula, to Jordan, to Iraq, to Syria, and even to Turkey. Clearly, additional refinement of geographical area is required, and the only remaining clue is "the land of Uz".

The word "Uz" occurs in the entire *Bible* only eight times.[11] In *Job* 1:1, "the land of Uz" is used as the home of Job, but without any direct location being specified. *Jeremiah* 25:20 refers to "all the kings of the land of Uz", but fails to locate Uz. *I Chronicles* 1:17 lists an Uz as being a descendant of Shem, which provides no real information regarding the land of Uz. *Genesis* 10:22-23 notes an Uz, who was the son of Aram, the son of Shem, and this appears to be the same Uz noted in *I Chronicles* 1:17. *Genesis* 22:21 notes an Uz, the son of Nahor, with the latter being the brother of the Prophet Abraham, peace be upon him. This Uz can be reliably placed at Harran (Haran)[12], on the Balikh River in southeastern Turkey[13], and this provides the first specific geographical candidate for Job's "land of Uz". *Genesis* 36:28 and *I Chronicles* 1:42 refer to an Uz, who is the son of Dishan, a Horite living in Seir (Edom)[14], which was an area in southern Jordan[15]. As such, southwestern Jordan, specifically the area southeast of the Dead Sea, becomes the second possible area for the location of Job. This latter possibility, i.e., that the land of Uz was located in Edom, which was located to the southeast of the Dead Sea, appears to be confirmed by the eighth and last reference to Uz in the *Bible*.

Lamentations 4:21 states:

> Rejoice and be glad, O daughter Edom, you that live in the land of Uz; but to you also the cup shall pass; you shall become drunk and strip yourself bare.

Who

If Job lived in the land of Uz, in Edom, southeast of the Dead Sea, who was he? Who were his people and tribe? What was his genealogy? Besidesextolling his faith and steadfastness during his trials and tribulations, why is the *Bible* so silent about this prophet of Allah? Why does the *Bible* say nothing about the background of Job?

Biblical References

The use of the name "Job" or "Job's" occurs 62 times in the *Bible*, including the Apocrypha. However, of these, 58 times the name appears in the book of *Job* which means that throughout the entire *Bible* and *Apocrypha*, the name "Job" occurs only four additional times. Further, these four references merely make a brief statement about the righteousness, steadfastness, or endurance of the Prophet Job.[16]

This is a rather amazing omission of detail regarding Job! Who was he, that the *Bible* cloaks his very person and individuality with such marked ommission/persistent invisibility? How does one begin to explain this Biblical silence, especially given the emphasis on genealogies and on tribal, clan, and family relationships typically found in the *Bible*? What motivates this lack of any personal detail? The answer to these questions comes in series of sequential considerations.

FIRST CONSIDERATION. The first consideration has already been noted, i.e., Job lived in the land of Uz, in Edom, which was southeast of the Dead Sea. In short, Job did not live in Palestine, the traditional home of the Israelite descendants of Jacob, peace be upon him. The question arises, was Job not an Israelite, i.e., he was not a descendant of Jacob?

SECOND CONSIDERATION. The second consideration has to do with the rather unique method in which Job's offspring inherited from him. Under the laws and traditions of the Israelites, daughters did not inherit from their father, unless there were no male heirs, and then only if they found husbands from their father's clan within their father's tribe.[17] The sole exception to be found in the entire *Old Testament* to this rule of inheritance is found in *Job* 42:13-15, in which Job specifically directed that his three daughters inherit along side of their seven brothers. Clearly, Job's bequeath to his daughters represents a non-Israelite custom, and strengthens the argument that Job was not an Israelite.

THIRD CONSIDERATION. The third consideration is Job's name. The name "Job" or "Job's" whenever it occurs in the *Bible*, is in reference to the prophet Job. The *Bible* does not mention any other person with this name. Why is this so? Why was the name that unusual and singular within the Biblical texts? Job was certainly a common name in Middle Eastern antiquity, being found in a variety of non-Biblical texts from the 19th to 14th centuries BCE.[18] If this was so, why is it that there was no one else in the *Bible* named Job? Was this name foreign to the Israelite descendants of Jacob?

FOURTH CONSIDERATION. The book of *Job* lists four friends or associates of Job. They were: Eliphaz, the Temanite[19]; Bildad, the Shuhite[20]; Zophar, the Naamathite[21]; and Elihu, the son of Barachel, the Buzite, of the family of Ram.[22] In addition, the book of *Job* gives the names of three of Job's daughters: Jemimah; Keziah: and Kerenhappuch.[23] There are a number of issues regarding the names of these four companions and three daughters of Job, each of which needs to be addressed.

Incidentally, the names of Bildad, Zophar, Barachel, Jemimah, Keziah, and Kerenhappuch occur nowhere else in the entire *Bible*. The name of Eliphaz occurs nine other times in the *Bible*, each time referring to the eldest son of Esau. The name of Elihu occurs four other times in the *Bible*, referring once each to: an Israelite of the sub-tribe of Ephraim; an Israelite of the sub-tribe of Manasseh; an Israelite of the tribe of Levi, and an Israelite of the tribe of Judah.[24]

What does one have here? Of the names associated with the four associates and three daughters of Job, six of the names are mentioned nowhere else in the entire *Bible*! The implications are obvious: these names were not used by the Israelite descendants of Jacob; and these names were foreign names to the Israelites. Furthermore, of the remaining two names, which do occur elsewhere in the *Bible*, Eliphaz is a name, which is only associated with the eldest son of Esau. In that respect, Esau is identified in *Genesis* 25:24-26 as being the elder brother of Jacob and as being the elder son of Isaac, peace be upon him. In addition, Esau is identified in *Genesis* 36:1,8-9 as being Edom, the eponymous ancestor of the Edomites. In short, Eliphaz is an Edomite name, which is consistent with Job residing in the land of Uz, in Edom.

Up to this point, there is strong circumstantial evidence, which suggests that Job, Job's daughters, and Job's friends had foreign, i.e., non-Israelite names. Further, in one of the two cases where a name can be tribally placed, i.e. that of Eliphaz, the name is an Edomite name. Still further, Job's bequeath to his daughters represents a non-Israelite custom/practice. Finally, Job apparently lived east of Palestine and in the land of Uz, which was part of Edom, located to the southeast of the Dead Sea in what is now southwestern Jordan. All of the foregoing facts or assumptions suggest that Job was a non-Israelite, and that he was an Edomite.

However, what about the name Elihu? As noted above, Elihu was an Israelite name, being variously associated with individuals from: the sub-tribe of Ephraim, the younger son of Joseph, peace be upon him, the son of Jacob; the sub-tribe of Manasses, the older son of Joseph, the son of Jacob; the tribe of Levi, the son of Jacob; and the tribe of Judah, the son of Jacob.[25] Quite simply, Biblical scholarship has long shown that the Elihu section of the book of *Job* is a later addition and insertion into an older substrata of material, and that this Elihu section can be dated no earlier than the third century BCE.[26] Thus, it can be seen that the only personal name, which shows an Israelite connection, is part of a section of *Job*, which was added many centuries after the original writing and so one may safely conclude that the personal names in the Job story clearly indicate non-Israelite origins, and probably Edomite origins.

FIFTH CONSIDERATION. Job's four friends or associates are identified not only by name, but also by clan or tribe. The four clan or tribal names given are that of Temanite, Shuhite, Naamathite, and Buzite. Each of these clan or tribal identifications needs to be examined in its own right.

The word "Temanite" or "Temanites" is mentioned only eight times in the *Bible*, while the word "Teman" occurs only 13 times.[27] Of the eight references to Temanite or to Temanites, six are references within *Job* to Eliphaz, while the other two references are to Temanites as a clan within the Edomite tribe.[28] Of the 13 references to Teman, eight simply refer to a geographic location, i.e., the land of the Temanites. The remaining five references refer to the clan of Teman (Temanites) among the Edomites or to Teman, the son of Eliphaz, the son of Esau (Edom).[29] Based on the above information, one can find that the first companion of Job, known as Eliphaz the Temanite, is identified as having been Eliphaz of the clan of Teman, the son of Eliphaz.[30] This latter Eliphaz is identified as having been the oldest son of Esau, the eponymous ancestor of the Edomites, out of Esau's wife, Adah.[31] (Esau's wife, Adah, is identified in *Genesis* 36:2 as being the daughter of "Elon the Hittite", but this is an obvious anachronism, as the Hittites cannot be placed anywhere near the Palestinian area as early in time as Job. It is more likely that *Genesis* 28:6-9 is correct in implying that Adah was a Canaanite.)

Within the entire *Bible*, the word "Shuhite" only occurs within the book of *Job*, and then only in specifying the clan or tribe of Bildad, the second of Job's four companions.[32] As such, attempts to identify the

Shuhite people boil down to the search for an eponymous ancestor. In that regard, there is only one candidate, i.e., Shuah, the son of Abraham out of his third wife, Keturah.[33] As such, the Shuhites can be seen as a tribe collateral to that of the Midianites (Madyans). Given this identification, Bildad is also quite clearly a non-Israelite. Like Eliphaz, Bildad becomes identified with those descendants of Abraham, who contributed to the formation of the Arab people.

Like the word "Shuhite", the word "Naamathite" occurs within the *Bible* only within the confines of the book of *Job*, and then only in specifying the clan or tribe of Zophar.[34] Once again, the identification of Naamathite becomes the search for an eponymous ancestor. Given the prior identifications regarding personal and clan names, the most likely person to have been the eponymous ancestor of the Naamathites appears to be Nahath. Nahath can be identified as the son of Reuel, the son of Esau (Edom) out of Esau's wife, Basemath, who was the daughter of Ismael, peace be upon him.[35] Weaving the facts with this information, one now has two of Job's companions identified as being Edomites, with one having an Ismaelite paternal grandmother. Further, all three of the companions identified so far are from the non-Israelite descendants of Abraham who contributed to the formation of the Arab people.

Next, one considers the word "Buzite". Once again, this word appears in the *Bible* only in the book of *Job*, and then only as a descriptor of Elihu.[36] In looking for an eponymous ancestor of the Buzites, one turns immediately to Buz. *Genesis* 22:21 notes a Buz, who was the son of Nahor, with Nahor being the brother of Abraham. This would probably indicate a location near Harran in southeastern Turkey, which does not fit with the information placing Job in Edom, i.e., southern Jordan. *I Chronicles* 5:14 refers to a Buz, who was an Israelite member of the tribe of Gad. However, *I Chronicles* 5:11-16 clearly places this Buz in Bashan, which would be in the extreme north of Jordan and in the area of the Golan in Syria. Again, the geography does not fit. However, neither does the chronology. As will be seen later, Job appears to have existed several centuries before the Israelite tribes carved out their traditional tribal areas in Palestine, and would thus, have existed several centuries before this particular Buz. Clearly, this Israelite Buz cannot be the eponymous ancestor of the clan of Buzites at the time of Job. Finally, *Jeremiah* 25:23 refers to a people called Buz, placing this people amidst a long list of different groups of people. Without quoting every ethnic group included in this list, extending from verse 18 through verse 26, it is helpful to note the exact wording of *Jeremiah* 25:23-24.

> Dedan, Tema, Buz, and all who have shaven temples; all the
> kings of Arabia and all the kings of the mixed peoples that
> live in the desert;

Each of the above clues from *Jeremiah* needs to be reviewed. First, Dedan refers to the Dedanites, i.e. the descendants of Dedan, the son of Jokshan, the son of Abraham out of his third wife, Keturah.[37] As such, the Dedanites were a tribe collateral to that of the Midianites and Shuhites. Their traditional home was the Hijaz of northwestern Saudi Arabia. Their area of control included the town of Dedan, and extended down as far south as Khaibar.[38] Second, Tema refers to one of the 12 sons of Ismael, Abraham's oldest son from his second wife, Hagar.[39] Traditionally, the land of Tema adjoined that of Dedan, in northwestern Saudi Arabia and included the city of Tema.[40] Third, there is a reference to shaven temples, which would contradict Israelite origin[41], and would indicate Bedouins.[42] There is also a reference to the kings of Arabia. Quite clearly, Buz is being included in *Jeremiah* as being one of the clans or tribes that would later coalesce as the Arab people.[43]

Finally, *Job* 32:2 states that the Buzites were "of the family of Ram". Now who was Ram? It may be noted that there are a number of different Israelites named Ram, who are referred to in the *Bible*, but quite simply Ram appears to be a mild corruption of the Arabized form of the name Reuel, i.e. Al-Rum. As noted earlier, Reuel was the son of Esau (Edom) from his wife, Basemath, who was the daughter of Ismael, the son of Abraham.[44] Interestingly, this same son of Esau is called Al-Rum by Al-Tabari[45], providing the Arabized form of the name.

SIXTH CONSIDERATION. Having finally gotten around to the concept of a corrupted form of a name, one can now consider the hypothesis that the name of Job actually appears four more times in the *Bible* than previously noted, but under a corrupted form of his name, i.e. Jobab. *Genesis* 36:33-34 and *I Chronicles* 1:44-45 report that when Bela, the son of Belor, died, he was succeeded as king of Edom by Jobab, the son of Zerah of Bozrah, who was succeeded upon his death by Husham of the Temanites.[46] *Genesis* 36:13 and *I Chronicles* 1:34-37 identify Zerah, the father of Jobab, as being the son of Reuel, the son of Esau and Basemath, the daughter of Ismael.

Al-Tabari

In one section of his monumental work on the history of the world, Al-Tabari offers a reported genealogy for the Prophet Job. This genealogy lists Job as being the son of Maws or Mawas. In turn, Maws is listed as having Razih or Raghwil as his father, and the daughter of the prophet Lot, peace be upon him, as his mother. In turn, Razih or Raghwil is listed as having Esau as his father. Further, Al-Tabari states that Job's wife was Liyya (this should probably be Dinah[47]—Liyya appears to be a variant of Dinah's mother's name), who was the daughter of Jacob (the son of Isaac) and of Leah. Still further, Al-Tabari lists two sons for Job: Hawmal; and Bishr, who subsequently became the father of 'Abdan.[48]

Genesis Vs. Al-Tabari

Assuming that Jobab, the son of Zerah, is the Prophet Job, one can then neatly contrast the proposed genealogies as found in *Genesis* and in Al-Tabari. This contrast is presented in Table 1 below, and reveals several striking similarities and a few differences.

Table 1: Genesis vs. Al-Tabari

GENESIS	AL-TABARI
Abraham	Abraham
Isaac	Isaac
Esau	Esau
Reuel	Razih or Raghwil
Zerah	Maws or Mawas
Jobab	Job

There is a perfect agreement between *Genesis* and Al-Tabari for the first three and for the sixth entries, assuming that Jobab is Job. The fourth entry appears problematic, but really isn't. Raghwil could just as easily be transliterated with an "e" instead of an "i", and with a "u" instead of a "w". This would render the name Raghuel, which becomes quite similar to Reuel. However, the author has no explanation for the discrepancies in the fifth entry in Table 1. Nonetheless, five of the six entries appear to be quite similar, if not totally identical. Furthermore, the number of generations between the given individuals remains the same in both lists. As such, it is suggested that the Prophet Job was the son of Zerah, the son of Reuel. Reuel's father was Esau (Edom), the eponymous ancestor of the Edomites, while Reuel's mother was Basemath, the daughter of

Ismael. That means Job appears to have descended from two lines from Abraham, both of which contributed to the later formation of the Arab people, and neither of which was of Israelite origin, i.e., having descent from Jacob, Esau's younger brother.

Job's Family Tree

Using the totality of the information so far presented, one can now begin to construct a speculative family tree of Job. This is done in Table 2 below. This family tree notes the relationship between Job and each of his four companions (Bildad, Eliphaz, Zophar, and Elihu), though some generations may be missing in the case of Job's companions, and a few of the identifications remain speculative in the said family tree. The tree further illustrates that Job was only three generations away from Esau and Jacob, four generations from Ismael and Isaac, and five generations from Abraham. Still further, it illustrates that Job was an Edomite, who traced his ancestry through his paternal grandmother to Ismael, thus tracing to two people (Edomites and Ismaelites), who contributed to the formation of the Arab people. Finally, it clearly indicates that Job was not an Israelite, i.e. a descendant of Jacob, although Job's wife was an Israelite.

Table 2: The Family Tree of Job

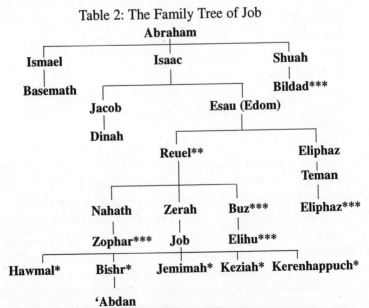

*   The mother was reportedly Dinah, the daughter of Jacob.
** The mother was reportedly Basemath, the daughter of Ismael.
*** One or more generations may be skipped between this entry and the one above it.

When

Having established a hypothetical family tree for Job, one is now in a better position to estimate the period in history when Job lived. However, in order to do so, one must start almost a millennia after Job, i.e., during the reign of King Solomon, peace be upon him. Almost all scholars place the commencement of the rein of King Solomon in the 10th century BCE, with estimates ranging from 992 to 961 BCE, and with the estimates tending to center around 970 BCE.[49] Using the date of 970 BCE as the start of Solomon's rein, one notes that Solomon began building his temple in the fourth year of his reign, which was 480 years after the Israelites came out of the land of Egypt under Prophet Moses, peace be upon him.[50] This would then place the exodus from Egypt as occurring around 1,446 BCE. Now, the Israelites reportedly lived in Egypt for 430 years,[51] marking the beginning of the Egyptian sojourn around 1,876 BCE.

Having established the start of the Egyptian sojourn as being about 1,876 BCE, one notes that Jacob lived in Egypt for 17 years, before dying at age 147.[52] This would indicate that Jacob was born 130 years prior to the start of the Egyptian sojourn, i.e., at about 2,006 BCE. Since Esau and Jacob were twins[53], this would also place Esau's birth at about 2,006 BCE. As noted previously, Job appears to have been only three generations away from Esau, suggesting that Job was born circa the 20th century BCE. As *Job* 42:16 says that Job lived for 140 years after his trial and restoration, one tentatively places Job's life as spanning the 19th century BCE and parts of the 20th and 18th centuries BCE as well.

Why

The when, where, and who of Job's life have now been discussed. However, one is left with one final question. Why is the *Bible* so sparing and parsimonious in the information it gives out about Job? Why does one need to sift through Biblical clues in the first place? Why does one need to assemble a jigsaw puzzle of details before arriving at the facts that: Job lived in Edom (southern Jordan); Job's friends and associates were among the forerunners (e.g., Edomites and Shuhites) of the Arab people; and Job himself was an Edomite, who carried 12.5% Ismaelite blood? The answer to each of these questions is as obvious as it is disturbing. The existence of Job as a prophet of Allah was a direct challenge and repudiation of the traditional Israelite concept of the Israelites being the "chosen people".

Equally cucial to the "chosen people" concept was the notion that they had an exclusive claim to a relationship with Allah.[54] According to the Israelites, this was a claim not shared by any other ethnic group. A prophet of Allah arising from a neighboring ethnic group, e.g., the Edomites, was a direct repudiation of this very conceptualization, especially since the Edomites traced their ancestoral roots to the elder son of Isaac, while the Israelites traced theirs to the younger son of Isaac. Further, this particular Edomite also carried Ismaelite blood, thus tracing through the first son of Abraham, while the Israelites could trace only through the second son of Abraham. Thus, the very presence of Job raised serious questions about whether the Israelites could have a legitimate and exclusive inheritance of Allah's covenant with Abraham. If the covenant were an exclusive inheritance, as the Israelites claimed, if Job were an Edomite of Ismaelite descent, and if Job were a prophet of Allah, then the obvious questions that pop up are: was it Ismael or Isaac or both, who inherited the covenant from Abraham; and if Isaac inherited it from Abraham, was it Esau or Jacob or both, who inherited the covenant from Isaac. These would be most disturbing questions to any Israelite who maintained the traditional Israelite notions of "chosen people" and of the exclusive inheritance of the covenant.[55]

What could be done to set aside this challenge? Job was obviously too famous and too well known[56], simply to be ignored by the writers and compilers of Jewish scriptures. His story as a prophet of Allah, who was tried with massive tribulations, who triumphed over those tribulations and over whatever temptations may have accompanied them, was already a part of both the Hebrew and the Arabic languages. Ignoring the historical Job would not make him go away And so, the story of Job had to be included in the Jewish scriptures. However, it was included only in a manner so as to nullify any identifying details of his ethnic background to Esau and Ismael.

Postscript

Having devoted this entire chapter to Biblical questions relating to Job's location, identity, and time, it is fitting to close this chapter with the accounts of Job as mentioned in the *Qur'an*.

> We have sent thee inspiration, as We sent it to Noah and the
> messengers after him: We sent inspiration to Abraham,
> Ismail, Isaac, Jacob and the tribes, to Jesus, Job, Jonah,
> Aaron, and Solomon, and to Dàvid We gave the Psalms.[57]

That was the reasoning about Us, which We gave to Abraham (to use) against his people: We raise whom We will, degree after degree: for thy Lord is full of wisdom and knowledge. We gave him Isaac and Jacob: all (three) We guided: and before him, We guided Noah, and among his progeny, David, Solomon, Job, Joseph, Moses, and Aaron: thus do We reward those who do good.[58]

And (remember) Job, when he cried to his Lord, "Truly distress has seized me. But Thou art the most merciful of those that are merciful." So We listened to him: We removed the distress that was on him, and We restored his people to him, and doubled their number—as a grace from Ourselves, and a thing for commemoration, for all who serve Us.[59]

Commemorate Our servant Job. Behold he cried to his Lord: "The evil one has afflicted me with distress and suffering!" (The command was given:) "Strike with thy foot: here is (water) wherein to wash, cool and refreshing, and (water) to drink." And We gave him (back) his people and doubled their number—as a grace from Ourselves, and a thing for commemoration, for all who have under-standing. "And take in thy hand a little grass, and strike therewith: and break not (thy oath)." Truly We found him full of patience and constancy, how excellent in Our service! Ever did he turn to Us.[60]

Chapter 9

A Concise Introduction to Islam
– Articles of Faith and Pillars of Practice

This concise essay introduces the non-Muslim reader to the basic beliefs and practices of Islam from a traditional Muslim perspective, and in doing so attempts to draw parallels between Islam and Christianity. It is in no way a scholarly debate, or an in-depth set of instructions. It is a brief handshake, made in the sincere hope that this will inspire the reader to seek a deeper knowledge of Islam, and an appreciation of the basic similarities and bonds between Christnity and Islam.

Allah

The use of the word "Allah" to mean "God" frequently sounds rather strange, esoteric, and foreign to Western ears. "Allah" is an Arabic word derived from the contraction of "Al" and "Ilahi", meaning "the God", or by implication "the One God". Linguistically, Hebrew and Arabic are related Semitic languages, and the Arabic "Allah" or "Al-Ilahi" is related to the Hebrew "El", meaning "God"[1], and "El-Elohim", meaning "God of Gods" or "the God".[2] It is these Hebrew words that are translated in the *Old Testament* as "God". Thus, one can see that the use of the word "Allah" is consistent, not only with the *Qur'an* and with Islamic tradition, but with the oldest Biblical traditions as well.

This basic similarity between the Arabic "Al-Ilahi", of which "Allah" is a contraction, and the Hebrew "El-Elohim" can be seen even more clearly when one considers the Arabic and Hebrew alphabets. Neither Arabic nor Hebrew have letters for vowels. Both languages have alphabets consisting only of consonants, and both rely on vowel markings, typically found only in formal writing, as a pronunciation guide. The English transliteration of the Arabic "Al-Ilahi" and of the Hebrew "El-

Elohim" have included these vowel markings. If one were to remove the
English transliteration of these vowel markings, the Arabic becomes "Al-
Ilh" and the Hebrew becomes "El-Elhm". If one were to remove the plural of respect, which is found only in the Hebrew, the Arabic remains "Al-
Ilh", while the Hebrew becomes "El-Elh". Finally, if one were to translit-
erate all Arabic "Alifs" as "a", and all Hebrew "Alifs" as "a", the Arabic
becomes "Al-Alh" and the Hebrew becomes "Al-Alh". In other words,
with the single exception that the Hebrew uses the plural of respect, "Al-
Ilahi", for which "Allah" is a contraction, and "El-Elohim", the Hebrew
translated as "God" in the English version of the *Old Testament*, are
absolutely identical terms in two closely related languages.

Islam

"Islam" is an Arabic word, which literally means "submission", i.e., submission to the will and pleasure of Allah. However, this is not a mere lip
service type of submission. Islam implies a total submission of the heart,
mind, and body. This type of total submission still finds expression in the
Jewish scriptures of the "received *Torah*."[3]

> You shall love the Lord your God with all your heart, and
> with all your soul, and with all your might.[4]

The Christian scriptures maintain that Jesus, peace be upon him[5],
echoed the above verse , and thus also mandated a total submission to
Allah. In addition, further expression of the need to submit to Allah can
be found in the *New Testament.*

> Submit yourselves therefore to God...Draw near to God,
> and he will draw near to you"

The need to submit totally to Allah finds its clearest expression in the
Qur'an, as translated in the following verse:[8]

> So if they dispute with thee, say: "I have submitted my
> whole self to Allah, and so have those who follow me."[9]

Unfortunately, the majority of the children of Israel did not
submit to Allah, resulting initially in the formation of Judaism, and
subsequently in the formation of Christianity. In that respect, the *Bible*
records that Prophet David, peace be upon him, spoke the following
words of revelation from Allah.

> I am the Lord your God, who brought you up out of the land

of Egypt. Open your mouth wide and I will fill it. But my people did not listen to my voice; Israel would not submit to me.[10]

As to the failure to submit to Allah, which resulted in the sequential formation of both Judaism and Christianity, the *Qur'an* records the following words of Allah.

The religion before (in the sight of) Allah is Islam (submission to His will): nor did the people of the book dissent therefrom except through envy of each other, after knowledge had come to them. But if any deny the signs of Allah, Allah is swift in calling to account.[11]

The believer in and practitioner of Islam is known as a Muslim. The words "Muslim" and "Islam" derives from the same Arabic root word and "Muslim" literally means "one who submits", i.e., one who wholly submits to Allah. While "submission" is the primary definition associated with the etymology of the word "Islam", there is also a secondary definition, which is "peace". Thus, it is only with full and complete submission to Allah that a Muslim experiences true spiritual peace.

While most non-Muslims typically believe that Islam began in the seventh century CE with the advent of the preaching of Prophet Muhammad, peace be upon him, Muslims adamantly reject this supposition. They believe that Islam began at the dawn of mankind with Adam, peace be upon him, and his wife being the first persons to practice Islam.

We had already, beforehand, taken the covenant of Adam, but he forgot: and We found on his part no firm resolve.[12]

However, Muslims also believe that Islam has been given to mankind as a progressive revelation. While the core of that revelation, i.e., that there is no god but Allah, has never changed throughout the course of time, the revelation was only completed and finalized with the last revelation given to the Prophet Muhammad.[13]

This day have I perfected your religion for you, completed my favor upon you, and have chosen for you Islam as your religion.[14]

The Articles of Faith

With the final revelation to Prophet Muhammad completed, the basic

belief system of Islam came to comprise five primary articles of faith.
(1) Belief in that there is no god but Allah. (2) Belief in all the messengers and prophets of Allah. (3) Belief in all the scripture and revelations
of Allah as they were delivered in their original form. (4) Belief in the
angels of Allah, without in anyway attributing to the angels any partnership or association with Allah. (5) Belief in life after death and in an ultimate Day of Judgment. These five articles of faith will be presented
briefly in the pages that follow.

Belief in Allah

The first article of faith in Islam is belief in Allah, glorified and exalted is
He. As the term "Allah" implies, the belief in Allah is a stringent and strict
monotheism. Allah is "the One God". There is no other. As such, Allah
is not the god of just one selected nation or ethnic group. Allah is the god
of all mankind, of all forms of life, of all creations, and of all worlds.

> Praise be to Allah, the cherisher and sustainer of the
> worlds.[15]

Allah is not simply a nationalistic or ethnic god among a plurality of
gods, as early Judaism appears to have maintained, and which at least one
reading of the following *Old Testament* verse appears to imply. In that
regard, it needs to be pointed out that the following verse, the first of the
so-called Ten Commandments, does not deny the existence of other gods,
but merely prioritizes which god is to be worshipped by the children of
Israel, and establishes a preferred tribal deity, i.e., "the god of Abraham,
Isaac, and Jacob", peace be upon them.

> I am the Lord your God, who brought you out of the land of
> Egypt, out of the house of slavery; you shall have no other
> gods before me.[16]

However, not only is Allah One without equal and without peer, He
is also One in His unity. His unity admits and allows no partners or associates. His unity leaves no room for any triune conceptualization of the
deity, which results in sectarian divisions and in endless theological
squabbling about issues such as: is it three persons in one substance, or
three persons of similar substance; how does one really define "person"
and "substance"; how does each of three "persons" in one "substance"
keep its separate identity, which "person" of the unified "substance" pre-

ceded which other "persons"; which "person" of the unified "substance" begat which other "person"; if one "person" begat another "person", did not the first "person" precede the second "person", implying a time when the second "person" did not exist; which "person" of the unified "substance" directed which other "person" to do what, e.g., to   create the world and universe, and does this not imply that one "person" is subordinate to another "person"; are the three "persons" of the unified "substance" equal or unequal; do each of the three "persons" of the unified "substance" share in the being of the other "persons", or are they rigidly separated; etc.

Issues such as the above have resulted in fruitless and repetitious debate, as well as multiple schisms, within Christianity for almost 2,000 years. Ritualistic and liturgical formulae and creeds, such as the statement that the Son proceeded from the Father and the Holy Spirit proceeded from the Father and the Son, raise far more questions than they answer.

In Islam, Allah is One, i.e., One without peer, and One in absolute unity. He is not One among many, nor even One among others, but One in total uniqueness. His very uniqueness defies total comprehension by the limited intellect of mortal man. He is without beginning and without end, and there is nothing comparable to Him. Allah is the One God, besides Whom there is no other. The most perfect, beautiful, and sublime expression of this Oneness of Allah is to be found in the the *Qur'an Sura* 112, entitled *Al Ikhlas* (The Purity of Faith):

> In the name of Allah, most gracious, most merciful. Say:
> He is Allah, the One and Only; Allah, the eternal,
> absolute; He begetteth not, nor is He begotten; and there
> is none like unto Him.[17]

Belief in the Prophets and Messengers of Allah

BELIEF IN ALL THE PROPHETS AND MESSENGERS. Muslims believe in all the messengers and prophets of Allah. Further, they believe that Allah has provided a messenger to every people. At one time or another, every people or nation of people has received revelation from Allah through its own messenger of Allah. There are many verses in the *Qur'an*, which attest to this basic truth.[18] Perhaps, the following verses are among the most direct in this respect:

> Before thee We sent (messengers) to many nations, and We
> afflicted the nations with suffering and adversity, that they
> might learn humility.[19]

> Verily, We have sent thee in truth, as a bearer of glad
> tidings, and as a warner: and there never was a people,
> without a warner having lived among them (in the past).[20]

> To every people (was sent) a messenger: when their mes-
> senger comes (before them), the matter will be judged
> between them with justice, and they will not be wronged.[21]

> For We assuredly sent amongst every people a messenger,
> (with the command), "Serve Allah, and eschew evil": of the
> people were some whom Allah guided, and some on whom
> error became inevitably (established). So travel through the
> earth, and see what was the end of those who denied (the
> truth).[22]

Many of these messengers and prophets may no longer be known
to modern man. However, numerous prophets and messengers are
directly mentioned in the *Qur'an*, including, among others, Adam, Noah,
Abraham, Lot, Isma'il, Isaac, Jacob, Joseph, Job, Moses, Aaron, David,
Solomon, Jonah, John the Baptist, Jesus, and Muhammad, peace be upon
them all. There were many prophets and messengers, and a Muslim is not
free to pick and choose among the prophets and messengers of Allah.
A Muslim must acknowledge with equal respect all the prophets
and messengers of Allah of whom he is aware, e.g., specifically those
mentioned in the *Qur'an*.

> Those who deny Allah and His messengers, and (those
> who) wish to separate Allah from His messengers, saying:
> "We believe in some but reject others": and (those who)
> wish to take a course midway—they are in truth (equally)
> unbelievers; and We have prepared for unbelievers a
> humiliating punishment.[23]

THE NATURE OF THE MESSAGE. Each prophet and messenger
was granted inspiration and revelation from Allah. As time passed,
because of the nature of the progressive revelation of Allah, earlier

revelations were sometimes abrogated, modified, or expanded.[24] However, it must be stressed that Islam vehemently rejects the notion that Allah in any way evolved. The evolution under discussion is limited to the revelation that Allah has sent. In short, the revelation of Allah evolved, consistent with man's evolving readiness to receive that revelation. The following verses of the *Qur'an* serve to highlight and confirm this concept of progressive revelation:

> O People of the Book! There hath come to you Our messenger, revealing to you much that ye used to hide in the book, and passing over much (that is now unnecessary): There hath come to you from Allah a (new) light and a perspicuous book—wherewith Allah guideth all who seek His good pleasure to ways of peace and safety, and leadeth them out of darkness, by His will, unto the light—guideth them to a path that is straight.[25]

> None of Our revelations do We abrogate or cause to be forgotten, but We substitute something better or similar: knowest thou not that Allah hath power over all things.[26]

> This *Qur'an* is not such as can be produced by other than Allah; on the contrary it is a confirmation of (revelations) that went before it, and a fuller explanation of the book— wherein there is no doubt—from the Lord of the worlds.[27]

> We did send messengers before thee, and appointed for them wives and children: and it was never the part of a messenger to bring a sign except as Allah permitted (or commanded). For each period is a book (revealed). Allah doth blot out or confirm what He pleaseth: with Him is the mother of the book.[28]

However, consistent throughout all these revelations, which were given to different prophets at different times, the central theme was the Oneness of Allah. Only Allah is worthy of worship. Not withstanding the messenger, the setting, or the progressive character of the revelation, the fundamental truth of the Oneness of Allah was the pivotal point of the message provided by Allah. This fact is explicitly stated by Allah in the following verse from the *Qur'an*:

> Not a messenger did We send before thee without this
> inspiration by Us to him: that there is no god but I;
> therefore worship and serve Me.[29]

MAKE NO DISTINCTIONS AMONG THEM. Not only are
Muslims to believe in all of the prophets and messengers of Allah, but
they are specifically commanded by Allah to make no hierarchical
distinctions among His prophets and messengers, even though Allah may
have bestowed certain gifts upon one prophet or messenger and He may
have preferred one prophet or messenger to another.[30] A Muslim has
neither the religious freedom nor the knowledge to elevate one messenger above another. A Muslim is to honor all of Allah's messengers and
prophets equally. Unfortunately, some Muslims, in their zeal to honor
Prophet Muhammad appear to lose sight of this Qur'anic injunction.
However, the non-Muslim observer of such zealousness should not be
misled by the behavior or statements of Muslims, which appear to
contradict the non-discriminatory way in which all Muslims are to respect
and honor all of Allah's prophets and messengers. The words of Allah, as
recorded in the *Qur'an*, are quite clear:

> Say ye: "We believe in Allah, and the revelation given to us,
> and to Abraham, Ismail, Isaac, Jacob, and the tribes, and
> that given to Moses and Jesus, and that given to (all)
> prophets from their Lord: we make no difference between
> one and another of them: and we bow to Allah (in Islam).[31]

> The messenger believeth in what hath been revealed to him
> from his Lord, as do the men of faith. Each one (of them)
> believeth in Allah, His angels, His books, and His messen-
> gers. "We make no distinction (they say) between one and
> another of His messengers." And they say: "We hear, and
> we obey: (We seek) Thy forgiveness, our Lord, and to Thee
> is the end of all journeys."[32]

> To those who believe in Allah and His messengers
> and make no distinction between any of the messengers,
> We shall soon give their (due) rewards: for Allah is oft-
> forgiving, most merciful.[33]

Furthermore, the words of Prophet Muhammad on this subject are equally clear and unambiguous. As narrated by both Abu Sa'id Al-Khudri[34] and Abu Huraira[35], and as recorded by Al-Bukhari[36], Prophet Muhammad specifically instructed his companions to refrain from assigning to any one prophet, including himself, superiority over any other of Allah's prophets.

THE PROPHETS AND MESSENGERS ARE MEN. It needs to be emphasized here that in Islam, there is no room for any triune god, or any attempt to dress polytheism in the clothing of monotheism. The prophets and messengers of Allah are not in any way, shape, or form to be considered as "partners" with Allah. Islam is the religion perfected by Allah, not by Prophet Muhammad, or by any other prophets or messengers of Allah. The prophets and messengers, while chosen by Allah, were merely instruments for the transmission of the revelation and were devoid of any divine or semi-divine character. In the words attributed to Jesus in the *Bible:*

> Very truly, I tell you, servants are not greater than their master, nor are messengers greater than the one who sent them.[37]

The messengers and prophets of Allah were simply men upon whom Allah had conferred His inspiration. This was true of Prophet Muhammad and every prophet and messenger who preceded him:

> Before thee, also, the messengers We sent were but men, to whom We granted inspiration: if ye realise this not, ask of those who possess the message. Nor did We give them bodies that ate no food, nor were they exempt from death.[38]

In the case of Prophet Muhammad this is even more emphatically attested by the following verses of the *Qur'an*:

> Muhammad is no more than a messenger: many were the messengers that passed away before him. If he died or were slain, will ye then turn back on your heels? If any did turn back on his heels, not the least harm will he do to Allah; but Allah (on the other hand) will swiftly reward those who (serve him) with gratitude.[39]

Say: "Glory to my Lord! Am I aught but a man—a messenger. What kept menback from belief when guidance came to them, was nothing but this: they said "Has Allah sent a man (like us) to be (His) messenger.[40]

Say: "I am but a man like yourselves, (but) the inspiration has come to me that your God is One God: whoever expects to meet his Lord, let him work righteousness, and, in the worship of his Lord, admit no one as partner."[41]

Various Ahadith[42] also affirm the complete humanity of Prophet Muhammad, while denying any pretense of divinity. The following two examples are noteworthy in that respect.

At the time of the Prophet there was a hypocrite who rendered so much harm to the believers that some of them summoned the others to ask the help of the Prophet against him. When the Prophet, peace be upon him, heard of it, he said: "No man may seek my help. Only the help of Allah is worthy of being sought"[43]

'Umar reported that the Prophet, peace be upon him, said: "Do not aggrandize me as the Christians aggrandized the son of Maryam. I am but a creature. Call me the creature of Allah, His servant and messenger."[44]

Having stressed the point that the prophets and messengers were only men, it also needs to be acknowledged that the prophets were men of extraordinary character, piety, spirituality, and faith. This Islamic view of the prophets and messengers stands in sharp contrast to the Judeo-Christian scriptures, in which the prophets are frequently portrayed as spiritual leaders with feet of clay, lusting and sinning as frequently as those to whom they preached. However, Allah, Himself, has assured mankind that no prophet could betray the revelation and inspiration given to him.

No prophet could (ever) be false to his trust.[45]

Does this mean that the prophets were perfect? Of course not, as nothing is perfect other than Allah. Does this mean that the prophets were never tempted? No, as Allah's own words indicate that they might be:

> *Perchance thou mayest* (feel the inclination) to give up a part of what is revealed unto thee, and thy heart feeleth straitened lest they say, "Why is not a treasure sent down unto him, or why does not an angel come down with him?" But thou art there only to warn! It is Allah that arrangeth all affairs![46]

Does this mean that a prophet could never make a mistake? No, as clearly stated in the *Qur'an* with regard to: an example of rushing to judgment between two disputants by Prophet David[47]; and an example of Prophet Muhammad ignoring the questioning of a blind man interested in Islam, due to his preoccupation in attempting to persuade a person of substance and influence into Islam.

> (The Prophet) frowned and turned away, because there came to him the blind man (interrupting), but what could tell thee but that perchance he might grow (in spiritual understanding)? Or that he might receive admonition, and the teaching might profit him? As to one who regards himself as self-sufficient, to him dost thou attend; though it is no blame on thee if he grow not (in spiritual understanding). But as to him who came to thee striving earnestly and with fear (in his heart), of him wast thou unmindful. By no means (should it be so)! For it is indeed a message of instruction: therefore let whoso will keep it in remembrance."[48]

However, such mistakes were a far cry from the immorality frequently attributed to the prophets by the *Bible*, and do not imply that the prophets and messengers made mistakes when it came to points of religious doctrine and belief. Clearly, despite occasional minor mistakes, the prophets were exemplary individuals, and were excellent guides to follow. This very point is stated in the *Qur'an*, where Allah talks about the examples of Abraham and Muhammad:

> Abraham was indeed a model. Devoutly obedient to Allah, (and) true in faith, and he joined not gods with Allah. He showed his gratitude for the favors of Allah, Who chose him, and guided him to a straight way. And We gave him good in this world, and he will be, in the hereafter, in the ranks of the righteous. So We have taught thee the inspired

(message), "Follow the ways of Abraham the true in faith, and he joined not gods with Allah."[51]

We have indeed in the messenger of Allah a beautiful pattern (of conduct) for any one whose hope is in Allah and the final day, and who engages much in the praise of Allah.[52]

As such, Muslims do utilize the model, i.e. sayings and behavior (Hadith; plural is Ahadith), of Prophet Muhammad as an example that should be followed and as being religiously authoritative, without elevating such sayings or behavior to the status of having the same significance or importance as the literal words of Allah, i.e., the *Qur'an*.

THE SEAL OF THE PROPHETS. While Muslims are forbidden to differentiate among the prophets and messengers of Allah in any hierarchical manner, and while all such prophets and messengers are to be seen as only men, however virtuous, the *Qur'an* specifically states that Prophet Muhammad was the last of the prophets and messengers of Allah. In that respect, Allah refers to Prophet Muhammad as the "seal of the prophets". This phrase is sometimes understood by non-Muslims and by Westerners to imply some sort of hierarchical significance to the prophethood of Muhammad. However, such an understanding is erroneous. Just as the last thing to be placed on a formal document is the signatory seal, Prophet Muhammad is to be considered as "the seal of the prophets", meaning that he is the last prophet and messenger of Allah. With the revelation given to Prophet Muhammad, the revelation of Allah has ended, earlier revelations have been modified or abrogated, and Islam has been perfected.

Muhammad is not the father of any of your men, but (he is) the messenger of Allah, and the seal of the prophets: and Allah has full knowledge of all things.[53]

Belief in the Books of Allah

Muslims believe in all of the Books of Allah. This includes both the *Qur'an* and the earlier Books revealed by Allah to His various messengers. While all of Allah's prophets received divine inspiration and revelation, some of them were given an actual Book of revelation. Those, who were given such a Book, are frequently referred to as the messengers of Allah.[54] The *Qur'an* notes five such Books of revelation: the Book given to Abraham[55]; the Book (*Torah* or Law) given to Moses[56]; the Book (*Zabur* or *Psalms*) given to David[57]; the Book (*Injil* or Gospel) given to Jesus[58]; and the Book (*Qur'an*) given to Muhammad.[59] Muslims believe that all these Books, as they were delivered in their original form to the messengers who then imparted them to mankind, were the actual, literal words of Allah. However, the operative phrase is "as they were delivered in their original form".

THE CORRUPTION OF EARLIER BOOKS. The Book of Abraham is no longer known to exist, and no trace of such a book has been left to modern man. However, the book of *Jubilees*, a Jewish religious writing of the third or second century BCE, seems to refer to that Book of Abraham, when it notes that, upon his death, Jacob left his books and the books of his fathers, i.e. Isaac and Abraham, to his son Levi.[60]

As regards the Book of Moses, the "received *Torah*", as found in the current Biblical books of *Genesis, Exodus, Leviticus, Numbers,* and *Deuteronomy*, is a far cry from the original *Torah*, although traces and elements of the original *Torah* may continue to be found, scattered here and there in the "received *Torah*". In fact, Biblical analysis by Christian scholars has clearly demonstrated that: these five books of the "received Torah" did not reach their present form until late in the fifth century BCE, i.e. around 1,000 years after Moses; and that these books are compilations from earlier written sources, known as *J, E, P,* and *D*.[61]

Likewise, the current Biblical book of *Psalms* is a poor resemblance of the original *Psalms* of David, although occasional chapters or verses in the "received *Psalms*" may be part of the original *Psalms*. Interestingly, this Islamic belief finds significant support from Christian scholars and commentators on the *Psalms*.[62]

Finally, it must be noted that the original *Gospel* of Jesus can nowhere be found in the corpus of the *Bible*, although various sayings attributed to Jesus in the *Bible* may represent preserved fragments from the original Gospel or *Injil*. The original *Gospel* of Jesus would have been a word-for-word repetition of the words of Allah to Jesus. In that regard, it may have been similar to *Q* (a lost collection of the sayings of Jesus utilized by *Matthew, Luke,* and *Thomas*) or to the apocryphal *Gospel* of *Thomas*, both of which were books of the sayings of Jesus. In contrast, the current canonical gospels of *Matthew, Mark, Luke,* and *John* are basically small biographies of Jesus. The canonical gospels are merely the writings about Jesus of anonymous authors, to whom the later

Christian churches assigned the names of various disciples of Jesus or followers of the disciples of Jesus. They certainly are not books that claim to be the word-for-word rendition of Jesus wherein he quotes the words of Allah.[63]

Numerous passages in the *Qur'an* refer to man's distortion and alteration of the previous Books of revelation from Allah.[64] These passages consistently note that the received Books that are utilized by the People of the Book, i.e., by Jews and Christians, do not conform to the original revelations that were given. The following verses from the *Qur'an* are among the more direct in addressing this distortion of the prior Books of Allah:

> Can ye (O ye men of faith) entertain the hope that they will believe in you?—seeing that a party of them heard the word of Allah, and perverted it knowingly after they understood it...Then woe to those who write the book with their own hands, and then say: "This is from Allah," to traffic with it for a miserable price!—woe to them for what their hands do write, and for the gain they make thereby.[65]

> There is among them a section who distort the book with their tongues: (as they read) you would think it is a part of the book, but it is no part of the book; and they say, "That is from Allah," but it is not from Allah: it is they who tell a lie against Allah, and (well) they know it.[66]

> And remember Allah took a covenant from the People of the Book, to make it known and clear to mankind, and not to hide it; but they threw it away behind their backs, and purchased with it some miserable gain! And vile was the bargain they made![67]

> But because of their breach of their covenant, We cursed them, and made their hearts grow hard: they change the words from their (right) places and forget a good part of the message that was sent them, nor wilt thou cease to find them—barring a few—ever bent on (new) deceits: but forgive them, and overlook (their misdeeds): for Allah loveth those who are kind. From those, too, who call

them-selves Christians, We did take a covenant, but they forgot a good part of the message that was sent them: so We estranged them, with enmity and hatred between the one and the other, to the Day of Judgment. And soon will Allah show them what it is they have done.[68]

No just estimate of Allah do they make when they say: "Nothing doth Allah send down to man (by way of revelation)": say: "Who then sent down the book which Moses brought?—a light and guidance to man: but ye make it into (separate) sheets for show, while ye conceal much (of its contents): therein were ye taught that which ye knew not— neither ye nor your fathers." Say: "Allah (sent it down)": then leave them to plunge in vain discourse and trifling.[69]

THE INVIOLABILITY OF THE *QUR'AN*. In contrast to the prior Books of revelation, the incorruptibility of the *Qur'an* is guaranteed by Allah Himself. The revelation of Allah to Prophet Muhammad through a span of about 22 years is preserved without blemish in the *Qur'an*. As such, the *Qur'an* remains a true and unadulterated recording of the literal words of Allah. As recorded in the *Qur'an*, Allah's own promise to Prophet Muhammad illustrates that the integrity of the *Qur'an* will remain inviolate for all time.

And recite (and teach) what has been revealed to thee of the book of thy Lord: none can change His words, and none wilt thou find as a refuge other than Him.[70]

Nay, this is a glorious *Qur'an* (inscribed) in a tablet preserved.[71]

In closing this brief discussion of the Muslim's belief in the Books of Allah, it needs to be reemphasized that the *Qur'an* is a true and accurate recording of Prophet Muhammad quoting verbatim the words delivered to him from Allah. Therefore, the *Qur'an* does not contain the words of Muhammad, but of Allah. The *Qur'an* does not even consist of the words of Muhammad as inspired by Allah. Likewise, the *Qur'an* is not Muhammad's interpretation of the words or message of Allah.[72] The

Qur'an is simply the words of Allah.

Belief in the Angels of Allah

ANGELS AS A CLASS OF CREATION. Muslims believe in the angels of Allah, without attributing to them any partnership whatsoever with Allah. The angels are no more than creations of Allah. In that respect, the angels can be compared to the jinn and to man.

> 'A'isha reported that Allah's Messenger (may peace be upon him) said: "The angels were born out of light and the jinns were born out of the spark of fire and Adam was born as he has been defined (in the *Qur'an*) for you (i.e., he is fashioned out of clay).[73]

Given the above Hadith and the confusion that typically exists among non-Muşlims and Westerners about the Islamic view of these three classes of creation, as well as the differences between the Muslims and those of the Judeo-Christian persuasion on the role of Satan, it may be profitable to digress for a moment. This is appropriate, in order to consider briefly the similarities and differences found among these three classes of creations, i.e. the angels, the jinn, and mankind.

OF ANGELS, *JINN*, AND MEN. As the above Hadith reveals, the angels were created from light, the jinn from fire[74], and mankind, through Adam, from clay.[75]

> We created man from sounding clay, from mud molded into shape; and the jinn race, We had created before, from the fire of a scorching wind.[76]

> He created man from sounding clay like unto pottery, and He created jinns from fire free of smoke... [77]

These three classes of beings are part of the creations of Allah.. While it may be true that the angels and the *jinn* have been granted certain powers by Allah, which have not been granted to man, the angels and *jinn* still remain no more than mere creatures of Allah. None of the three classes can claim any divinity, and none are to be considered associates or partners of Allah. Such a conceptualization would constitute a direct denial of the Oneness of Allah, and thus is expressly forbidden in

Islam. Likewise, one may not pray to any of the creations of Allah, whether angel or other, not even to the extent of asking such a creature to make intercession between oneself and Allah. One prays directly to Allah, without intermediaries.

> How many so ever be the angels in the heavens, their inter-
> cession will avail nothing except after Allah has given leave
> for whom He pleases and that he is acceptable to Him.[78]

Of these three classes of creation, Allah has endowed only the *jinn* and mankind with free will. Among both the jinn and mankind there were and are believers and non-believers, i.e., those who choose to sub-mit to Allah and those who do not. This distinction between believers and non-believers cannot be said to exist among the angels. All angels are believers, because they are not free to choose otherwise. Therefore, with this in view, there can be no "fallen angels" as portrayed in the Judeo-Christian tradition.

SATAN OR *IBLIS*. If there are no "fallen angels", how does Islam account for Satan? According to the *Qur'an*, Satan, also known as *Iblis*, was a particularly powerful *jinn*. This identification of Satan with the *jinn* can be made both directly and indirectly. The indirect identification is based upon those Qur'anic passages, in which Iblis refers to himself as having been created from fire by Allah[79], which links the creation of *Iblis* with the creation of the *jinn*. However, one does not have to rely upon this indirect identification. A direct identification of *Iblis* as being one of the jinn is specifically stated in the *Qur'an*:

> Behold! We said to the angels, "Bow down to Adam": they
> bowed down except *Iblis*. He was one of the *jinns*, and he
> broke the command of his Lord.[80]

The story of the "fall" of Iblis or Satan is told in greater detail in other passages of the *Qur'an*.[81] In summary, after creating Adam from clay, Allah ordered the angels to bow down to Adam. The angels did, but not so Iblis. Iblis, who happened to be in a company of angels at that time, refused to bow down, claiming that he was better than Adam. Adam had only been fashioned from clay, while *Iblis* had been created from fire. As such, Iblis believed that he was Adam's superior, and his own arrogance and pride resulted in his choosing to disobey Allah. Caught disobeying his Creator, and about to be punished for his disobedience, *Iblis* begged

that the punishment be postponed until the Day of Judgment. Allah granted him his request, and *Iblis* then vowed to spend his time between then
and the Day of Judgment in attempting to lead astray mankind and the
jinn; away from true submission to Allah. However, it is a great mercy to
mankind that Allah specifically stipulated that *Iblis* would have no power
over those who submit fully to their Creator:

> Behold! thy Lord said to the angels: "I am about to create
> man, from sounding clay, from mud molded into shape;
> when I have fashioned him (in due proportion) and breathed
> into him of My spirit, fall ye down in obeisance unto him."
> So the angels prostrated themselves, all of them together;
> not so Iblis: he refused to be among those who prostrated
> themselves. (Allah) said: "O *Iblis*! What is your reason for
> not being among those who prostrated themselves?" (*Iblis*)
> said: "I am not one to prostrate myself to man, whom Thou
> didst create from sounding clay, from mud molded into
> shape." (Allah) said: "Then get thee out from here: for thou
> art rejected, accursed. And the curse shall be on thee till the
> Day of Judgment." (*Iblis*) said: "O my Lord! give me
> then respite till the day the (dead) are raised." (Allah)
> said: "Respite is granted thee—till the day of the time
> appointed." (*Iblis*) said: "O my Lord! because Thou hast put
> me in the wrong, I will make (wrong) fair-seeming to them
> on the earth, and I will put them all in the wrong—except
> Thy servants among them, sincere and purified (by Thy
> grace)." (Allah) said: "This (way of my sincere servants)
> is indeed a way that leads straight to Me. For over My
> servants no authority shalt thou have, except such as put
> themselves in the wrong and follow thee." And verily, hell
> is the promised abode for them all![82]

NAMES OF THE ANGELS. Four angels are mentioned by name in
the *Qur'an*. They are Gabriel (*Jibril*)[83], Michael[84], Harut[85], and Marut[86].
Of these four, both Gabriel[87] and Michael[88] are mentioned in the *Bible*.
Of linguistic interest, one notes that both Gabriel (Hebrew = Gabri'el)
and Michael (Hebrew = Myka'el) incorporate in Hebrew the Semitic
root word "El" at the end of their names. Thus, the name Gabriel can be
translated as "man of God (Allah)" or "God (Allah) has shown Himself
strong", while Michael can be translated as "who is like God (Allah)?"[89],

implying that there is none other than Allah, and thus emphasizing the Oneness of Allah.

THE ROLE OF THE ANGELS. The *Qur'an* specifically mentions several different roles fulfilled by the angels of Allah. These roles include, but are not limited to: removing the souls from men after death[90]; recording every deed of man, both good and bad, in order to provide a record, by which each man will be judged on the Day of Judgment[91]; protecting men[92]; running errands of mercy[93]; praying for forgiveness from Allah for all of mankind[94]; providing occasional trials to test mankind[95]; praising and worshipping Allah[96]; and serving as the transmitters of Allah's revelation to His prophets and messengers.[97]

GABRIEL. The *Qur'an* identifies Gabriel as being the messenger angel, who serves as the one who provides the words of Allah to His prophets and messengers.

> Say: whoever is an enemy to Gabriel—for he brings down
> the (revelation) to thy heart by Allah's will, a confirmation
> of what went before, and guidance and glad tidings for
> those who believe—whoever is an enemy to Allah and His
> angels and prophets, to Gabriel and Michael—Lo! Allah is
> an enemy to those who reject faith.[98]

It may be noted that this same role of being the bearer of Allah's revelation and inspiration is assigned to Gabriel in several passages in the *Bible*, including those from both the *Old* and *New Testament* [99]. As such, the concept of Gabriel as the messenger angel, who brings Allah's revelation and inspiration to His prophets and messengers, is a concept that is common to Judaism, Christianity, and Islam.

Having established that the scriptures of Judaism, Christianity, and Islam all hold that it is Gabriel, who, among the angels, transmits Allah's divine revelation to His human messengers and prophets, one is now in a position to further identify Gabriel according to certain titles. These titles are occasionally used in the *Qur'an* in place of Gabriel's name, especially when discussing Gabriel's role as the transmitter of Allah's revelation. In several passages in the *Qur'an*[100], Gabriel is simply referred to by the title of "*Al-Ruh*", which can be translated as "the spirit". Somewhat more specifically, Gabriel is referred to as "*Al-Ruh Al-Amin*".

> Verily this is a revelation from the Lord of the worlds: with

it came down the Spirit of Faith and Truth— [101]

In the above quotation from the meaning of the *Qur'an*, "*Al-Ruh Al-Amin*" has been rendered as "Spirit of Faith and Truth". A somewhat more literal translation might be "Spirit of Trustworthiness". However, the most appropriate translation is perhaps simply "Spirit of Truth".

Several Biblical passages in the gospel of *John* address the concept of the "Spirit of Truth". Traditional Christian interpretation identifies this "Spirit of Truth" with the Holy Spirit.

> And I will ask the Father, and he will give you another Advocate, to be with you forever. This is the Spirit of truth, whom the world cannot receive, because it neither sees him nor knows him. You know him, because he abides with you, and he will be in you.[102]

> When the Advocate comes whom I will send to you from the Father, the Spirit of truth who comes from the Father, he will testify on my behalf.[103]

> When the Spirit of truth comes, he will guide you into all the truth; for he will not speak on his own, but will speak whatever he hears, and he will declare to you the things that are to come.[104]

These Biblical passages clearly associate the Spirit of Truth with the bringing of Allah's revelation and inspiration, and it is noted that the Spirit of Truth "will not speak on his own, but will speak whatever he hears" from Allah. In other words, these verses from *John*: clearly imply that the Spirit of Truth, i.e. the Holy Spirit, is subordinate to Allah, and is not a partner with Him, in that the Spirit of Truth "will not speak on his own, but will speak whatever he hears" from Allah; and assign the same function, i.e. the bringing of revelation, to Gabriel and to the Spirit of Truth, i.e., the Holy Spirit. Thus, it is implied that Gabriel is the Spirit of Truth, and that the Spirit of Truth is the Holy Spirit. If Gabriel were the bearer of revelation, if the Spirit of Truth were the bearer of revelation, and if the Holy Spirit were the Spirit of Truth, then Gabriel is the Holy Spirit. The mathematical logic of this identification can be readily summarized as: G (Gabriel) = B (bearer of revelation); ST (Spirit of

Truth) = B (bearer of revelation); HS (Holy Spirit) = ST (Spirit of Truth); therefore G (Gabriel) = HS (Holy Spirit).

This identification is seen quite clearly in the *Qur'an*, merely by contrasting two verses, each of which discusses the bearer of Allah's revelation to Prophet Muhammad. In the first verse, Gabriel is identified by name as being the bearer of revelation to Prophet Muhammad. In the second verse, Gabriel is identified by his title, i.e. the Holy Spirit, as being the bearer of revelation to Muhammad. In that second verse, "*Al-Ruh Al-Qudusi*" is translated quite literally as "Holy Spirit".

> Say: whoever is an enemy to Gabriel—for he brings down the (revelation) to thy heart by Allah's will, a confirmation of what went before. And guidance and glad tidings for those who believe—[105]

> Say, the Holy Spirit has brought the revelation from thy Lord in truth, in order to strengthen those who believe, and as a guide and glad tidings to Muslims.[106]

In summary, Gabriel is none other than the Holy Spirit. While traditional Christianity has elevated Gabriel, under his title of Holy Spirit, to a partnership with his creator, i.e., Allah, in a triune godhead, Islam reaffirms the Oneness of Allah, vigorously resisting any polytheistic ideology, and continues to see Gabriel as merely an angel of Allah who transmits His messages to mankind.

Belief in the Day of Judgment

As is the case in Judaism and Christianity, belief in an eventual Day of Judgment is a central article of belief in Islam. While there are certain similarities among the Jewish, Christian, and Islamic conceptions of the Day of Judgment, there are also distinct differences. An in-depth analysis of the Day of Judgment from the Islamic perspective, not to mention from the vantage of comparative religions, is outside the scope and framework of this essay. As such, only a few issues concerning the Islamic belief in the Day of Judgment will be covered.

THE TIME. As repeatedly stated in the *Qur'an*, the timing of the Day of Judgment is knowledge that rests solely with Allah.[107] No man, no jinn, no angel, and no prophet or messenger has the least knowledge about its precise timing. During his ministry, Prophet Muhammad was asked repeatedly about the timing of the Day of Judgment. In response to

such questioning, Allah provided the following revelations to Prophet
Muhammad through the angel Gabriel.

> They ask thee about the (final) Hour—when will be its
> appointed time? Say: "The knowledge thereof is with my
> Lord (alone): none but He can reveal as to when it will
> occur. Heavy were its burden through the heavens and the
> earth. Only, all of a sudden will it come to you." They ask
> thee as if thou wert eager in search thereof: say: "The
> knowledge thereof is with Allah (alone), but most men
> know not."[108]

> They ask thee about the Hour –"When will be its appointed
> time?" Wherein art thou (concerned) with the declaration
> thereof? With thy Lord is the limit fixed therefor. Thou art
> but a warner for such as fear it.[109]

> Men ask thee concerning the Hour: say, "The knowledge
> thereof is with Allah (alone)": and what will make thee
> understand?—perchance the hour is nigh![110]

> Say: "As to the knowledge of the time, it is with Allah
> alone: I am (sent) only to warn plainly in public."[111]

As a brief digression, it is instructive to note the similarity between the wording of these revelations to Prophet Muhammad and the Biblical report of the
words of Jesus on the same issue:

> But about that day and hour no one knows, neither the
> angels of heaven, nor the Son, but only the Father.[112]

Even with the inappropriate capitalization of the word "son"[113] by the
Bible translators, the Biblical statement is remarkably similar in conceptual content to those recorded in the *Qur'an*.

THE PRECURSORS. Notwithstanding the fact that no one knows
the timing of the Day of Judgment except Allah, the coming of the Day
of Judgment is inevitable.[114]

> The Hour will certainly come: therein is no doubt: yet most
> men believe not.[115]

> Verily, the doom of thy Lord will indeed come to pass—
> there is none can avert it—on the Day when the firmament
> will be in dreadful commotion, and the mountains will fly
> hither and thither.[116]

> The unbelievers think that they will not be raised up (for
> judgment), say: "Yea, by my Lord, ye shall surely be raised
> up: then shall ye be told (the truth) of all that ye did. And
> that is easy for Allah."[117]

THE JUDGMENT. In the Jewish tradition, the Final Judgment is based upon one's acts and deeds. The issue of faith or belief does not really figure in the equation. In the Christian tradition, the Final Judgment is based upon one's faith. While lip service is sometimes paid to the issue of the righteousness and piety of one's life on earth, the bottom line remains that if one has sufficient faith, one "passes"--if not, one "fails". Unfortunately, this doctrine is often used by Christians for rationalizing the commission of sinful or questionable behavior, "No matter what my behavior is in this instance, my faith will still save me."

The Islamic view of the Final Judgment stands in sharp contrast to that of both Judaism and Christianity. In Islam, belief is a necessary condition for final reward and salvation, but it is not a sufficient condition, in and of itself. If belief were present during earthly life, judgment then devolves on the merits and demerits of the individual to be judged. At this point, the individual's book of deeds in life, as previously listed by the recording angels, firmly enters into the equation.[118] Given human nature, it is to the extreme good fortune of mankind, that this analysis of one's merits and demerits is tempered by the abundant mercy of Allah. However, unbelief is a sufficient condition, in and of itself, for punishment and damnation.[119]

> And the earth will shine with the glory of its Lord: the
> record (of deeds) will be placed (open); the prophets and the
> witnesses will be brought forward; and a just decision
> pronounced between them; and they will not be wronged (in
> the least). And to every soul will be paid in full (the fruit)
> of its deeds; and (Allah) knoweth best all that they do. The
> unbelievers will be led to hell in crowd: until, when they
> arrive there, its gates will be opened. And its keepers will
> say, "Did not messengers come to you from among your-

selves rehearsing to you the signs of your Lord, and warning you of the meeting of this Day of yours?" The answer will be: "True: but the decree of punishment has been proved true against the unbelievers!" (To them) will be said: "Enter ye the gates of hell, to dwell therein: and evil is (this) abode of the arrogant!" And those who feared their Lord will be led to the garden in crowds: until behold, they arrive there; its gates will be opened; and its keepers will say: "Peace be upon you! Well have ye done! Enter ye here, to dwell therein." They will say: "Praise be to Allah, Who has truly fulfilled His promise to us, and has given us (this) land in heritage: we can dwell in the garden as we will: how excellent a reward for those who work (righteousness)!"[120]

Further, one notes that each person is judged on his own merits and demerits. Unlike the Christian concept of Final Judgment, there is no salvation through the sacrifice of another, and there is no "atonement in the blood". Each person must stand on his/her own before Allah to answer for his/her own conduct and belief.

On that day shall no intercession avail except for those for whom permission has been granted by (Allah) most gracious and whose word is acceptable to Him.[121]

Again, what will explain to thee what the Day of Judgment is? (It will be) the day when no soul shall have power (to do) aught for another: for the command, that day, will be (wholly) with Allah.[122]

REWARD AND PUNISHMENT. The traditional Christian perspective of the judgment of Allah is that it is a "pass-fail" test. One either passes, i.e. receives heaven, or one fails, i.e., enters hell. The Islamic view is rather more sophisticated and complex, and emphasizes a level of fairness beyond that seen in the Christian perspective. In that regard, it is first noted that some individuals may first be punished in hell for a while, before Allah's mercy allows them to enter heaven. Second, in the Islamic belief system, heaven is multi-leveled, as is hell. While the gulf between "passing" and "failing" is enormous, and the consequences of that gulf are beyond the actual comprehension of the human mind, there are different degrees of reward in heaven, and different degrees of punishment in hell.

> Such in truth are the believers: they have grades of dignity with their Lord, and forgiveness, and generous sustenance...[123]

In this way, each person "gets every good that it earns, and it suffers every ill that it earns".[124]

The rewards of heaven and the punishment of hell are both physical and spiritual. With regard to the bliss of heaven, one notes the following passages from the *Qur'an*.

> Verily the companions of the garden shall that day have joy in all that they do; they and their associates will be in groves of (cool) shade, reclining on thrones (of dignity); (every) fruit (enjoyment) will be there for them; they shall have whatever they call for; "Peace!"—a word (of salutation) from a Lord most merciful.[125]

> And he will be in a life of bliss, in a garden on high, the fruits whereof (will hang in bunches) low and near. "Eat ye and drink ye, with full satisfaction; because of the (good) that ye sent before you, in the days that are gone!"[126]

> Verily for the righteous there will be a fulfillment of (the heart's) desires; gardens enclosed, and grapevines; companions of equal age; and a cup full (to the brim).[127]

> The righteous (will be) amid gardens and fountains (of clear-flowing water). (Their greeting will be): "Enter ye here in peace and security." And We shall remove from their hearts any lurking sense of injury: (they will be) brothers (joyfully) facing each other on thrones (of dignity). There no sense of fatigue shall touch them, nor shall they (ever) be asked to leave.[128]

> But the sincere (and devoted) servants of Allah—for them

is a sustenance determined, fruits (delights); and they (shall enjoy) honor and dignity, in gardens of felicity, facing each other on thrones (of dignity): round will be passed to them a cup from a clear-flowing fountain, crystal-white, of a taste delicious to those who drink (thereof), free from headiness; nor will they suffer intoxication therefrom. And besides them will be chaste women; restraining their glances, with big eyes (of wonder and beauty). As if they were (delicate) eggs closely guarded.[129]

The *Qur'an* describes the curse and punishment of hell in even more graphic terms, as witnessed in the following verses:

(The stern command will say): "Seize ye him and bind ye him, and burn ye him in the blazing fire. Further, make him march in a chain, whereof the length is seventy cubits! This was he that would not believe in Allah most high, and would not encourage the feeding of the indigent! So no friend hath he here this day. Nor hath he any food except the corruption from the washing of wounds, which none do eat but those in sin."[130]

Truly hell is as a place of ambush—for the transgressors a place of destination: they will dwell therein for ages. Nothing cool shall they taste therein, nor any drink, save a boiling fluid and a fluid, dark, murky, intensely cold—a fitting recompense for them...for no increase shall We grant you, except in punishment.[131]

In front of such a one is hell, and he is given for drink, boiling fetid water. In gulps will he sip it, but never will he be near swallowing it down his throat: death will come to him from every quarter, yet will he not die: and in front of him will be a chastisement unrelenting.[132]

Summary

To summarize briefly, the five articles of Islamic faith are as follows:
   • Muslims believe that there is no god but Allah and that only Allah is worthy of worship. The essential Oneness of Allah precludes His

having any associates or partners.

• Muslims believe in all the messengers and prophets of Allah without differentiating hierarchically among them, and without elevating them beyond their human nature.

• Muslims believe in all the scriptures and revelations from Allah as they were delivered in their original form. However, only the last book from Allah, i.e., the *Qur'an*, continues to exist on earth in its original and pristine form.

• Muslims believe in the angels of Allah while realizing that they are no more than one of Allah's creations.

• Muslims believe in life after death, in an ultimate Day of Judgment, and in a hereafter containing both a heaven and a hell.

• Muslims believe in the timeless knowledge of Allah, and in His power to plan and execute His will.

These five articles of faith are succinctly listed in the following verse from the *Qur'an*.

> It is not righteousness that ye turn your faces towards east or west; but it is righteousness—to believe in Allah and the Last Day, and the angels, and the book, and the messengers...[133]

The Pillars of Practice

Given the five articles of faith enumerated above, the application of faith in daily life can be summarized into what has been called the Five Pillars of Islam:

• The first pillar is *Shahadah,* the testimonial or declaration of faith, i.e., "*I testify that there is no god but Allah, and I testify that Muhammad is the messenger of Allah*".

• The second pillar is to perform the *Salat,* five obligatory daily prayers.

• The third pillar is to fast during the Islamic month of *Ramadan.*

• The fourth pillar is *Zakkat,* a mandatory payment to approved charity of a set percentage of one's financial surplus.

• The fifth pillar is to make the *Hajj* pilgrimage to Makkah at least once in one's adult lifetime, if one is financially and physically capable of doing so.

Shahadah

The first pillar of practice is the *Shahadah*, or testimonial of faith. In simple English translation, the *Shahadah* consists of saying: "I testify that there is no god but Allah, and I testify that Muhammad is the messenger of Allah". It would suffice to say that anyone who sincerely says the *Shahadah* with comprehension and understanding is a Muslim.

Given the previous discussion of the etymology of the word "Allah", most Christians and Jews who bother to think about the *Shahadah* would probably conclude that they would have no difficulty saying and meaning the first part of the *Shahadah*, i.e. "there is no god but Allah". However, those Christians who actually believe in a triune godhead should be warned that the first part of the *Shahadah* incorporates by implication the concept of "La Sharika", i.e. "no partners or associates" with Allah. The Oneness of Allah is absolute, and there is no maneuvering room or "fudge factor" with regard to this concept.

However, the stumbling block in the *Shahadah* for most Christians and Jews consists of testifying to the fact that Muhammad was the messenger of Allah. While it must be emphasized that this phrase does not imply that Prophet Muhammad was the only messenger of Allah, this phrase still remains a gulf separating Islam from Christianity and from Judaism. Each Christian and Jew who is reading this essay may find his or her own way to bridge this gulf.

A final point needs to be made about the *Shahadah*. In accepting Prophet Muhammad as a messenger of Allah, one must by implication accept the *Qur'an* as the revealed words of Allah.

Salat

PRAYER. The second pillar of practice is to perform the daily prayers of worship, i.e., *Salat*. The importance of establishing regular prayer is repeatedly stressed in the *Qur'an*. A few of those Qur'anic injunctions are quoted below.

> And be steadfast in prayer; practice regular charity; and bow down your heads with those who bow down (in worship).[134]

> Guard strictly your (habit) of prayers, especially the middle prayer; and stand before Allah in a devout (frame of mind).[135]

Say: "Allah's guidance is the (only) guidance, and we have been directed to submit ourselves to the Lord of the worlds—to establish regular prayers and to fear Allah: for it is to Him that we shall be gathered together."[136]

And establish regular prayers at the two ends of the day and at the approaches of the night: for those things that are good remove those that are evil: be that the word of remembrance to those who remember (their Lord):[137]

Establish regular prayers—at the sun's decline till the darkness of the night, and the morning prayer and reading: for the prayer and reading in the morning carry their testimony. And pray in the small watches of the morning: (it would be) an additional prayer (or spiritual profit) for thee: soon will thy Lord raise thee to astation of praise and glory.[138]

Therefore be patient with what they say, and celebrate (constantly) the praises of thy Lord before the rising of the sun, and before its setting; yea, celebrate them for parts of the hours of the night, and at the sides of the day: that thou mayest have (spiritual) joy.[139]

O ye who believe! Bow down, prostrate yourselves, and adore your Lord; and do good; that ye may prosper.[140]

So establish regular prayer and give regular charity; and obey the messenger; that ye may receive mercy.[141]

So (give) glory to Allah, when ye reach eventide and when ye rise in the morning; yea, to Him be praise, in the heavens and on earth; and in the late afternoon and when the day begins to decline.[142]

Turn ye back in repentance to Him, and fear Him: establish regular prayers, and be not ye among those who join gods with Allah—[143]

Several points need to be emphasized with regard to *Salat*. First and foremost, *Salat* is obligatory, not voluntary. Second, *Salat* is primarily a prayer of worship, and is not a prayer of supplication or of personal communication, which is called *Dua*, although *Dua* may be appended to or incorporated into the *Salat*. Third, *Salat* takes a set form. Fourth, there are five set-times every day during which *Salat* must be offered. In what follows, some of these points are further clarified.

Salat is obligatory on every Muslim who has reached ten years of age.[144] However, there are certain exceptions to and modifications of this rule. Without going into in-depth, explanatory detail, it is noted that there are those who are excused from, and in some cases even prohibited from, performing Salat. These include the feeble minded, the mentally insane[145], and those in certain states of ritual impurity (e.g., menstruating women[146], post-partum women[147], etc.). Further, the obligatory nature of Salat is eased for those upon whom Salat would be especially difficult, e.g. the traveler[148], the person who is in a state of personal danger from his or her surroundings[149], the seriously ill[150], etc. In such cases, if certain conditions are met, Salat may be shortened, or may be modified as to the nature of the ritual positions assumed in performing Salat, or two different Salat may be combined, meaning that they could be said consecutively, instead of waiting for the appointed time of each.

> When ye travel through the earth, there is no blame on
> you if ye shorten your prayers, for fear the unbelievers
> may attack you: for the unbelievers are unto you open
> enemies.[151]

Salat is a prayer of worship. It is an act of worshipping Allah, glorified and exalted is He. For Christians, who are used to conceptualizing prayer as a time of personal communication with the deity, Salat may seem somewhat impersonal and lacking in personal gratification. In this regard, it must be re-emphasized that Salat is an obligatory act of worshipping Allah. However, Salat is not a substitute for personal communication with Allah, nor is it a replacement for supplicating to Allah. Such personal communication and supplication is known in Islam as Dua, and can be made at any time of the day or night. Salat is not a substitute for Dua. They are two different concepts and two different acts. The former is a required act of worship, while the latter is voluntary, and has a more personal meaning.

WORSHIP. As repeatedly stressed earlier, Salat is an act of worship. Obviously, Salat is not the only act of worship that can and should be made, but it is an obligatory one. As noted in the Qur'an, the very purpose of man's existence is to serve and worship Allah.

> Not a messenger did We send before thee without this
> inspiration sent by Us to him: that there is no god but I;
> therefore worship and serve Me.[152]

Did I not enjoin on you, O ye children of Adam, that ye should not worship Satan; for that he was to you an enemy avowed?—And that ye should worship Me, (for that) this was the straight way?[153]

That is Allah, your Lord! There is no god but He, the creator of all things; then worship ye Him; and He hath power to dispose of all affairs.[154]

I have only created *jinns* and men, that they may serve Me.[155]

The Fasting (*Sawm*)

The third pillar of practice is *Sawm*, i.e., fasting, during the Islamic month of *Ramadan*. The *Qur'an* directly prescribes and addresses the issues of this third pillar of practice:

O ye who believe! Fasting is prescribed to you as it was prescribed to those before you, that ye may (learn) self-restraint...*Ramadan* is the (month) in which was sent down the *Qur'an*, as a guide to mankind, also clear (signs) for guidance and judgment (between right and wrong). So every one of you who is present (at his home) during that month should spend it in fasting...[156]

RAMADAN AND THE ISLAMIC CALENDAR. Unlike the solar calendar of the West, the Islamic calendar is a lunar calendar of 12 months. Of these lunar months, the eighth is *Sha'ban*, the ninth is *Ramadan*, and the tenth is *Shawwal*. Further, because the Islamic calendar is lunar, each Islamic year is approximately 11 days short of a solar year. Thus, every year on the Gregorian calendar, *Ramadan* occurs about 11 days earlier than the year before. *Ramadan* begins on the sighting of the first sliver of the crescent of the new moon following the month of *Sha'ban*. It continues for the next 29 or 30 days depending on the sighting of the first sliver of the crescent of the next new moon.

WHY FAST. Why do Muslims fast during the month of *Ramadan*? There are a number of benefits from such fasting: (1) spiritual purification; (2) potential health benefits, especially in a Western society tending towards corpulence; (3) increased self-discipline and self-restraint; (4) increased focus on and study of one's religion; (5) a heightened sense of Muslim community, with Muslims across the world fasting together; (6) an increased empathy for the poor and hungry. However, none of these is the reason why Muslims fast during *Ramadan*. They fast simply because it has been ordained by Allah. This directive is eloquently stated in the in the *Qur'an* as follows:

> O ye who believe! Fasting is prescribed to you as it was prescribed to those before you, that ye may (learn) self-restraint—(fasting) for a fixed number of days; but if any of you is ill or on a journey, the prescribed number (should be made up) from days later. For those who can do it (with hardship), is a ransom, the feeding of one that is indigent but he that will give more, of his own free will—it is better for him. And it is better for you that ye fast, if ye only knew. *Ramadan* is the (month) in which was sent down the *Qur'an*, as a guide to mankind, also clear (signs) for guidance and judgment (between right and wrong). So every one of you who is present (at his home) during that month should spend it in fasting. But if any one is ill, or on a journey, the prescribed period (should be made up) by days later. Allah intends every facility for you; He does not want to put you to difficulties. (He wants you) to complete the prescribed period, and to glorify Him in that He has guided you; and perchance ye shall be grateful.[157]

THE FAST. As to the fast itself, fasting begins each day at the first light of dawn, prior to the time of the first prayer (*Salat Al-Fajr*), and continues until the completion of sunset, i.e. the time of fourth prayer (*Salat Al-Maghrib*). As such, the day of fasting is longer when *Ramadan* occurs in the summer, and shorter when *Ramadan* occurs in the winter. During the time of fasting, food, drink, sexual activity, tobacco, gum, and the ingestion of any and all substances are prohibited. Frivolous and worldly talk is discouraged, and Muslims are to be especially vigilant in focusing on the spiritual aspects of their lives. Each day during *Ramadan*, a Muslim is encouraged to read 1/30th of the *Qur'an*, so that by the completion of the month of *Ramadan*, the entire *Qur'an* has been read with a receptive and meditative attitude. Furthermore, throughout the entire month of *Ramadan,* it is preferable for Muslims to participate in a series of supplementary prayers (*tarawih*) each night, following the last daily prayer (*Salat Al-'Isha*).

REVELATION IN *RAMADAN*. Over and above fasting, Ramadan holds a special place in the Islamic calendar and history, for tradition holds that it was during the last ten days of the month of *Ramadan* that revelation was first given to the Prophet Muhammad. Within Islam, the time of this first revelation is referred to as the Night of *Qadr* (*Lailatul Al-Qadr*), i.e., the night of power. A chapter in the *Qur'an* by the name of *Al-Qadr* reads:

> We have indeed revealed this (message) in the Night of Power. And what willexplain to thee what the Night of Power is? The Night of Power is better thana thousand months. Therein come down the angels and the Spirit by Allah'spermission, on every errand: peace!...this until the rise of morn![158]

Tradition further holds that every *Ramadan* following the initial Night of *Qadr*, and throughout the remainder of the lifetime of the Prophet Muhammad, the angel *Jibril* (Gabriel) would rehearse the *Qur'an* with him.

The Alms (*Zakat*)

Zakat refers to obligatory charity. Both obligatory and voluntary charity are concepts that are repeatedly endorsed in the *Qur'an* as shown in the following quotations:

> And be steadfast in prayer and regular in charity...[159]

> ...it is righteousness—to believe in Allah and the Last Day, and the angels, and the Book, and the messengers; to spend of your substance, out of love for Him, for your kin, for orphans, for the needy, for the wayfarer, for those who ask, and for the ransom of slaves...[160]

> And spend of your substance in the cause of Allah, and make not your own hands contribute to (your) destruction; but do good; for Allah loveth those who do good.[161]

They ask thee what they should spend (in charity), Say: Whatever ye spend that is good, is for parents and kindred and orphans and those in want and for wayfarers. And whatever ye do that is good—Allah knoweth it well.[162]

They ask thee how much they are to spend; say: "What is beyond your needs." Thus doth Allah make clear to you His signs: in order that ye may consider—[163]

O ye who believe! spend out of the bounties We have provided for you...[164]

For those who give in charity, men and women, and loan to Allah a beautiful loan, it shall be increased manifold (to their credit), and they shall have (besides) a liberal reward.[165]

And spend something (in charity) out of the substance which We have bestowed on you, before death should come to any of you and he should say, "O my Lord! why didst Thou not give me respite for a little while? I should then have given (largely) in charity, and I should have been one of the doers of good."[166]

So fear Allah as much as ye can; listen and obey; and spend in charity for the benefit of your own souls. And those saved from the covetousness of their own souls—they are the ones that achieve prosperity. If ye loan to Allah a beautiful loan, He will double it to your (credit), and He will grant you forgiveness: for Allah is most ready to appreciate (service), most forbearing—[167]

ZAKAT VS. TITHING. Zakat has often been compared by Western writers to the Judeo-Christian concept of tithing. However, such a comparison is highly misleading for several reasons. In what follows, the concept of Zakat is explained by contrasting it with tithing, which was mandated in several passages in the received Torah.[168] In making these comparisons, the following contrasts are generalizations, which ignore the special rules that apply to agricultural produce, livestock, etc.

However, these are considerations, which would affect few Occidentals:

(1) Tithing is based upon one's yearly income, while *Zakat* is based upon one's financial surplus which has been held for one year.

(2) Tithing is obligatory on every Christian and Jew who has any income, although this is honored by Christians more as the exception rather than the rule. In contrast, *Zakat* is obligatory only upon those Muslims with a financial surplus.

(3) Tithing is based upon a formula of giving 10.0% of one's income. In fact, the word "tithe" comes from the Old English, meaning "the tenth part". In contrast, *Zakat* is based upon a formula of giving 2.5% of one's financial surplus.

(4) Tithes are to be given to the relevant ecclesiastical authority, i.e., the church for Christians, where the money is used to support various building programs (e.g., bricks and mortar for new churches), to pay ministerial and staff salaries, and to otherwise cover the expenses of running the church. Only if the church has a financial surplus does some portion of the tithes go to charity. (In ancient Judaism, the entire tithe was meant for the support of the Levites and the priestly class[169]). In contrast, it is preferred that *Zakat* go directly from the hand of the one who is giving to the hand of the person in need. This implies that every Muslim has a responsibility to know those in need. In addition, there are certain approved programs to which *Zakat* can be given.

Two hypothetical examples may better illustrate the contrast between *Zakat* and tithing. As a first example, consider a Christian family consisting of father, mother, and three children, whose yearly income is $15,000. After deducting reasonable expenses, such as rent, food, medical bills, educational bills, etc., the family will probably have no economic surplus, and will probably be in debt. Under a strict interpretation of the Judeo-Christian concept of tithing, the family is still obligated to turn over $1,500 each year to the church, thus increasing their debt load. In contrast, consider a Muslim family of five with exactly the same income and expenses. Under the rules of *Zakat*, since there is no economic surplus, no *Zakat* is due from the family. Further, because the family has incurred debt in maintaining a subsistence level of existence, the family is actually eligible to receive *Zakat* from those who have a financial surplus.

As a second example, take a Christian family consisting of a father, a mother, and two children, whose yearly income is $100,000. By the rules of tithing, the family should give $10,000, presumably to the church. In contrast, consider a Muslim family of four with exactly the same income and expenses. Reasonable living expenses (rent, food, clothing, transportation, mandatory taxes, mandatory social security payments—assuming an American family, medical bills, etc.) might easily run up to $60,000, leaving an economic surplus of $40,000. If the family were able to hold that financial surplus for one full year, they would then need to pay $1,000 in *Zakat* to someone in need.

ZAKAT VS. SADAQAH. Besides the *Zakat*, which is obligatory charity, Muslims are prompted by the *Qur'an* to contribute an additional charity, called *Sadaqa*. But unlike *Zakat*, which is mandatory, *Sadaqa* is entirely voluntary.

Hajj

The fifth pillar of the practice of Islam is the pilgrimage to Makkah to perform the rites of *Hajj* at their appointed times during the Islamic month of *Dhul-Hijjah*. Performance of the *Hajj* is incumbent upon every adult Muslim, male and female, who has the financial and physical ability to do so. This obligation is specified in the following passage from the *Qur'an*, in which Makkah is referred to by an older variant of its name, i.e., *Bakka*:

> The first house (of worship) appointed for men was that at Bakka; full of blessing and of guidance for all kinds of beings; in it are signs manifest; (for example), the Station of Abraham; whoever enters it attains security; pilgrimage thereto is a duty men owe to Allah—those who can afford the journey; but if any deny faith, Allah stands not in need of any of His creatures.[170]

The prescribed pilgrimage to Makkah traces its origin to Prophet Ibrahim (Abraham). Following the building of the *Ka'ba* (literally "cube"; the *Ka'ba* is also known as Sacred House and Ancient House) at Makkah by Prophet Ibrahim and his son Isma'il[171], Allah prescribed on the Muslims the pilgrimage to Makkah as an obligatory duty:

> Behold! We gave the site, to Abraham, of the (Sacred) House, (saying): "Associate not anything (in worship) with

Me; and sanctify My House for those who compass it round, or stand up, or bow, or prostrate themselves (therein in prayer). And proclaim the pilgrimage among men: they will come to thee on foot and (mounted) on every kind of camel, lean on account of journeys through deep and distant mountain highways; that they may witness the benefits (provided) for them, and celebrate the name of Allah, through the days appointed, over the cattle which He has provided for them (for sacrifice): then eat ye thereof and feed the distressed ones in want. Then let them complete the rites prescribed for them, perform their vows, and (again) circumambulate The Ancient House". Such (is the pilgrimage): whoever honors the sacred rites of Allah, for him it is good in the sight of his Lord...[172]

Although the rites of the *Hajj* are rich in symbolic meaning, as will be seen below, the correct performance of the *Hajj* can never be reduced to mere ritual. One must also have the right attitude and conduct in performing *Hajj*. But above all, a correct intention should necessarily be the forerunner in the performance of *Hajj*.

For *Hajj* are the months well known. If anyone undertakes that duty therein, let there be no obscenity, nor wickedness, nor wrangling in the *Hajj*. And whatever good ye do, (be sure) Allah knoweth it. And take a provision (with you) for the journey, but the best of provisions is right conduct. So fear Me, O ye that are wise.[173]

THE SYMBOLIC MEANING OF *HAJJ*. There are a number of rituals of *Hajj* (the major pilgrimage) and *'Umra* (the minor pilgrimage). Each ritual, the performance of the ritual, and the order or progression of the rituals is based upon the manner in which Prophet Muhammad performed Hajj in 632 CE. These rituals may seem foreign and somewhat incomprehensible to non-Muslims. However, most of these rituals have a symbolic meaning that can be traced back either to the events in the life of Adam or to events in the life of Abraham. In what follows, several of these rituals are explained, as well as their relevant symbolic origins. The rituals which will be considered are those of *Arafat, Hadi, Maqam Ibrahim, Ramy, Sa'e, Talbiyah, Tawaf,* and *Zamzam.*

ARAFAT. The ritual of *Arafat* is performed on the ninth of *Dhul*

Hijjah, and is the most important of the rituals of *Hajj*. It is recorded that the Prophet Muhammad said, " *Hajj* is *Arafat*".[174] *Arafat* is an area about 12 miles from Makkah, and includes Jebel Al-Rahman, i.e., the Mount of Mercy.

The origins of the Arafat ritual go back to Adam and Eve.

> We said: "O Adam! Dwell thou and thy wife in the Garden; and eat of the bountiful things therein as (where and when) ye will; but approach not this tree, or ye run into harm and transgression." Then did Satan make them slip from the (Garden), and get them out of the state (of felicity) in which they had been. We said: "Get ye down, all (ye people), and with enmity between yourselves. On earth will be your dwelling place and your means of livelihood—for a time."[175]

After their expulsion from the Garden of Eden Adam and Eve were placed on earth, but they were separated by a vast distance. Because of their supplications and prayers to Him, Allah allowed them to find each other and to reunite at the Mount of Mercy in *Arafat*.

As such, the ritual of *Arafat* consists of constantly approaching Allah in prayers of supplication, in giving praise and thanksgiving, and in reciting the *Qur'an*. This activity continues throughout the time between noon and sunset on the ninth of *Dhul Hijjah*. In this way, *Hajj* commemorates the thanksgiving offered by Adam and Eve upon their reunion on earth.

Arafat is also quite important to Muslims, because it was on the day of *Arafat*, i.e., the ninth of *Dhul Hijjah,* that Allah sent the final revelation to Prophet Muhammad that perfected and completed the religion of Islam.[177] This revelation finds verbatim expression in the *Qur'an*, the key phrase of which is translated as follows:

> This day have I perfected your religion for you, completed My favor upon you, and have chosen for you Islam as your religion.[178]

HADI. Hadi refers to a sacrificial animal, and the ritual of *Hadi* consists of making an animal sacrifice in Mina on the 10th of *Dhul Hijjah.* For each individual, the sacrifice consists of one lamb or goat. However, seven *Hajjis* may join together to sacrifice either one camel or one cow, instead of making individual sacrifices. Originally, the meat from the sacrifice was given to the poor of Makkah, as well as being eaten by the *Hajjis*. With approximately 2,000,000 *Hajjis* making the *Hajj* every year, it is physically impossible for 2,000,000 individual sacrifices to be carried out, with meat being distributed to the poor of Makkah. Today, most *Hajjis* purchase a sacrificial animal, which is then sacrificed for them at modern automated slaughtering houses in Mina. The meat from this sacrifice is stored in refrigerators and then distributed to the poor throughout the Muslim world.

The act of sacrifice on the 10th of *Dhul Hijjah* has its origins in the stories of Prophet Abraham. The Biblical account of the relevant event is found in *Genesis*, and is quoted below (boldface added).

> After these things God tested Abraham. He said to him, "Abraham!" And he said, "Here I am." He said, "Take your son, **your only son**, Isaac, whom you love, and go to the land of Moriah, and offer him there as a burnt offering on one of the mountains that I shall show you." So Abraham rose early in the morning, saddled his donkey, and took two of his young men with him, and his son Isaac; he cut the wood for the burnt offering, and set out and went to the place in the distance that God had shown him. On the third day Abraham looked up and saw the place far away...When they came to the place that God had shown him, Abraham built an altar there and laid the wood in order. He bound his son Isaac, and laid him on the altar, on top of the wood. Then Abraham reached out his hand and took the knife to kill his son. But the angel of the Lord called to him from heaven, and said, "Abraham, Abraham!" And he said, "Here I am." He said, "Do not lay your hand on the boy or do anything to him; for now I know that you fear God, since you have not withheld your son, your only son, from me." And Abraham looked up and saw a ram, caught in a thicket by its horns. Abraham went and took the ram and offered it up as a burnt offering instead of his son.[179]

The Islamic tradition regarding the sacrifice of Abraham is in essential agreement with the *Genesis* account, but there are a few important differences. First, the Islamic tradition holds that the sacrifice was made in Mina, not in Moriah. Second, the Islamic tradition holds that it was Isma'il not Isaac who was to be sacrificed. The Islamic tradition maintains that there have been numerous corruptions of the *Bible* over time, and that the references to Isaac in *Genesis* 22 are examples of such corruptions of the original text. In that regard, Muslim scholars note that *Genesis* 22 twice refers to the intended sacrificial victim as being Abraham's "only son". As *Genesis* 16:15 clearly states that Isma'il was born when Abraham was 86 years old, and as *Genesis* 21:5 clearly states that Isaac was not born until Abraham was 100 years old, it stands to reason that Isma'il was Isaac's senior by 14 years, and that the only time Abraham had an only son was after the birth of Isma'il and before the birth of Isaac. (Note: this cannot be explained away by positing that Isma'il died before the sacrifice, because *Genesis* 25:7-9 clearly states that both Isma'il and Isaac buried their father, Abraham.)

As Abraham sacrificed a ram at Mina in exchange for Isma'il so *Hajjis* sacrifice a lamb as part of their *Hajj*.[180]

MAQAM IBRAHIM. While the Ka'ba has been built and rebuilt on several occasions, the *Qur'an* specifically states that the foundations of the Ka'ba were built by Abraham and Isma'il:

> And remember Abraham and Ismail raised the foundations
> of the House (with this prayer): "Our Lord! Accept (this
> service) from us: for Thou art the all-hearing, the all-know-
> ing."[181]

According to Islamic tradition, Abraham had to stand on a rock on the ground, in order to lift a rock high enough to place it on the highest row of rocks comprising the walls of the Ka'ba.[182] The rock on which Abraham stood is known as Maqam Ibrahim (the station of Abraham). In remembrance of this event, the *Qur'an* directs Muslims to pray behind the *Maqam Ibrahim*.

> Remember We made the House a place of assembly for men
> and a place of safety; and take ye the station of Abraham as
> a place of prayer; and We covenanted with Abraham and
> Ismail that they should sanctify My House for those who
> compass it round, or use it as a retreat, or bow, or prostrate
> themselves (therein in prayer).[183]

As such, upon completion of *Tawaf* (see below), a Muslim is direct-ed to offer prayer behind *Maqam Ibrahim*.

RAMY. As already noted, Islamic tradition holds that Abraham was directed to sacrifice his son, Isma'il and that this sacrifice was to take place at Mina. Islamic tradition further holds that on his way from Makkah to Mina with Isma'il, Abraham was several times tempted by Satan not to sacrifice Isma'il. As each such temptation was presented, Abraham rejected the temptation, and symbolically drove Satan off by throwing small stones at him.[184]

This aspect of the Abrahamic tradition in symbolized in *Hajj* by the act of Ramy, or the stoning of a series of three stone pillars (*Jamarat Al-'Aqaba, Jamarat Al-Wusta, and Jamarat Al-Sughra*) in Mina. The first act of *Ramy* occurs on the 10th of *Dhul Hijjah*, when one arrives back in Mina from Muzdalifeh. At this time, only the largest (*Jamarat Al-'Aqaba*) of the three stone pillars is stoned, and one throws seven small stones, one at a time, each the size of a large pea. With each throw, one says "*Allahu Akbar*".[185] On the 11th, 12th, and possibly 13th of *Dhul Hijjah*, one repeats the act of *Ramy*. However, on these days, all three stone pillars are stoned, beginning with *Jamarat Al-Sughra*, and ending with *Jamarat Al-'Aqabah*. Each pillar is stoned seven times during each stoning, and with each throw, one says "*Allahu Akbar*".

SA'E. The act of *Sa'e* is also a symbolic event in the Abrahamic tradition. According to the Biblical account of *Genesis* 21:8-13, after the weaning of Isaac, which would make Isma'il about 16 years old, Sarah grew jealous of Isma'il when she saw him playing with Isaac. As such, she requested that Abraham drive Hagar and Isma'il away. Abraham was reportedly distressed by this request, but Allah assured Abraham that he should follow Sarah's request. The Biblical story then continues in Genesis with the following account (boldface added).

> So Abraham rose early in the morning, and took bread and a skin of water, and gave it to Hagar, **putting it on her shoulder, along with the child,** and sent her away. And she departed, and wandered about in the wilderness of Beersheba. When the water in the skin was gone, **she cast the child under one of the bushes.** Then she went and sat down opposite him a good way off, about the distance of a bowshot; for she said, "Do not let me look on the death of the child." And as she sat opposite him, she lifted up her voice and wept. And God heard the voice of the boy; and the angel of God called to Hagar from heaven, and said to her, "What troubles you, Hagar? Do not be afraid; for God has heard the voice of the boy where he is. Come, **lift up**

the boy and hold him fast with your hand, for I will make a great nation of him." Then God opened her eyes and she saw a well of water. She went, and filled the skin with water, and gave the boy a drink.[186]

In the above quotation, boldface type has been added to key phrases, which illustrate the impossibility of the *Genesis* account of Isma'il being about 16 years old at the time. Hagar variously carries Isma'il on her shoulder, casts him under a bush, and lifts him up and holds him fast with one hand. These simply are not actions one does with a 16-year-old. Rather, they are actions one might do with an infant. This observation serves as the introduction to the Islamic tradition regarding the above event.

The Islamic tradition preserves an independent account of the separation of Hagar and Isma'il from Abraham. Among the differences to be found in the Islamic tradition are that the event takes place when Isma'il is an infant, before he is weaned, and many years before the birth of Isaac. Abraham does not send his wife and son out of the camp on their own but, on the contrary, accompanies them to a place where he eventually leaves them with his wife's (Hagar's) consent. The place is not Beersheba, but is Makkah, which was then an isolated, barren, and desert valley, devoid of civilization. At Makkah, Abraham leaves Hagar and Isma'il with only a skin of water and a bag of dates, entrusting their care and survival to Allah. Abraham soon thereafter returns to Sarah in the Negev of Palestine.[187]

As in the Biblical account, Hagar's skin of water is soon emptied, and she and her infant son begin to suffer early dehydration and starvation. This continues to the point where Hagar's milk supply dries up, and she is no longer able to nurse Isma'il, and Isma'il begins his death throes. At that point, Hagar frantically begins to look around her for any possible help. Seeing a hill (Safa) a little way in the distance, she desperately climbs to the top of the hill to look for any possible caravan that might be passing by. Seeing none, she climbs down the hill. However, rather than returning to Isma'il she walks to an adjoining hill (Marwah) about 450 meters from Safa. Along the way, despite her weakened physical condition, she inexplicably begins to run for part of the way. Climbing Marwah, she again finds no sign of a passing caravan. She then retreats from Marwah, only to climb Safa again. Still, there is no sign of possible help. In her frantic and desperate state, she then climbs Marwah for a second time, climbs Safa for a third time, climbs Marwah for a third time, climbs Safa for a fourth time, and finally climbs Marwah for a fourth time. Each time she walks between the two hills from Safa to Marwah, she inexplicably runs for part of the distance.[188]

The above account of Hagar traveling back and forth between Safa and Marwah for a total of seven times provides the symbolic meaning of Sa'e. Thus, *Sa'e* consists of climbing up Safa, and then traveling back and forth between Safa and Marwah seven times, running part of the way each time one goes from Safa to Marwah. *Sa'e* ends on the fourth ascent of Marwah. During both *'Umrah* and *Hajj*, the *Hajji* is required to perform the act of *Sa'e* at set times, thus commemorating and symbolically re-enacting Hagar's desperate attempt to save Isma'il. (Note: for the ease of close to two million *Hajjis* attempting to perform *Sa'e* at roughly the same time, the Kingdom of Saudi Arabia has enclosed both hills and the distance between them within the two story structure of the Grand Mosque. Thus, counting the roof surface, there are three levels on which *Hajjis* may simultaneously perform *Sa'e*.) The rite of *Sa'e* is consistent with the following verse from the *Qur'an* 2:158:

> Behold! Safa and Marwah are among the symbols of Allah.
> So, if those who Visit the House in the season or at other
> times, should compass them round, it is no sin in them. And
> if anyone obeyeth his own impulse to good—be sure that
> Allah is He Who recognizeth and knoweth.[189]

As to what happened when Hagar ascended Marwah for the last time, that part of the narrative is presented below under the topic of *Zamzam*.

TALBIYAH. While journeying to Makkah, and at frequent and various times during the course of *Hajj*, the *Hajjis* are encouraged to recite the *Talbiyah*.

> *Labbayk Allahumma Labbayk. Labbayk La Sharika Laka*
> *Labbayk. Innal Hamda Wannimata Laka Walmulk. La*
> *Sharika Lak.*

The *Talbiyah* can be roughly translated as follows.

> Here I am, O Allah, at Your service, here I am. Here I am,
> You (are One, and) have no partner, here I am. Truly, all
> praise and provision are Yours, and so is the dominion and
> sovereignty. You (are One, and) have no partner.

TAWAF. Tawaf consists of circumambulating the *Ka'ba* seven times in a counter-clockwise direction. Islamic tradition holds that the act of Tawaf, at what would later become the eventual site of the *Ka'ba*, was first practiced as an act of worship of Allah by Adam.[190] During both *'Umra* and *Hajj*, the *Hajji* is required to perform *Tawaf* at certain set times

> Behold! We gave the site to Abraham, of the (Sacred) House, (saying): "Associate not anything (in worship) with Me; and sanctify My House for those who compass it round, or stand up, or bow, or prostrate themselves (therein in prayer).[191]

> Then let them complete the rites prescribed for them, perform their vows, and (again) circumambulate The Ancient House.[192]

It should be noted that counter-clockwise circumambulation also finds expression in the Jewish tradition, reaching back at least 3,000 years into the distant past. In that regard, one notes the rituals surrounding the Feast of Booths or Tabernacles (Hebrew = "Sukkot"), also known as the Festival of Ingathering (Hebrew = "Hag ha-Asif"). The Feast of Booths was the celebration of the fall fruit and olive harvest in ancient Israel, lasted for seven days, and was the most important of the three pilgrim festivals in ancient Israel.[193] According to the rituals prescribed for this feast in the *Mishna* tractate Sukka (part of the *Talmud*), the Jewish priests made a daily circumambulation of the altar at the temple in Jerusalem (or of the synagogue dais in non-temple times) and a seven-fold circuit of the altar at the temple in Jerusalem (or of the synagogue dais in non-temple times) on the last day of the festival.[194]

ZAMZAM. Returning to the Islamic account of Hagar and Isma'il having been left in Makkah by Abraham, the report of that story had previously been ended with the account of Hagar having climbed Marwah for the fourth time. One can now continue the narrative by noting that when Hagar stood on Marwah for the fourth time, she heard a voice. Looking down into the valley by where Isma'il was dying under the scrub bush, she saw the angel Gabriel standing there. Gabriel then struck the ground with the heel of his foot. Where his foot hit, water came gushing up out of the ground. Despite her precarious and weakened state, Hagar struggled down off Marwah, and rushed to Isma'il and to the newly formed Well of *Zamzam*. She scooped the running water into her water skin, and drank her fill. Miraculously, her milk supply returned, and she suckled Isma'il who was unexpectedly revived by his mother's milk.[195]

The Biblical account in *Genesis* limits the above narrative to a single verse, which is quoted below.

> Then God opened her eyes and she saw a well of water. She went, and filled theskin with water, and gave the boy a drink.[196]

As can be seen, the *Genesis* account is extremely sparse, and omits much of the detail found in the Islamic tradition. However, *Psalms* refers to the Well of *Zamzam*, although not by name, and specifically locates it in Baca, an early variant of the name Makkah.

> Happy are those whose strength is in you, in whose heart are the highways to Zion. As they go through the valley of Baca they make it a place of springs; the early rain also covers it with pools.[197]

Rather miraculously, the Well of *Zamzam* continues to exist some 4,000 years after its founding by the angel Gabriel, and it continues to be a source of plentiful water, serving close to two million *Hajjis* each year, as well as serving the residents of Makkah. With the expansion of the Grand Mosque over the years, the Well of *Zamzam* has come to be located within the actual walls of the Grand Mosque, and is about half way between the *Ka'ba* and Safa.

In remembrance of Allah, having saved Hagar and Isma'il, through Gabriel founding the Well of *Zamzam*, it is tradition that *Hajjis* drink from the Well of *Zamzam* immediately after performing prayers behind the *Maqam Ibrahim*, which is done immediately after performing *Tawaf*.

Summary

The sum total of the above introduction to Islam has necessarily been quite concise. The interested reader can expand his knowledge by turning to additional sources of information on Islam. Of these, the most important is a good English translation of the meaning of the *Qur'an*. In that regard, the author suggests that of 'Abdullah Yusuf 'Ali[198], that of Muhammad Taqi-ud Din Al-Hilali and Muhammad Musin Khan[199], or that published by Saheeh International.[200] Of these three, the typical American reader will probably be most comfortable with the translation of 'Abdullah Yusuf 'Ali, which is the most "user friendly" when it comes to the English language and vocabulary employed. Though not of the same caliber as the three translations mentioned above, Pickthall's translation[201] is at least adequate

In addition to securing a good English translation of the meaning of the *Qur'an*, the interested reader is advised to contact Mosques in his local area. Many Mosques maintain a speakers' bureau, while others offer informal classes explaining Islam to new converts and to non-Muslims interested in Islam. In almost any Mosque, one will find Muslims who are happy to take the time to talk about Islam to those who are interested in it or merely curious about it.

Notes

NOTES

Chapter 1. Parallels between Christianity and Islam

1. See author's preface regarding the use of the term "Allah".
2. A) *Exodus* 20:1-21. B) *Deuteronomy* 5:1-22.
3. See the author's preface regarding the use of the phrase "peace be upon him".
4. *Matthew* 22:37-39.
5. Growing out of the Anabaptist movement, the Mennonites were a conservative Christian denomination. However, there was a range of Mennonite conservatism, varying from the relatively less conservative General Conference Mennonites, through the decided more conservative Old Mennonites, to the extremely conservative Amish. My own childhood environment was primarily one shaped by the General Conference and Old Mennonite traditions.
6. See for example, the following: A) Smith WC (1943); B) Smith WC (1957); C) Smith WC (1964); and D) Smith WC (1965).
7. 'Ali A.Y. (2000).
8. The numbers given in this list may vary somewhat from those that would be obtained from the Arabic original of the *Qur'an*, secondary to the translator's use of parenthetical insertions of a name, and the use of a name when the actual Arabic gives a pronoun. However, these discrepancies are minor, and do not affect the overall conclusions that should be drawn.
9. This count includes all use of the name "Jesus", as well as those cases in which "Christ" is used without "Jesus".
10. *Qur'an* 15:28-29. Also, see parallel versions in *Qur'an* 32:7-9; 38:71-72; and 55:14.
11. *Qur'an* 2:31a.
12. *Qur'an* 7:19-25.
13. *Qur'an* 5:27-30.
14. *Qur'an* 5:20-26.
15. *Qur'an* 37:139-148.
16. *Qur'an* 3:38-41.
17. *Qur'an* 3:42-48.
18. *Qur'an* 3:44.
19. *Qur'an* 3:49.
20. *Luke* 1:35,39-56.
21. *Qur'an* 3:35-37.
22. *Exodus* 6:16-20.
23. *Qur'an* 3:44.
24. *The Gospel of the Birth of Mary*. In Platt RH, Brett JA.
25. *The Protevangelion of James* 8:2. In Platt RH, Brett JA.
26. *The Protevangelion of James* 8:3-4. In Platt RH, Brett JA.
27. *The Gospel of the Birth of Mary* 5:4-6:7 and *The Protevangelion of James* 8:6-16. In Platt RH, Brett JA.

28. *Qur'an* 19:27-32.
29. *The First Gospel of the Infancy of Jesus Christ* 1:2. In Platt RH, Brett JA.
30. *Qur'an* 3:47-49.
31. *Qur'an* 5:110.
32. *The First Gospel of the Infancy of Jesus Christ* 15:6. In Platt RH, Brett JA.

Chapter 2. Judaism, Christianity and Islam

1. See the author's preface regarding the use of the phrase "peace be upon him".
2. Actually, there are differences between the Jewish and Christian perspectives on the origins of these three religions. However, these differences are mainly confined to the perceived relationship of Judaism and Christianity. As this relationship is of less concern to the present author than that of Islam to Judaism and of Islam to Christianity, the author has elected to present a combined Judeo-Christian perspective, which reflects a Christian bias.
3. *Genesis* 5:1-29. (Alternatively, some sources list the name of Qaynan between that of Arpachshad and Shelah. A) Al-Tabari MH (1987). B) *Jubilees* 8:1-6. In Charles RH (1969).
4. See the author's preface regarding why the term "Allah" has been employed.
5. *Genesis* 6:18.
6. *Genesis* 6:11-22.
7. *Genesis* 9:8-17.
8. *Genesis* 10:1; 11:10-26.
9. *Genesis* 17:9-14.
10. *Genesis* 17:4-8,18-19,21.
11. *Genesis* 26:1-5.
12. *Genesis* 25:29-34; 27:1-40; 28:13-16; *Exodus* 2:24.
13. *Genesis* 32:28.
14. Schonfield HJ (1967).
15. *I Kings* 6:1.
16. *I Kings* 6:2.
17. Josephus F (1988).
18. A) Mack BL (1996). B) Schonfield HJ (1967).
19. Schonfield HJ (1967).
20. Within Judaism, the office of the priesthood was inherited on patrilineal lines from the Prophet Aaron, peace be upon him. Aaron was of the tribe of Levi, and those members (Levites) of the tribe of Levi, who were not male-line descendants of Aaron had various, non-priestly roles and offices associated with the temple cult in Jerusalem.
21. Schonfield HJ (1967).
22. *Haggai* 1:1; 2:1.
23. *Haggai* 1:1; 2:1-3.
24. *Ezra* 6:3.
25. A) Josephus F (1988). B) Schonfield HJ (1967).
26. A) Leon-Dufour X (1983). B) Schonfield HJ (1967). C) Sandison GH. D) Josephus F (1988).
27. Schonfield HJ (1967).

28. A) Schonfield HJ (1967). B) Leon-Dufour X (1983). C) Sandison GH. D) Josephus F (1988).

29. A) Josephus F (1988). B) Mack BL (1996). C) Sandison GH. D) Leon-Dufour X (1983). E) Stegemann H (1998). F) Dupont-Sommer A (1967).

30. A) Duncan GB (1971). B) Josephus F (1988). C) Sandison GH. D) --- (1998p). E) Leon-Dufour X (1983). F) Dupont-Sommer A (1967).

31. Mack BL (1996).

32. A) Mack BL (1996). B) Sandison GH.

33. See the chapter entitled "The Crucifixion: A Question of Identity".

34. See the chapter entitled "The Baptism of Jesus: The Origin of the 'Sonship' of Jesus".

35. As it would be anathema to Muslims to use the term "Allah" within the context of this and some of the following points being discussed, the author has fallen back on the use of the term "God" in these instances.

36. *John* 1:1-18.

37. *Qur'an* 42:13.

38. *Qur'an* 40:78.

39. *Qur'an* 2:40,63,83,92-93,125; 3:81; 4:153-155; 5:12-14,70; 20:80-83,115; 33:7; 43:46-49.

40. *Qur'an* 2:125.

41. *Qur'an* 3:81.

42. *Qur'an* 33:7.

43. *Qur'an* 6:42,130-131; 10:47,74; 16:36,63,84,89; 17:71; 35:24.

44. *Qur'an* 6:42.

45. *Qur'an* 10:47.

46. *Qur'an* 16:36.

47. *Qur'an* 35:24.

48. *Qur'an* 2:106; 3:2-3,23,50,93; 4:44,160; 5:3,15; 6:145-146; 10:37; 13:38-39; 16:101; 17:106; 25:32; 26:5; 76:23.

49. *Qur'an* 2:106; 6:145-146; 13:38-39; 16:101.

50. *Qur'an* 17:106; 25:32; 76:23.

51. *Qur'an* 4:43.

52. *Qur'an* 5:90-91.

53. *Qur'an* 2:106.

54. *Qur'an* 13:38-39.

55. *Qur'an* 10:37.

56. *Qur'an* 16:101.

57. *Qur'an* 2:37.

58. *Qur'an* 5:3.

59. *Qur'an* 21:25.

60. *Qur'an* 4:164-165; 16:36.

61. *Qur'an* 3:19; 5:12-13,32,42-44; 42:13-14; 45:16-17.

62. Christians and Jews are both referred to as People of the Book, with the Book referring to the scriptural revelations initially given by Allah to the Jews and Christians, which these people then distorted and altered.

63. *Qur'an* 2:75-79; 3:23-24,71,78,187; 4:46; 5:12-13,15,41,44; 6:91; 10:93; 11:110; 15:90; 41:45; 62:5.

64. *Qur'an* 3:19.

65. *Qur'an* 42:13-14.

66. *Qur'an* 3:161a.

67. *Qur'an* 3:45-47,59; 19:16-35; 112:1-4.
68. *Qur'an* 3:45-47.
69. *Qur'an* 3:59; 6:2;7:11-12; 15:26-33; 17:61; 18:50; 32:7; 37:11; 38:71-76; 55:14.
70. *Qur'an* 3:59.
71. *Qur'an* 4:171; 5:17,75; 6:83-90; 43:57-59.
72. *Qur'an* 3:45; 5:72,75.
73. A) *Qur'an* 4:157. B) See the chapter entitled "The Crucifixion: A Question of Identity".
74. A) *Qur'an* 4:171; 5:72-75; 9:30; 43:57-59; 112:1-4. B) See the chapter entitled "The Baptism of Jesus: The Origin of the 'Sonship' Of Jesus".
75. A) *Qur'an* 3:45-49; 61:6. B) See the chapter entitled "The Mission and Ministry of Jesus".
76. *Qur'an* 3:50-51; 61:6.
77. *Qur'an* 61:6.
78. *Qur'an* 43:63-65.
79. *Qur'an* 5:14.
80. *Qur'an* 57:27.
81. *Qur'an* 28:52-53.
82. A) *Qur'an* 2:136,253,285; 3:84; 4:150-152. B) This point is developed more fully in the chapter entitled "A Concise Introduction to Islam: Articles of Faith and Pillars of Practice".
83. A) *Qur'an* 3:144; 17:93-94; 18:110. B) This point is developed more fully in the chapter entitled "A Concise Introduction to Islam: Articles of Faith and Pillars of Practice".
84. *Qur'an* 38:86-87.

Chapter 3. The Books of Revelation and Scripture

1. See author's preface regarding why the term "Allah" has been employed.
2. The author utilizes the division and names of books as found in the Christian *Bible*. It should be noted that Judaism proposes a somewhat different division (24 books) and naming process for these books, which it claims as scripture, although the sum total of these books equates with the *Old Testament* of the *Christian Bible*. The difference in count between 24 and 39 books is simply a process of differentiating where books begin and end. For example, the synagogal canon of Judaism combines *I* and *II Chronicles* into one book, combines *Ezra* and *Nehemiah* into a single book, etc.
3. The Hebrew word *"Tanakh"* consists of and is formed by placing in sequence the first letter from each of the following three words: *"Torah"*, *"Nevi'im"*, and *"Ketuvim"*.
4. A) Silberman LH (1971). B) Sundberg AC (1971). C) Sarna NM (1998).
5. *Qur'an* 4:163; 17:55; 21:105.
6. See the author's preface regarding the use of the phrase "peace be upon him".
7. *Qur'an* 3:3,48,50,65,93; 5:43-46,66,68,110; 7:157; 9:111; 48:29; 61:6.
8. *Revelation*.
9. *Acts of the Apostles*.

10. *Romans, I* and *II Corinthians, Galatians, Ephesians, Philippians, Colossians, I* and *II Thessalonians, I* and *II Timothy, Titus, Philemon, Hebrews, James, I* and *II Peter, Jude,* and *I, II,* and *III John.*

11. *Matthew, Mark, Luke,* and *John.*

12. A) Laymon CM (1971b). B) Mack BL (1996).

13. Sundberg AC (1971).

14. *Qur'an* 3:3,48,65; 5:46-47,66,68,110; 7:157; 9:111; 48:29; 57:27.

15. For purposes of analyzing provenance in this article, the end of revelation will be assumed to correspond to the end of the life of the person receiving the revelation.

16. In Arabic, the full title is Khalifah Rasul Allah, which may be translated as "successor to the messenger of Allah", i.e. the earthly successor to Muhammad as temporal ruler of the Muslim Ummah (nation or community).

17. Duncan GB (1971).

18. Leslie EA (1929a).

19. *I Kings* 6:1.

20. A) Simpson DC (1929). B) Lewlie EA (1929a). C) Rohl DM (1995). D) Duncan GB (1971). E) Herbert G (1962). F) Finegan J (1952). G) Terrien S (1964). H) Wright GE (1960). I) Beck HF (1971). J) Asimov I (1968). K) Noth M (1960).

21. A) Duncan GB (1971). B) Leslie EA (1929a). C) Hyatt JP (1971).

22. Sources used in constructing Figure #2 include the following. A) Marks JH (1971). B) Gray J (1971). C) Milgrom J (1971). D) Guthrie HH (1971). E) Gottwald NK (1971).

23. A) Milgrom J (1971). B) Gottwald NK (1971).

24. A) Marks HJ (1971). B) Robinson TH (1929). C) Eiselen FC (1929). D) Gottwald NK (1971).

25. Sources used in constructing Figure #3 include the following. A) Duncan GB (1971). B) Hyatt JP (1971). C) Marks HJ (1971). D) Robinson TH (1929). E) Eiselen FC (1929). F) Leslie EA (1929a).

26. A) Marks HJ (1971). B) Robinson TH (1929).

27. Joseph was the son of Jacob, who was the son of Isaac, who was the son of Abraham.

28. Ishmael was the son of Abraham out of Hagar (Hajar).

29. Midian (Madyan) was the son of Abraham out of Keturah (Qantura, Qaturah).

30. *Genesis* 37:25-30, 36; 39:1.

31. A) Reumann J (1971). B) Sarna NM (1998).

32. A) Reumann J (1971). B) Sarna NM (1998).

33. Reumann J (1971).

34. Stegemann H (1998).

35. A) Duncan GB (1971). B) Leslie EA (1929a).

36. Silberman LH (1971).

37. *Qur'an* 4:163; 17:55; 21:105.

38. *Qur'an* 21:79-80; 34:10-11.

39. Rohl DM (1995).

40. *Psalms* 8; 19:1-6; 33; 65; 100; 103-105; 111; 113-115; 117; 134-136; 145-150.

41. *Psalms* 46; 48; 76; 87.

42. *Psalms* 29; 47; 93; 95-99.

43. *Psalms* 3-7; 13; 17; 22; 25; 26; 28; 31; 35; 38-39; 42-43; 51; 54-57; 59; 61; 63-64; 69-71; 86; 88; 102; 109; 120; 130; 140-143.

44. *Psalms* 12; 44; 58; 60; 74; 79; 80; 83; 90; 106; 123; 126; 137.

45. *Psalms* 11; 16; 23; 62; 125; 129; 131.

46. *Psalms* 30; 32; 34; 41; 65-67; 92; 116; 124; 138.

47. *Psalms* 2; 18; 20-21; 45; 72; 89; 101; 110; 132; 144.

48. *Psalms* 1; 37; 49; 73; 112; 127-128; 133.

49. *Psalms* 15; 24; 50; 75; 85; 118; 121.

50. *Psalms* 84; 122.

51. For example, the unknown editor attributed *Psalms* 3-9, 11-32, and 34-41 to David, *Psalms* 42 and 44-49 to the descendants of Korah, *Psalms* 51-65 and 68-70 to David, and *Psalms* 73-83 to Asaph. Concerning other individual hymns within the *Psalms*, some have and some do not have an attribution of authorship assigned by the unknown editor. Among those others who have been assigned authorship are Solomon, Moses, Ethan the Ezrahite, Heman the Ezrahite, and Jeduthun. The last three named individuals were choir leaders at the Jerusalem Temple.

52. Originally, the individual chapters of *Psalms* were simply individual hymns that were used at the Jerusalem Temple and at other religious shrines during festivals and acts of worship. As time passed, these individual hymns were grouped into various collections or hymnbooks.

53. This hymnbook basically corresponds to *Psalms* 2-41.

54. This hymnbook basically corresponds to *Psalms* 42-50.

55. This hymnbook basically corresponds to *Psalms* 51-72.

56. This hymnbook basically corresponds to *Psalms* 73-83.

57. Toombs LE (1971).

58. Toombs LE (1971).

59. Duncan GB (1971).

60. If one accepts the events described in *Matthew* 2:16-18 as being historically reliable, a most risky assumption as can be seen by reading the chapter entitled "One Size Fits All", the implication would be that Jesus could not have been born before 6 BCE, since Herod supposedly had all the children age two and under killed.

61. A) Baird W (1971). B) Schonfield HJ (1967).

62. A) Josephus F (1988). B) Asimov I (1969). C) Baird W (1971). D) Duncan GB (1971). E) Leon-Dufour X (1983).

63. See, for example, *John* 1:14. "And the Word became flesh and lived among us, and we have seen his glory, the glory as of a father's only son, full of grace and truth."

64. The word "gospel" is from the Greek "eu-aggelion", where "eu" means "good" or "well" and "aggelion" means "to announce", i.e. "good news". The term used in the *Qur'an* is "Injil".

65. See, for example, *Galatians* 1:11-12. "For I want you to know, brothers and sisters, that the gospel that was proclaimed by me is not of human origin; for I did not receive it from a human source, nor was I taught it, but I received it through a revelation of Jesus Christ."

66. Sundberg AC (1971).

67. A) Duncan GB (1971). B) Davies JN (1929a). C) Moffatt J (1929). D) Sundberg AC (1971). E) Pherigo LP (1971). F) Asimov I (1969). G) Mack BL (1996). H) Nineham DE (1973). I) Leon-Dufour X (1983). J) Kee HC (1971). K) Fenton JC (1973). L) Baird W (1971). M) Shepherd MH (1971).

68. His reference was to *Mark*, for which he attributed authorship to a translator for Peter, one of the disciples of Jesus. Of note, the reference by Papias clearly states that the author of *Mark* never met Jesus, and was not one of the followers of Jesus. Further, Papias stated that he preferred the oral traditions to the written gospels with which he was familiar.

69. Sundberg AC (1971).

70. See the chapter entitled "The Crucifixion: A Question of Identity" for a listing of these "apocryphal" gospels.

71. Figure #4 is based upon information provided by the following sources: A) Filson FV (1971). B) Wilson RM (1971).

72. Mack BL (1996).

73. A) Robinson JM (1971a). B) Robinson JM (1971b). C) Koester H (1971a). D) Mack BL (1996).

74. A) Filson FV (1971). B) Kee HC (1971). C) Baird W (1971). D) Burch EW (1929). E) Leon-Dufour X (1983). F) Koester H (1971b).

75. A) Koester H (1971a). B) Robinson JM (1971b). C) Koester H (1971b). D) Mack BL (1996).

76. Mack BL (1996).

77. Mack BL (1996).

78. For example, the *Q* material of *Matthew* 5:3 has parallels with the *Testament of Benjamin* 1:26-27, the *Testament of Judah* 4:31, and the *Testament of Gad* 2:15. As a second example, the *Q* material of *Matthew* 5:11-12 has parallels with the *Testament of Levi* 4:26 and the *Testament of Joseph* 1:20-21. As to these quotations from the *Testaments of the Twelve Patriarchs*, see Platt RH, Brett JA.

79. Mack BL (1996).

80. A) Duncan GB (1971). B) Davies JN (1929a). C) Moffatt J (1929). D) Sundberg AC (1971). E) Pherigo LP (1971). F) Asimov I (1969). G) Mack BL (1996). H) Nineham DE (1973). I) Leon-Dufour X (1983).

81. A) Duncan GB (1971). B) Sundberg AC (1971). C) Kee HC (1971). D) Leon-Dufour X (1983). E) Mack BL (1996). F) Fenton JC (1973).

82. A) Mack BL (1996). B) Kee HC (1971). C) Filson FV (1971). D) Burch EW (1929).

83. A) Mack BL (1996). B) Baird W (1971). C) Filson FV (1971). D) Burch EW (1929).

84. A) Mack BL (1996). B) Asimov I (1969). C) Duncan GB (1971). D) Baird W (1971). E) Sundberg AC (1971). F) Some scholars argue that there was an earlier version of Luke, which can be called proto-Luke, which was composed around 60 CE, and which began with the baptism of Jesus, just as Mark had. Caird GB (1972).

85. Shepherd MH (1971).

86. A) Mack BL (1996). B) Duncan GB (1971). C) Shepherd MH (1971). D) Leon-Dufour X (1983).

87. Mack BL (1996).

88. Canonized a saint by the Roman Catholic Church, Titus Flavius Clemens (Clement) was a 2nd and 3rd CE century president of the Christian catechetical school at Alexandria. His written works include: *Protreptikos*; *Paidagogos*; *Stromateis*; *A Discourse Concerning the Salvation of Rich Men*; *Exhortation to Patience or Address to the Newly Baptized*; *Excerpta ex Theodoto*; *Eclogae Propheticae*; and *Hypotyposeis*. Fredericksen LF et al. (1998).

89. Shepherd MH (1971).

90. A) Mack BL (1996). B) Garvie AE (1929).

91. A) Shepherd MH (1971). B) Moffat J (1929).

92. Garvie AE (1929).

93. See the chapter entitled "The Baptism of Jesus" for a fuller explanation of this alteration.

94. The editorial addition consists of the words: "For the kingdom and the power and the glory are yours forever. Amen."

95. Shepherd MH (1971).
96. A) Shepherd MH (1971). B) Moffat J (1929).
97. *Matthew* 16:17-20 immediately follows Peter's alleged confession that Jesus was "the Messiah, the Son of the living God". These verses then read: "And Jesus answered him, 'Blessed are you, Simon son of Jonah! For flesh and blood has not revealed this to you, but my Father in heaven. And I tell you, you are Peter, and on this rock I will build my church, and the gates of Hades will not prevail against it. I will give you the keys to the kingdom of heaven, and whatever you bind on earth will be bound in heaven, and whatever you loose on earth will be loosed in heaven.' Then he sternly ordered the disciples not to tell anyone that he was the Messiah."
98. Robertson AT (1929).
99. In other words, can the book of scripture be traced directly to the one who reportedly received the revelation in the first place?
100. Time between the end of the revelation and the initial compilation of the complete book of scripture.
101. Time between the end of the revelation and the final compilation of the complete book of scripture.
102. This figure assumes the Masoretic text manuscript of 895 CE is the "final" compilation. However, in reality, the "final" compilation is not yet complete, as Biblical scholars continue to make changes in the text as new archaeological finds are discovered and analyzed. As such, this figure could just as easily read: "3,400 years and counting".
103. This figure assumes the Masoretic text manuscript of 895 CE is the "final" compilation. However, in reality, the "final" compilation is not yet complete, as Biblical scholars continue to make modifications in the text. As such, this figure could just as easily read: "2,970 years and counting".
104. Changes continue to be made in the text by Biblical scholars, and the figure could read: "1,960+ years and counting".

Chapter 4. The Baptism of Jesus

1. *Qur'an* 112:1-4.
2. *Qur'an* 19:88-93.
3. A) Duncan GB (1971). B) Davies JN (1929a). C) Moffatt J (1929). D) Sundberg AC (1971). E) Pherigo LP (1971). F) Asimov I (1969). G) Mack BL (1996). H) Nineham DE (1973). I) Leon-Dufour X (1983).
4. See author's preface regarding the use of the phrase "peace be upon him".
5. A) Duncan GB (1971). B) Sundberg AC (1971). C) Kee HC (1971). D) Leon-Dufour X (1983). E) Mack BL (1996). F) Fenton JC (1973).
6. A) Mack BL (1996). B) Asimov I (1969). C) Duncan GB (1971). D) Baird W (1971). E) Sundberg AC (1971). F) Some scholars argue that there was an earlier version of Luke, which can be called proto-Luke, which was composed around 60 CE, and which began with the baptism of Jesus, just as Mark had. Caird GB (1972).
7. This story, recorded only in Luke, has suspicious similarities with an autobiographical story told by Josephus about an event in his life at age 14. Findlay JA (1929).
8. The use of "John" in the title has no relationship to John the Baptist, who was most definitely not the author of this book.

9. A) Mack BL (1996). B) Duncan GB (1971). C) Shepherd MH (1971). D) Leon-Dufour X (1983).

10. See footnotes #1, 3, 4, and 5.

11. *Mark* 1:1-11.

12. *Matthew* 1:1-2:23.

13. *Luke* 1:26-38; 2:1-38.

14. *Luke* 2:41-51.

15. *John* 1:1-18.

16. See author's preface regarding the use of the term "Allah".

17. *Matthew* 1:18,20,23; 2:15.

18. *John* 1:1-5.

19. *Luke* 3:1.

20. A) Josephus F (1988). B) Asimov I (1969). C) Baird W (1971). D) Duncan GB (1971). E) Leon-Dufour X (1983).

21. *Matthew* 3:4-5; *Mark* 1:4-5; *Luke* 3:2-3; *John* 2:28.

22. *Luke* 3:2-3.

23. *John* 2:28-29.

24. *Luke* 3:21-22.

25. Conzelmann H (1969). Pages 77-78.

26. *Luke* 3:21-22.

27. Cameron R (1982).

28. Wingren G (1998).

29. Cameron R (1982).

30. --- (1998i).

31. *Gospel of the Ebionites*. In Epiphanius: *Panarion* 30.13.7-8. In Cameron R (1982). Page 105.

32. *Exodus* 4:22.

33. *Hosea* 11:1-3,10-11.

34. *Jeremiah* 31:9.

35. *Jeremiah* 31:20.

36. *Psalms* 2:7. Here, the reference is to King David.

37. *Psalms* 89:26-27. Here, the reference is to King David.

38. *II Samuel* 7:13-14. Here, the reference is to King Solomon, son of King David.

39. *Job* 1:6. See footnote in *The Holy Bible: New Revised Standard Version*. Nashville, Thomas Nelson, Inc., 1989.

40. *Job* 1:6.

41. *Deuteronomy* 14:1.

42. *Ecclesiasticus* 4:10. In Charles RH (1971). *Ecclesiasticus* is also known as *The Book of Sirach*, *Ben-Sira*, and the *Wisdom of Jesus Ben-Sira*.

43. Leon-Dufour X (1983).

44. Conzelmann H (1969). Page 76.

45. According to the *Qur'an*, Jesus' status as a prophet who had received revelation from Allah greatly preceded his baptism from John the Baptist. In fact, the *Qur'an* establishes that the prophethood of Jesus began in his infancy. "But she pointed to the babe. They said: 'How can we talk to one who is a child in the cradle?' He said: 'I am indeed a servant of Allah: He hath given me revelation and made me a prophet...'" *Qur'an* 19:29-30.

46. A) Conzelmann H (1969). Pages 86, 128. B) Fuller RH (1965). Pages 169-170. C) Hahn F (1969). Pages 293-294.

47. A) Hahn F (1969). Pages 293-294, 336-338, 382. B) Fuller RH (1965). Pages 86, 128. C) Conzelmann H (1969). Pages 86, 128.

48. *Qur'an* 19:30.

49. Paul appeared to promote the concept of the pre-existence of Jesus, and expressed such sentiments in written form during the sixth decade of the first century CE. Laymon CM (1971a). However, the early evolution of the concept of the pre-existence of Jesus within the Pauline churches, was not expressed in the gospel tradition until about six decades after Paul's writings. This concept of the pre-existence of Jesus is also stated by the anonymous author of *Hebrews* 1:1-4, at some point prior to 96 CE. Quanbeck WA (1971).

50. *Qur'an* 4:171.

51. *Qur'an* 10:68.

52. *Qur'an* 25:1-2.

53. *Qur'an* 43:57-59.

Chapter 5.   The Crucifixion

1. *Qur'an* 4:157-158.

2. Josephus F (1988). Pages 264-265.

3. Tacitus: *Annals*. In Pagels E (1979). Page 70.

4. See the author's preface regarding the use of the phrase "peace be upon him" in this book.

5. Vigorous debates can be generated among Christians, as to whether the site of the crucifixion was Gordon's Calvary or the site presently hosting the Basilica of the Holy Sepulcher.

6. There are two issues regarding the date of the crucifixion. First, in what year during Pontius Pilate's government was the crucifixion? Second, is the chronology of the Synoptic or Johanine tradition to be followed in placing the crucifixion in relation to the Jewish Passover?

7. See the author's preface regarding the use of the term "Allah" in this book.

8. Pagels E (1979). A) Canonized as a saint by the Roman Catholic Church, Ignatius or Ignatius Theophoros was the bishop of Antioch (Syria). In 107 or 108 CE, Ignatius was arrested by the Romans, and transported to Rome. Between that time and his death around 110 CE, Ignatius wrote a series of letters in which he attacked the proposition that Jesus' suffering and death were an illusion. Beiler JG (1998). B) Canonized as a saint by the Roman Catholic Church, Polycarp was a 2nd century CE bishop of Smyrna. His writings included *Letter to the Philippians*, in which he vigorously attacked the argument that Christ's suffering and death were illusory. --- (1998l). C) Canonized a saint by the Roman Catholic Church, Justin was a 2nd century CE Christian philosopher. His works include *Apologies* and *Dialogue with Trypho*. --- (1998k). D) Canonized as a saint by the Roman Catholic Church, Irenaeus was the late 2nd century CE bishop of Lyon. Irenaeus is best remembered for his five-volume *Adversus Haereses*, which was basically an attack against Christian Gnosticism. Wingren G (1998). E) Quintus Septimus Florens Tertullianus (Tertullian) was a late 2nd and early 3rd century CE Christian theologian, who later defected to the Montanist heresy. His written works included *Apologeticum, Adversus Marcionem, Ad Uxorem, De Patientia, Adversus Hermogenem, Adversus Valentinianos, De Resurrectione Carnis, De Baptismo, De Anima,* and numerous other books. Wilkin RL (1998). F) Canonized as a saint by the Roman Catholic Church, Hippolytus was born around 170 CE and died around 235 CE. He was a Christian martyr, and was the first anti-pope. He is remembered for his voluminous writings against heresies, including *Philosphumena*. --- (1998j).

9. Ignatius: *Trallians* 10:1. In Pagels E (1979). Page 83.

10. Danielou J, Marrou H (1964).

11. In many cases, the emerging orthodoxy of Christianity did its utmost to suppress and destroy all copies of these gospels. In some cases, the destruction of these books by the emerging orthodoxy of Christianity succeeded. In such cases, one knows of these books only because they were mentioned by an early Christian writer.

12. This list is compiled from the following sources: A) Platt RH, Brett JA. B) Cameron R (1982). C) Pagels E (1979). D) Robinson JM (1990). E) Hennecke E, Schneemelcher W, Wilson RM (1963).

13. *The Gospel of Barnabas*. In Ragg L, Ragg L (1974).

14. A) Platt RH, Brett JA. B) --- (1998e). C) Sundberg AC (1971). D) Koester H (1982).

15. Canonized a saint by the Roman Catholic Church, Titus Flavius Clemens (Clement) was a 2nd and 3rd CE century president of the Christian catechetical school at Alexandria. His written works include: *Protreptikos*; *Paidagogos*; *Stromateis*; *A Discourse Concerning the Salvation of Rich Men*; *Exhortation to Patience or Address to the Newly Baptized*; *Excerpta ex Theodoto*; *Eclogae Propheticae*; and *Hypotyposeis*. Fredericksen LF et al. (1998).

16. Oregenes Adamantius (Origen) was a 3rd century CE president of the Christian catechetical school at Alexandria. He was a pupil of Clement of Alexandria (see immediately preceding footnote), and was the author of *Hexapla, De Principiis, Contra Celsum, On Prayer*, and numerous commentaries on various books of the *Bible*. Chadwick H (1998).

17. Eusebius Pamphili was a 4th century CE bishop of Caesarea. He was the author of the monumental *Ecclesiastical History, Chronicle*, and various apologies and commentaries. --- (1998c).

18. Canonized a saint by the Roman Catholic Church, Eusebius Hieronymus (Jerome) was a Catholic priest, private secretary to Pope Damasus, monastery founder, and translator. His written works include the *Vulgate Bible, Liber Locorum, Liber Interpretationis Hebraicorum Nominum, Liber Hebraicarum Quaestionum in Genesim*, and various commentaries. Burghardt WJ (1998).

19. A) Schneemelcher W: General Introduction. In Hennecke E, Schneemelcher W, Wilson RM (1963). B) Platt RH, Brett JA.

20. A) Rahim MA (1974). B) Abdullah M (1996).

21. --- (1998h).

22. --- (1998m).

23. Lernet-Holenia AM (1998).

24. Lernet-Holenia AM (1998).

25. *Gospel of Barnabas* 215-217. In Ragg L, Ragg L (1974)..

26. *Gospel of Barnabas* 217. In Ragg L, Ragg L (1974).

27. *Gospel of Barnabas* 217-218. In Ragg L, Ragg L (1974).

28. *Gospel of Barnabas* 219-221. In Ragg L, Ragg L (1974).

29. --- (1998d).

30. Hennecke E, Schneemelcher W, Wilson RM (1963).

31. *Two Books of Jeu*. In Hennecke E, Schneemelcher W, Wilson RM (1963). Page 261.

236

32. Brashler J (1990).
33. *Apocalypse of Peter* 81:4-32; 82:1-3,17-23,27-33. In Robinson JM (1990).
34. Gibbons JA (1990).
35. --- (1998b).
36. *The Second Treatise of the Great Seth* 55:10-20,30-35; 56:1-13,18-19,23-25. In Robinson JM (1990). Page 365.
37. Canonized a saint by the Roman Catholic Church, Aurelius Augustinus (Augustine) was bishop of Hippo (Africa) from 396 to 430 CE, and is generally acclaimed by the traditional church as being the greatest Christian theologian of the early era. His literary works include *Confessions, De Trinitate, De Civitate Dei*, etc. Burnaby J (1998).
38. Cameron R (1982).
39. *Acts of John* 97-99,101. In Cameron R (1982). Pages 94-96.
40. A) Moffat J (1929). B) Robertson AT (1929). C) Burch EW (1929). D) Peritz IJ (1929). E) Scott EF (1929). F) Davies JN (1929b) G) Davies JN (1929a). H) Findlay JA (1929). I) Garvie AE (1929). J) Kee HC (1971). K) Pherigo LP (1971).L) Baird W (1971). M) Shepherd MH (1971). N) Wilson RM (1971). O) Filson FV (1971). P) Sundberg AC (1971). Q) Duncan GB (1971). R) Marsh J (1972). S) Caird GB (1972). T) Nineham DE (1973). U) Fenton JC (1973). V) Hamilton W (1959). W) Mack BL (1996). X) Koester H (1982). Z) Robinson JM, Koester H (1971). ZZ) Cameron R (1982).
41. Shepherd MH (1971). Page 722. This issue of the exact chronology of the crucifixion in relation to the Jewish Passover, as well as the chronology of John vs. the chronology of the synoptic gospels, has divided Christian theologians for centuries, and lies outside the scope of the present article.
42. *John* 18:1-12.
43. A) *Luke* 22:47 refers to the arresting force as "a crowd". B) *Mark* 14:43 refers to the arresting force as "a crowd with swords and clubs, from the chief priests, the scribes, and the elders", implying the temple police force. C) *Matthew* 26:47 refers to the arresting force as "a large crowd with swords and clubs, from the chief priests and the elders of the people", implying the temple police force.
44. On the flight of the disciples see *Matthew* 26:56 and *Mark* 14:50-2.
45. *Luke* 22:50-51.
46. *John* 18:13-16.
47. *Matthew* 26:57; *Mark* 14:53; *Luke* 22:54.
48. *Matthew* 26:57-58; *Mark* 14:53-54; *Luke* 22:54-55; *John* 18:15-16.
49. *Matthew* 26:69-75.
50. *Luke* 22:55-62.
51. *Mark* 14:66-72.
52. *John* 18:17-18,25-27.
53. A) Danielou J, Marrou H (1964). B) Asimov I (1969). C) Leon-Dufour X (1983). D) Schonfield HJ (1967). E) --- (1998p). F) Bornkamm G (1998).
54. A) Josephus F (1988). B) Leon-Dufour X (1983).
55. A) --- (1998p). B) Asimov I (1969).
56. *Luke* 6:15; *Acts* 1:13.
57. *Matthew* 10:4; 26:14; *Mark* 3:19; 14:10; *Luke* 6:16; 22:3; *John* 6:71; 12:4; 13:2; 13:26.
58. A) Dupont-Sommer A (1967). B) Leon-Dufour X (1983).
59. Josephus F (1988).
60. A) *Luke* 2:1-3. B) Josephus F (1988). C) Bornkamm G (1998).

61. A) *Acts* 5:37. B) Josephus F (1988). C) Bornkamm G (1998). D)Leon-Dufour X (1983).

62. *Acts* 5:37.

63. A) Josephus F (1988). B) Leon-Dufour X (1983).

64. A) Josephus F (1988). B) Bornkamm G (1998).

65. *Matthew* 26:71.

66. *Mark* 14:67.

67. A) *Matthew* 26:71. See footnote "o" in ---: *The Holy Bible: New Revised Standard Version*. Nashville, Thomas Nelson, 1989. B) Stegemann H (1998). C) The statement of *Matthew* 2:23, in which Nazorean is linked with someone from Nazareth, is "far-fetched" and confuses the Hebrew "Nazir" (consecrated, holy, abstainer) with the Hebrew "Netzer" (sprout or shoot). Kee HC (1971).

68. Stegemann H (1998).

69. Stegemann H (1998).

70. A) Leon-Dufour X (1983). B) --- (1998f).

71. A) Schonfield HJ (1967). B) --- (1998f).

72. *Judges* 13:1-24; 16:13-17.

73. *I Samuel* 1:1-22.

74. A) Strugnell J (1998). In discussing John the Baptist, John Strugnell states: "His dress of an austere camel's hair garment was the traditional garb of the prophets, and his diet of locusts and wild honey represented either strict adherence to Jewish purity laws or the ascetic conduct of a Nazirite (a Jew especially vowed to God's service)." B) Schonfield HJ (1967).

75. *Acts* 21:17-26.

76. *Acts* 21:17-26.

77. The story of the raising of Lazarus from the dead is told in *John* 11:38-44. As that narrative makes clear, Jesus was in too close of a physical proximity to the corpse to have been a Nazorean.

78. A) Josephus F (1988). B) Schonfield HJ (1967). C) Wilson I (1985).

79. *Matthew* 27:11-26; *Mark* 15:6-15; *Luke* 23:13-25; *John* 18:38-40.

80. *Matthew* 27:11,15-26.

81. Procla is identified as the wife of Pilate in the following apocryphal writings, all of which can be located in Platt RH, Brett JA. A) *Letter of Herod to Pilate the Governor*. B) *Letter of Pilate to Herod*. C) *The Trial and Condemnation of Pilate*, also known as *The Paradosis of Pilate*.

82. The identification of Jesus as the given name of Barabbas appears in various ancient texts of Matthew, including Greek versions, Syriac, and others. It was also reported by Origen, the third century apostolic father. A) Fenton JC (1973). B) --- (1998a).

83. A) --- (1998a). B) Leon-Dufour X (1983). C) Asimov I (1969). D) Schonfield HJ (1967). E) Fenton JC (1973). F) Pherigo LP (1971).

84. *Matthew* 16:17. In the *NRSV*, the translators have gone all the way, and have rendered the name "Simon son of Jonah". In the earlier *RSV*, the translators have simply said "Simon Bar-Jona".

85. A) --- (1998a). B) Leon-Dufour X (1983). C) Asimov I (1969). D) Fenton JC (1973). E) Pherigo LP (1971).

86. For the sake of Muslim readers, the author notes that the phrase "son of the Father" does not imply any "begotten" status. In that regard, see the chapter entitled "The Baptism of Jesus".

87. *Matthew* 27:17.

88. *Matthew* 27:17-26.

89. *Matthew* 27:11.
90. A) Leon-Dufour X (1983). B) Schonfield HJ (1967).
91. *Mark* 15:8-9,11.
92. *Matthew* 26:69-70.
93. Platt RH, Brett JA.
94. A) Hennecke E, Schneemelcher W, Wilson RM (1963). Page 484. B) Platt RH, Brett JA. Page 279. C) --- (1998g).
95. --- (1998n).
96. *Matthew* 27:32-36.
97. *Mark* 15:21-24.
98. *Luke* 23:26,32-33.
99. Norwood FA (1971).
100. --- (1998b).

Chapter 6. The Mission and Ministry of Jesus

1. See the author's preface regarding the use of the phrase "peace be upon him".
2. See the author's preface regarding the use of the term "Allah".
3. See the chapter entitled "Judaism, Christianity, and Islam: Origins and Relationships" for a fuller exposition of this concept.
4. *Qur'an* 3:45a, 48-49a.
5. *Qur'an* 43:57-59.
6. *Matthew* 10:5-6. Of note, the parallel accounts of this commissioning to be found in *Mark* 6:6b-13 and *Luke* 9:1-6 conveniently leave out the restrictions found in *Matthew*'s narrative.
7. *Matthew* 15:21-28.
8. The descendants of the Israelite tribe of Benjamin are also typically referred to as being Jews.
9. *Matthew* 7:6.
10. *The Gospel of Thomas*. In Robinson JM (1990). Page 136. An alternative translation can be found in Guillaumont A, Puech HC, Quispel G, Till W, 'Abd Al-Masih Y (1959).
11. As to the alleged crucifixion of Jesus, see the chapter entitled "The Crucifixion: A Question of Identity".
12. *Luke* 7:1-7,9-10. The Matthean parallel can be found in *Matthew* 8:5-13. However, the account in Matthew fails to record the special circumstances involved, whereby Jesus makes an exception to the usual limits of his ministry.
13. See the chapter entitled "The Crucifixion: A Question of Identity" for a discussion of the issues involved in the Biblical presentation of the alleged crucifixion of Jesus.
14. Presumably, the 11 disciples refer to the 12 disciples minus Judas Iscariot.
15. *Matthew* 28:16-20.
16. *Acts* 9:1-9.
17. *Acts* 2:38.
18. Eusebius Pamphili was a 4th century CE bishop of Caesarea. He was the author of the monumental *Ecclesiastical History*, *Chronicle*, and various apologies and commentaries. --- (1998c).
19. Davies JN (1929b).

20. The disciples and elders grouped together in Jerusalem are traditionally referred to as the Jerusalem church. However, they were not a "church". They continued to congregate and pray at the Jewish temple, and obviously maintained themselves as being part of the "house of Israel". They were not a new religion, i.e. Christianity, but were instead among those Jews who had returned to proper submission to Allah. (See the chapter entitled "Judaism, Christianity, and Islam: Origins and Relationships".)

21. *Acts* 9:26.

22. *Acts* 15:1-5; 21:17-26; *Galatians* 2:1-9. Remember that the book of *Acts* was written by the Pauline tradition and school, and thus presents a very biased report of the conflict between Paul and the early "church" at Jerusalem. For example, *Acts* 21:17-26 purports to show that the Jerusalem "church" backed Paul. However, the fact of the matter was, as recorded in that very passage, that the elders of the Jerusalem "church" made Paul undergo the temporary rites of being a Nazarite, indicating that he was made to purify himself and to pay penance for what he had been doing.

23. *Acts* 11:19.

24. Fenton JC (1973). Page 453.

25. Hamilton W (1959). Page 109.

26. *Luke* 24:45-49.

27. *Acts* 11:1-18; 15:1-5; 21:17-26; *Galatians* 2:1-9.

28. *Acts* 11:19.

29. See the chapter entitled "The Crucifixion: A Question of Identity".

30. *Acts* 1:4-5,8-9.

31. *Acts* 11:1-19; 15:1-5; 21:17-26; *Galatians* 2:1-9.

32. *John* 14:25-31. The reader of this passage should note that the alleged words of Jesus specifically state that Jesus is subordinate to "the Father", i.e. to Allah. In short, this passage is also a direct refutation of the concept of the trinity.

33. *John* 16:7.

34. *Psalms* 51:11; *Mark* 12:36; *Acts* 1:16; 4:25.

35. *Acts* 28:25.

36. *Isaiah* 63:10-11.

37. *Luke* 2:25-26.

38. *Luke* 1:15

39. *Luke* 1:41.

40. *Luke* 1:67.

41. *Luke* 1:35.

42. *Matthew* 1:20; 3:11; *Mark* 1:8; *Luke* 3:16,22; 4:1: 10:21; *John* 1:33; *Acts* 10:38.

43. *Mark* 13:11; *Luke* 12:12; *John* 20:22; *Acts* 1:2.

44. *John* 20:22.

45. *Acts* 1:1-2.

46. For a fuller discussion of these issues, see the chapter entitled "A Concise Introduction to Islam: Articles of Faith and Pillars of Practice".

47. *John* 14:26; 16:7b.

48. *Qur'an* 2:87,136,253; 3:45-59; 4:157-159,163,171-172; 5:17,46,72-75,78,110-118; 6:85; 9:30-31; 19:19-35,88-93; 21:91; 23:50; 33:7; 42:13; 43:57-65; 57:27; 61:6,14.

49. *Qur'an* 2:136.

50. *Qur'an* 2:253.

51. *Luke* 24:50.

52. *Acts* 1:3.

53. *Qur'an* 3:45a,48-49a.

Chapter 7.   One Size Fits All

1. Leon-Dufour X (1983).
2. Leon-Dufour X (1983).
3. See the author's preface regarding the use of the term "Allah".
4. See the author's preface regarding the use of the phrase "peace be upon him".
5. *Matthew* 1:22.
6. *Matthew* 2:5.
7. *Matthew* 2:15.
8. *Matthew* 2:17.
9. *Matthew* 2:2:23.
10. *Matthew* 3:3.
11. A) Sundberg AC (1971). B) Duncan GB (1971). C) Mack BL (1996). D) Kee HC (1971). E) Fenton JC (1973). F) Leon-Dufour X (1983). G) Filson FV (1971). H) Peritz IJ (1929).
12. A) Leon-Dufour X (1983). B) Kee HC (1971). C) Davies JN (1929b). D) Hamilton W (1959). E) Koester H (1982).
13. A) Leon-Dufour X (1983). B) Kee HC (1971). C) Filson FV (1971). D) Burch EW (1929). E) Cadbury HJ (1929). F) Moffatt J (1929). G) Grobel K (1971). H) Robertson AT (1929). I) Koester H (1982).
14. A) Davies JN (1929b). B) Kee HC (1971). C) Moffatt J (1929). D) Koester H (1982).
15. A) Kee HC (1971). B) Filson FV (1971). C) Davies JN (1929b). D) Hamilton W (1959).
16. The word "Palestinian" is used here strictly as a geographical reference point, and has no ethnic meaning.
17. A) Filson FV (1971). B) Davies JN (1929b). C) Fenton JC (1973). D) Hamilton W (1959). E) Mack BL (1996). F) Koester H (1982).
18. A) Filson FV (1971). B) Kee HC (1971). C) Leon-Dufour X (1983). D) Davies JN (1929b). E) Burch EW (1929). F) Wilson RM (1971). G) Fenton JC (1973). H) Hamilton W (1959). H) Koester H (1982).
19. A) Filson FV (1971). B) Fenton JC (1973).
20. *Matthew* 1:17.
21. *I Chronicles* 3:10-12.
22. *I Chronicles* 3:15-16.
23. Fenton JC (1973). Page 41.
24. *Matthew* 1:22-23.
25. *Isaiah* 7:14.
26. Kohlenberger III JR (1991).
27. *Matthew* 2:1.
28. *Matthew* 2:5-6.
29. *Micah* 5:2-5. This is from the Hebrew text, as this prophecy is not preserved in the Greek *Septuagint*. Fenton JC (1973).
30. *Matthew* 2:1; *Luke* 2:4-20.
31. *John* 7:37-44.
32. Kohlenberger III JR (1991).
33. *Matthew* 2:1-15,19-21.
34. *Matthew* 2:15.

35. Fenton JC (1973).

36. *Hosea* 11:1-5,10-11.

37. The fall of the northern Kingdom of Israel is typically dated at 723 to 722 BCE. Duncan GB (1971).

38. Current Israelies claim descent from the two tribes of the southern Kingdom of Judah, i.e. the tribes of Judah and of Benjamin, and from those Levites who inhabited the southern Kingdom of Judah. The 10 northern tribes were deported, scattered, dispersed, and lost to history, giving rise to the concept of the "10 lost tribes of Israel".

39. A) Kohlenberger III JR (1991). B) Certain apocryphal gospels speak of the infancy of Jesus in Egypt, but these books were written after *Matthew*, and cannot be said to be independent of *Matthew*.

40. *Deuteronomy* 18:15-19.

41. *Matthew* 2:16-18.

42. *Jeremiah* 31:15-18.

43. *Genesis* 30:22-24.

44. *Genesis* 29:31-35.

45. *Genesis* 41:50-52; 48:1.

46. Frost SB (1971).

47. *Matthew* 2:6; *Micah* 5:2.

48. Fenton JC (1973).

49. *Exodus* 1:15-2:10.

50. *Matthew* 2:23.

51. Kohlenberger III JR (1991).

52. *Numbers* 6:1-21.

53. A) Strugnell J (1998). B) Schonfield HJ (1967).

54. Kohlenberger III JR (1991).

55. A) Kee HC (1971). B) Fenton JC (1973).

56. A) Leon-Dufour X (1983). B) Kee HC (1971).

57. Kee HC (1971). Page 612.

58. *Matthew* 3:1-3.

59. Fenton JC (1973). Of note, *Mark* makes use of the same verse from *Isaiah* at the same point in the life of Jesus, and also utilizes the *Septuagint*. Probably, *Matthew* was simply quoting from *Mark*, without bothering to check *Mark*'s reference.

60. *Isaiah* 40:3.

61. *Matthew* 4:13-16.

62. *Isaiah* 9:1-2.

63. Leon-Dufour X (1983).

64. See the chapter entitled "The Mission and Ministry of Jesus".

65. *Joshua* 19:10-16.

66. *Joshua* 19:32-39.

67. *Matthew* 10:5-6; 15:21-28.

68. *Matthew* 8:17.

69. *Isaiah* 53:3-4.

70. *Matthew* 11:7,9b-10.

71. Actually, *Matthew* is probably merely following the lead of *Mark* in making this change. See *Mark* 1:2, where this passage is incorrectly attributed to *Isaiah*, but is not placed into the mouth of Jesus.

72. *Malachi* 3:1,5a,6a.

73. *Matthew* 12:17-21.

74. Fenton JC (1973).

75. *Isaiah* 42:1-4.

76. See the chapter entitled "The Mission and Ministry of Jesus".

77. *Matthew* 12:39-40.

78. *Jonah* 1:17.

79. This is an assumption that the author makes only within the context of the present discussion, and then only to make a point that the reference to Jonah cannot apply to the alleged crucifixion and resurrection, even if one accepts that such events happened. See the essay entitled "The Crucifixion: A Question of Identity" for the argument from Christian scripture that it was not the prophet Jesus who was crucified.

80. The Jews at the time of Jesus began counting the start of a new day at sunset. So, at sunset on Friday, the day of Saturday began.

81. Or on Saturday and Sunday nights, using the Jewish formula for reckoning the start of a new day at sunset.

82. At sunset on the Western day of Friday, the Jewish night of Saturday begins. At sunrise on the Western day of Saturday, the Jewish day of Saturday begins. At sunset on the Western day of Saturday, the Jewish night of Sunday begins. At sunrise on the Western day of Sunday, the Jewish day of Sunday begins.

83. If the alleged crucifixion of Jesus actually took place (see chapter entitled "The Crucifixion: A Question of Identity), Jesus would have had to have been placed in the tomb prior to sunset on Friday, because Jewish law prohibited Jews from manual labor, especially with a corpse, on the Sabbath, which began at sunset on Friday.

84. *Matthew* 28:1-10 maintains that the alleged resurrection took place around dawn on Sunday. *Luke* 24:1-3 maintains that the alleged resurrection took place before "early dawn". *John* 20:1-10 maintains that the alleged resurrection took place on Sunday "while it was still dark". From all of this, with the passage from *John* being the clearest evidence, it is clear that the gospel account of the alleged resurrection maintains that there was no time after sunrise on Sunday that Jesus was allegedly still in the tomb.

85. Kee HC (1971).

86. *Luke* 11:29-30.

87. *Matthew* 13:10-13. Similar material and sentiments can be seen in *Mark* 4:10-12 and in *Luke* 8:9-10. As such, this passage can be seen as Markan in origin, even though *Matthew* has greatly elaborated the Markan original.

88. *Matthew* 13:14-16.

89. A) Fenton JC (1973). B) Kee HC (1971).

90. *Isaiah* 6:8-10.

91. Ackroyd PR (1971).

92. *Matthew* 13:34-35. Some texts of *Matthew* identify the prophet as being Isaiah. However, as will be seen, the *Old Testament* passage is not from *Isaiah*, but from *Psalms*.

93. Kee HC (1971).

94. *Psalms* 78:1-4.

95. *Matthew* 15:7-9.

96. *Mark* 7:6-8.

97. Fenton JC (1973).

98. *Isaiah* 29:13-14.

99. *Matthew* 21:1-11; *Mark* 11:1-11; *Luke* 19:28-40; *John* 12:12-19.

100. *Matthew* 21:4-5.

101. *Matthew* 21:2-3.

102. *Matthew* 21:7.

103. *Zechariah* 9:9-10.

104. A) Harvey DW (1971). B) Kee HC (1971). C) Fenton JC (1973).

105. *Mark* 11:1-11; *Luke* 19:28-40; *John* 12:12-19.

106. *Matthew* 21:12-16.

107. *Matthew* 21:16.

108. Fenton JC (1973).

109. *Psalms* 8:2.

110. *Matthew* 21:42-44.

111. *Psalms* 118:22-23.

112. *Mark* 12:1-12; *Luke* 20:9-19.

113. *Matthew* 26:31-32.

114. *Mark* 14:27-31.

115. *Zechariah* 13:7.

116. *Matthew* 26:57-75; *Mark* 14:53-72; *Luke* 22:54-62; *John* 18:12-27. As to those who would say that Peter's subsequent denial constituted "scattering" and "desertion", see "The Crucifixion: A Question of Identity" for the counter argument that Peter never denied Jesus.

117. *John* 18:12-16.

118. *Matthew* 26:14-16; 27:3-6.

119. *Matthew* 27:7-10.

120. Kohlenberger III JR (1991).

121. *Jeremiah* 18:2-3; 19:1; 32:6-7.

122. Kohlenberger III JR (1991).

123. *Zechariah* 11:12-14.

124. Carstensen RN (1971).

125. *Zechariah* 11:7-14.

126. *Qur'an* 5:14.

Chapter 8. The Prophet Job (Ayyoub)

1. See author's preface regarding the use of the term "Allah".

2. See author's preface regarding the use of the phrase "peace be upon him".

3. A) Anderson H (1971). B) Lofthouse WF (192). C) --- (1998o). D) Flaherty RL (1998).

4. Anderson H (1971).

5. Anderson H (1971).

6. Lofthouse WF (1929).

7. A) Asimov I (1968). B) Anderson H (1971). C) Flaherty RL (1998).

8. This latter view, i.e. that the original version of *Job* was written in Arabic or in proto-Arabic, was strongly espoused during the author's seminary education by Professor John Strugnell at the Harvard Divinity School.

9. *Job* 1:1.

10. *Job* 1:3.

11. Kohlenberger III JR (1991).

12. *Genesis* 11:31; 24:10.

13. --- (1971).

14. A) *Genesis* 36:21. B) *I Chronicles* 1:38.

15. ---: (1971).

16. Kohlenberger III JR (1991). The four references to Job, which exist outside of the book of *Job*, are *Ezekiel* 14:14, 20, *James* 5:11, and *Sirach* 49:9.

17. A) De Vaux R (1965). See discussion of succession and inheritance on pages 53-55. B) The specific exception of daughters being allowed to inherit when there is no male heirs and when they marry husbands from the clan of their father finds Biblical precedent in *Numbers* 27:1-8 and 36:1-9.

18. Flaherty RL (1998).

19. *Job* 2:11;4:1;15:1;22:1;42:7,9.

20. *Job* 2:11;8:1;18:1;25:1;42:9.

21. *Job* 2:11;11:1;20:1;42:9.

22. *Job* 32:2,6.

23. *Job* 42:14.

24. Kohlenberger III JR (1991). A) The nine other Biblical uses of the name Eliphaz can be found in *Genesis* 36:4,10-12,15-16 and in *I Chronicles* 1:35-36. B) The four other Biblical uses of the name Elihu can be found in *I Samuel* 1:1 and in *I Chronicles* 12:20; 26:7;27:18.

25. Genealogical connections among Ephraim, Manasses, Joseph, Levi, Judah, and Jacob are found in *Genesis* 35:22-26;48:1,14.

26. A) Anderson H (1971). B) Lofthouse WF (1929).

27. Kohlenberger III JH (1991).

28. *Genesis* 36:34 and *I Chronicles* 1:45.

29. *Genesis* 36:11,15,42 and *I Chronicles* 1:36,53.

30. *Genesis* 36:11,15 and *I Chronicles* 1:36.

31. *Genesis* 36:4,1012,15 and *I Chronicles* 1:35-36.

32. Kohlenberger III JR (1991).

33. *Genesis* 25:1-2 and *I Chronicles* 1:32.

34. Kohlenberger III JR (1991).

35. *Genesis* 36:3-4,10,13,17 and *I Chronicles* 1:37.

36. Kohlenberger III JR (1991).

37. *Genesis* 25:1-3.

38. --- (1971).

39. *Genesis* 25:12-15.

40. --- (1971).

41. *Leviticus* 19:27.

42. Welch AC (1929).

43. Frost SB (1971).

44. *Genesis* 36:1-4,9-10,13.

45. Al-Tabari MJ (1987).

46. This sequential listing of the kings of Edom clearly indicates that kingship was not hereditary among the Edomites, but was in some manner elective. In that regard, it is a little hard to imagine any people choosing a better king for themselves than Prophet Job.

47. *Genesis* 30:21.

48. Al-Tabari MJ (1987).

49. A) 'Ali 'AY (2000a). B) Simpson DC (1920). C) Leslie EA (1929a). D) Asimov I (1968). E) Rohl DM (1995). F) Duncan GB (1971). G) Beck HF (1971). H) Herbert G (1962). I) Finegan J (1952). J) Terrien S (1964). K) Wright GE (1960).

50. *I Kings* 6:1.

51. *Exodus* 12:40.

52. *Genesis* 47:28.

53. *Genesis* 25:24-26.

54. This "exclusive claim" was based upon their concept that the inheritance of the covenant between Allah and Abraham was exclusive to Isaac and then to Isaac's descendants through Jacob. In that regard, see *Genesis* 17:18-21.

55. These sorts of issues simply do not exist within Islam, as Allah's covenant with man is seen as being open to any man who sincerely believes in Him, regardless of ethnic or racial affiliation. In short, because Islam rejects the concept of exclusive inheritance of the covenant along ethnic lines, and because Islam rejects the concept of the "chosen people" as it was developed and formulated by the ancient Israelites, the ancestry of any particular prophet is of little concern to Muslims.

56. Asimov I (1968).

57. *Qur'an* 4:163.

58. *Qur'an* 6:83-84.

59. *Qur'an* 21:83-84.

60. *Qur'an* 38:41-44.

Chapter 9. A Concise Introduction to Islam

1. A) Toombs LE (1971). B) Schonfield HJ (1967).

2. A) Beavin EL (1971). B) Toombs LE (1971). C) Schonfield HJ (1967).

3. Islam acknowledges that a book of revelations, known as the *Torah*, was given by Allah to Moses. However, Islam maintains that the original *Torah* of Moses was adulterated by subsequent generations, and that the five books (*Genesis*, *Exodus*, *Leviticus*, *Numbers*, and *Deuteronomy*) presently known as the *Torah* are only a weak and frequently misleading echo of that original revelation.

4. *Deuteronomy* 6:5.

5. See the author's preface regarding use of the phrase "peace be upon him".

6. *Matthew* 22:37; *Mark* 12:30; *Luke* 10:27.

7. *James* 4:7-8.

8. Technically speaking, a verse of the *Qur'an* can only be quoted in its original Arabic and what is given here is a translation of the meaning of the verses.

9. *Qur'an* 3:20.

10. *Psalms* 81:10-11.

11. *Qur'an* 3:19. The phrase "People of the Book" denotes Jews and Christians, i.e. those who had received earlier books of revelation, but who had not kept those books of revelation in their original and pristine state.

12. *Qur'an* 20:115.

13. This concept is developed more fully in the chapter entitled "Judaism, Christianity, and Islam: Origins and Relationships".

14. *Qur'an* 5:3. This verse was part of the last revelation given to Prophet Muhammad shortly before his death.

15. *Qur'an* 1:2.

16. *Exodus* 20:2; *Deuteronomy* 5:6.

17. *Qur'an* 112:1-4.

18. *Qur'an* 6:42,130-131; 10:47,74; 16:36,63,84,89; 17:71;35:24.

19. *Qur'an* 6:42.

20. *Qur'an* 35:24.

21. *Qur'an* 10:47.

22. *Qur'an* 16:36.
23. *Qur'an* 4:150-151.
24. *Qur'an* 3:23,50,93; 4:44,160; 5:3,15-16; 6:145-146; 10:37; 13:38-39.
25. *Qur'an* 5:15-16.
26. *Qur'an* 2:106.
27. *Qur'an* 10:37.
28. *Qur'an* 13:38-39.
29. *Qur'an* 21:25.
30. *Qur'an* 2:136,253,285; 3:84; 4:150-152.
31. *Qur'an* 2:136.
32. *Qur'an* 2:285.
33. *Qur'an* 4:152.
34. Abu Sa'id Al-Khudri was a companion of the Prophet Muhammad. He was a member of the Khazraj tribe of Madina. He was 13 years old at the Battle of Uhud, for which reason the Prophet refused to let him fight. He died circa 652 CE in Madina. A total of 1,170 *Ahadith* have been attributed to him.
35. Abu Hurayrah 'Abd Al-Rahman Al-Dawsi was a companion of the Prophet Muhammad. Abu Hurayrah was a nickname, reflecting its bearer's love of kittens. Abu Hurayrah narrated more *Ahadith* than did any other companion of the Prophet. He died in Madina circa 677-680 CE at the age of 78 years.
36. Al-Bukhari MI. Hadith #3:594, 595; 4:620, 626; 6:162; 8:524; and 9:564.
37. *John* 13:16.
38. *Qur'an* 21:7-8.
39. *Qur'an* 3:144.
40. *Qur'an* 17:93b-94.
41. *Qur'an* 18:110.
42. A Hadith (plural = Ahadith) is a narration concerning a saying, action, tacit approval, etc. of the Prophet Muhammad, peace be upon him.
43. 'Abd Al-Wahhab M (1981). Page 43.
44. 'Abd Al-Wahhab M (1981). Pages 60-61. See also the parallel version of this Hadith in Al-Bukhari MI. Hadith #4:654.
45. *Qur'an* 3:161a.
46. *Qur'an* 11:12.
47. *Qur'an* 38:21-25.
48. *Qur'an* 80:1-12.
49. *Qur'an* 16:120-123; 60:4-6.
50. *Qur'an* 33:21.
51. *Qur'an* 16:120-123.
52. *Qur'an* 33:21.
53. *Qur'an* 33:40.
54. The word "messenger" can also be used to refer to the angel who, upon the instructions of Allah, glorified and exalted is He, gave the revelation to the prophet.
55. *Qur'an* 4:54; 53:36-37; 87:19.
56. *Qur'an* 2:87; 3:3; 5:44; 6:91,154; 11:17,110; 17:2; 23:49; 25:35; 28:43; 32:23; 37:114-118; 40:53; 41:45; 46:12; 53:36; 87:19.
57. *Qur'an* 4:163; 17:55; 21:105.
58. *Qur'an* 3:3,45-48; 5:46,110; 57:27.
59. *Qur'an* 3:7; 4:105,113,127,140; 5:48; 6:92; 7:2; 10:37; 11:1-4; 12:1-3; 13:1; 14:1; 16:64,89; 18:1,27; 27:1-6; 32:2-3; 38:29; 39:1-2,41; 40:2; 41:2-4; 56:75-80.
60. *Jubilees* 45:14-16. In Charles RH (1969).

61. See the chapter entitled "The Books of Revelation and Scripture: A Comparison of Judaism, Christianity, and Islam".

62. See the chapter entitled "The Books of Revelation and Scripture: A Comparison of Judaism, Christianity, and Islam".

63. See the chapter entitled "The Books of Revelation and Scripture: A Comparison of Judaism, Christianity, and Islam".

64. *Qur'an* 2:75-79,101; 3:23-24,71,78,187; 4:46; 5:12-15,41; 6:91; 11:110;15:90;41:45; 62:5.

65. *Qur'an* 2:75,79.

66. *Qur'an* 3:78.

67. *Qur'an* 3:187.

68. *Qur'an* 5:13-14.

69. *Qur'an* 6:91.

70. *Qur'an* 18:27.

71. *Qur'an* 85:21-22.

72. Such interpretation may be found at times in the Ahadith (the reported sayings and actions) of Muhammad, but never in the *Qur'an*. This distinction highlights one of the significant differences between the *Qur'an* and the Ahadith. A second distinction, which is of marked importance, is that Allah did not guarantee the perpetual incorruptibility of the Ahadith. In fact, there are numerous examples of distorted or even fabricated Ahadith. As such, all Ahadith need to be assiduously scrutinized to determine their accuracy and integrity of text and transmission, and no given Hadith can ever be held to be at the same level of sanctity as the *Qur'an*. Such analysis and determination comprise one branch of the Islamic sciences.

73. Al-Qushayri MH (Muslim) (1971):. Hadith #7134. 'A'isha was one of the wives of Prophet Muhammad.

74. *Qur'an* 7:11-12; 15:27; 38:76; 55:15. The most direct statements are to be found in 15:27 and in 55:15.

75. *Qur'an* 3:59; 6:2; 7:11-12; 15:26-33; 17:61; 18:50; 32:7; 37:11; 38:71-76; 55:14.

76. *Qur'an* 15:26-27.

77. *Qur'an* 55:14-15.

78. *Qur'an* 53:26.

79. *Qur'an* 7:11-12; 38:76.

80. *Qur'an* 18:50a.

81. *Qur'an* 7:11-18; 15:28-43; 17:61-65; 38:71-85.

82. *Qur'an* 15:28-43.

83. *Qur'an* 2:97-98; 66:4.

84. *Qur'an* 2:98.

85. *Qur'an* 2:102.

86. *Qur'an* 2:102.

87. *Daniel* 8:16; 9:21; *Luke* 1:19,26.

88. *Daniel* 10:13,21; 12:1; *Jude* 1:9; *Revelation* 12:7.

89. Leon-Dufour X (1983).

90. *Qur'an* 4:97; 6:61,93; 8:50; 47:27; 79:1-2.

91. *Qur'an* 50:16-17; 82:10-12.

92. *Qur'an* 82:10-12.

93. *Qur'an* 79:1-5.

94. *Qur'an* 42:5.

95. *Qur'an* 2:102.

96. *Qur'an* 42:5.

97. *Qur'an* 2:97; 16:2.
98. *Qur'an* 2:97-98.
99. *Daniel* 8:16; 9:21-27; *Luke* 1:11-38.
100. *Qur'an* 70:4; 78:38; 97:4.
101. *Qur'an* 26:192-193.
102. *John* 14:16-17.
103. *John* 15:26.
104. *John* 16:13.
105. *Qur'an* 2:97.
106. *Qur'an* 16:102.
107. *Qur'an* 7:187; 31:34; 33:63; 43:85; 67:26; 79:42-45.
108. *Qur'an* 7:187.
109. *Qur'an* 79:42-45.
110. *Qur'an* 33:63.
111. *Qur'an* 67:26.
112. *Matthew* 24:36; *Mark* 13:32.
113. For the original Biblical meaning of the "sonship" of Jesus, peace be upon him, see the chapter entitled "The Baptism of Jesus: The Origin of the 'Sonship' of Jesus."
114. *Qur'an* 34:3-5; 40:59; 51:5-6,12-14; 52:7-10; 56:1-7; 64:7.
115. *Qur'an* 40:59.
116. *Qur'an* 52:7-10.
117. *Qur'an* 64:7.
118. *Qur'an* 23:102-103; 27:89-90; 36:54; 39:70; 69:19-37.
119. *Qur'an* 39:71-72; 50:24-26.
120. *Qur'an* 39:69-74.
121. *Qur'an* 20:109.
122. *Qur'an* 82:18-19.
123. *Qur'an* 8:4.
124. *Qur'an* 2:286a.
125. *Qur'an* 36:55-58.
126. *Qur'an* 69:21-24.
127. *Qur'an* 78:31-34.
128. *Qur'an* 15:45-48.
129. *Qur'an* 37:40-49.
130. *Qur'an* 69:30-37.
131. *Qur'an* 78:21-26,30b.
132. *Qur'an* 14:16-17.
133. *Qur'an* 2:177a.
134. *Qur'an* 2:43.
135. *Qur'an* 2:238.
136. *Qur'an* 6:71b-72.
137. *Qur'an* 11:114.
138. *Qur'an* 17:78-79.
139. *Qur'an* 20:130.
140. *Qur'an* 22:77.
141. *Qur'an* 24:56.
142. *Qur'an* 30:17-18.
143. *Qur'an* 30:31.
144. A) Al-Azdi SA (Abu Daoud) (1990). Hadith #494-496. B) *Fiqh Al-Sunnah*. Volume 1, page 80.

145. *Fiqh Al-Sunnah*. Volume 1, page 80.
146. A) Al-Bukhari MI. Hadith #1:301,303,317,318. B) *Fiqh Al-Sunnah*. Volume 1, page 71.
147. *Fiqh Al-Sunnah*. Volume 1, page 71.
148. A) *Qur'an* 4:101. B) Al-Bukhari MI. Hadith #1:346. C) *Fiqh Al-Sunnah*. Volume 2, pages 112,115,119a.
149. A) *Qur'an* 4:101. B) Al-Bukhari MI. Hadith #4:101-103. C) *Fiqh Al-Sunnah*. Volume 2, pages 104a,105,108, 119a.
150. *Fiqh Al-Sunnah*. Volume 2, pages 103, 118.
151. *Qur'an* 4:101.
152. *Qur'an* 21:25.
153. *Qur'an* 36:60-61.
154. *Qur'an* 6:102.
155. *Qur'an* 51:56.
156. *Qur'an* 2:183,185a.
157. *Qur'an* 2:183-185.
158. *Qur'an* 97:1-5.
159. *Qur'an* 2:110a.
160. *Qur'an* 2:177b.
161. *Qur'an* 2:195.
162. *Qur'an* 2:215.
163. *Qur'an* 2:219b.
164. *Qur'an* 2:254a.
165. *Qur'an* 57:18.
166. *Qur'an* 63:10.
167. *Qur'an* 64:16-17.
168. E.g. *Deuteronomy* 14:22-29 and *Numbers* 18:21-32.
169. Leon-Dufour X (1983).
170. *Qur'an* 3:96-97.
171. A) *Qur'an* 2:127; 22:26. B) Al-Bukhari MI. Hadith #4:583-584
172. *Qur'an* 22:26-30a.
173. *Qur'an* 2:197.
174. See, for example, Al-Azdi SA (Abu Daoud) (1990). Hadith #1944.
175. *Qur'an* 2:35-36.
176. A) Al-Tabari MJ (1989). B) Matthews AD (1979).
177. Al-Bukhari MI. Hadith #1:43; 5:689; 9:373.
178. *Qur'an* 5:3, in part.
179. *Genesis* 22:1-4,9-13.
180. Certain other sacrifices are also permissible.
181. *Qur'an* 2:127.
182. Al-Bukhari MI. Hadith #4:583-584.
183. *Qur'an* 2:125.
184. Al-Tabari MJ (1987).
185. "Allah is greater".
186. *Genesis* 21:14-19.
187. Al-Bukhari MI. Hadith #4:583-584.
188. Al-Bukhari MI. Hadith #4:583-584.
189. *Qur'an* 2:158.
190. Al-Tabari MJ (1989).
191. *Qur'an* 22:26.

192. *Qur'an* 22:29.

193. The three pilgrim festivals, which required a pilgrimage to Jerusalem for male Jews, were: Pesah (Passover); Shavuot (Feast of Weeks, later Pentecost in the tradition of the Greek-speaking Jews and in the Christian tradition, which celebrated the wheat harvest); and Sukkot (Booths or Tabernacles).

194. A) Schonfield HJ (1967). B) Leiman SZ (1998).

195. Al-Bukhari MI. Hadith #4:583-584.

196. *Genesis* 21:19.

197. *Psalms* 84:5-6.

198. 'Ali 'AY (1992b).

199. Al-Hilali MT, Khan MM (1993).

200. --- (1997).

201. Pickthall MM.

Bibliography

BIBLIOGRAPHY

--- (1971): Maps. In Laymon CM (1971b).

--- (1997): *The Qur'an: Arabic Text with Corresponding English Meaning.* Jeddah, Abul-Qasim Publishing House.

--- (1998a): Barabbas. In *Encyclopaedia Britannica CD 98.*

--- (1998b): Basilides. In *Encyclopaedia Britannica CD 98.*

--- (1998c): Eusebius of Caesarea. In *Encyclopaedia Britannica CD 98.*

--- (1998d): Gnosticism. In *Encyclopaedia Britannica CD 98.*

--- (1998e): Letter of Barnabas. In *Encyclopaedia Britannica CD 98.*

--- (1998f): Nazirite. In *Encyclopaedia Britannica CD 98.*

--- (1998g): Pontius Pilate. In *Encyclopaedia Britannica CD 98.*

--- (1998h): Saint Damasus I. In *Encyclopaedia Britannica CD 98.*

--- (1998i): Saint Epiphanius of Constantia.
In *Encyclopaedia Britannic CD 98 .*

--- (1998j): Saint Hippolytus of Rome. In *Encyclopaedia Britannica CD 98.*

--- (1998k): Saint Justin Martyr. In *Encyclopaedia Britannica CD 98.*

--- (1998l): Saint Polycarp. In *Encyclopaedia Britannica CD 98.*

--- (1998m): Sixtus V. In *Encyclopaedia Britannica CD 98.*

--- (1998n): Stations of the cross. In *Encyclopaedia Britannica CD 98.*

--- (1998o): The book of Job. In *Encyclopaedia Britannica CD 98.*

--- (1998p): Zealots. In *Encyclopaedia Britannica CD 98.*

'Abd Al-Wahhab M (1981): *Kitab Al-Tawhid.*
In Al-Faruqi IR (trans): *Kitab Al-Tawhid.* Malaysia, Polygraphic Press Sdn. Bhd.

Abdullah M (1996):
What Did Jesus Really Say? Ann Arbor, IANA.

Ackroyd PR (1971):
The book of *Isaiah.* In Laymon CM (1971b).

Al-Azdi SA (Abu Daoud) (1990): *Kitab Al-Sunan.*
In Hasan A (trans.): *Sunan Abu Dawud.* New Delhi, Kitab Bhavan.

Al-Bukhari MI: *Kitab Al-Jami' Al-Sahih.* In Khan MM (trans.):
The Translation of the Meanings of Sahih Al-Bukhari. Medina, ---.

Al-Hilali MT, Khan MM (1993):

Interpretation of the Meanings of the Noble Qur'an in the English Language. Riyadh, Maktaba Dar-as-Salam.

'Ali. AY, (2000a): Commentary. In 'Ali A. Y. (2000b).

'Ali . AY, (2000b): *The Meaning of the Holy Qur'an.*

Beltsville, Amana Publications.

Al-Qushayri MH (Muslim) (1971): *Al-Jami' Al-Sahih.*

In Siddiqi 'AH (trans.): *Sahih Muslim.* ---, ---.

Al-Tabari MH (1987): *The History of al-Tabari: Volume II.*

Prophets and Patriarchs. Albany, State U. of New York Press.

Al-Tabari MH (1989): *The History of al-Tabari: Volume I.*

General Introduction and From the Creation to the Flood.

Albany, State U. of New York Press.

Anderson H (1971): The book of *Job.* In Laymon CM (1971b).

Asimov I 1968): *Asimov's Guide to the Bible: Volume I.*

The Old Testament. New York, Avon Books.

Asimov I (1969): *Asimov's Guide to the Bible: Volume II.*

The New Testament. New York, Avon Books.

Baird W (1971): The gospel according to *Luke.*

In Laymon CM (1971b).

Beavin EL (1971): *Ecclesiasticus.* In Laymon CM (1971b).

Beck HF (1971): *The History of Israel: Part I.*

From the beginnings to the exile. In Laymon CM (1971b).

Beiler JG (1998):

Saint Ignatius of Antioch. In *Encyclopaedia Britannica CD 98.*

Bornkamm G (1998):

The Christ and Christology. The gospel tradition:

Times and environment. In *Encyclopaedia Britannica CD 98.*

Brashler J (1990): Introduction to the *Apocalypse of Peter.*

In Robinson JM (1990).

Burch EW (1929): The structure of the synoptic gospels.

In Eiselen FC, Lewis E, Downey DG (1929).

Burghardt WJ (1998):
Saint Jerome. In *Encyclopaedia Britannica CD 98*.

Burnaby J (1998):
Augustine. In *Encyclopaedia Britannica CD 98*.

Cadbury HJ (1929): The language of the *New Testament*.
In Eiselen FC, Lewis E, Downey DG (1929).

Caird GB (1972): *Saint Luke*. Baltimore, Penguin Books.

Cameron R (1982): *The Other Gospels: Non-Canonical Gospel Texts*.
Philadelphia, Westminster Press.

Carstensen RN (1971): The book of *Zechariah*.
In Laymon CM (1971b).

Chadwick H (1998): Origen. In *Encyclopaedia Britannica CD 98*.

Charles RH (1969): *The Apocrypha and Pseudepigrapha of the Old
Testament in English: Volume II.*
Pseudepigrapha. Oxford, Oxford University Press.

Charles RH (1971): *The Apocrypha and Pseudepigrapha of the Old
Testament in English: Volume I. Apocrypha.*
Oxford, Oxford University Press.

Conzelmann H (1969): *An Outline of the Theology of the New
Testament.* New York, Harper & Row.

Danielou J, Marrou H (1964): *The Christian Centuries: Volume I.
The First Six Hundred Years.* New York, McGraw-Hill Book Co.

Davies JN (1929a): *Mark.* In Eiselen FC, Lewis E, Downey DG (1929).

Davies JN (1929b): *Matthew.* In Eiselen FC, Lewis E, Downey DG (1929).

De Vaux R (1965): *Ancient Israel: Volume 1. Social Institutions.*
New York, McGraw-Hill.

Duncan GB (1971): *Chronology.* In Laymon CM (1971b).

Dupont-Sommer A (1967): *The Essene Writings from Qumran.*
Cleveland, The World Publishing Company.

Eiselen FC (1929): *The Pentateuch*—Its origin and development.
In Eiselen FC, Lewis E, Downey DG (1929).

Eiselen FC, Lewis E, Downey DG (1929): *The Abingdon Bible
Commentary.* New York, Abingdon-Cokesbury Press.

Fenton JC (1973): *Saint Matthew.* Baltimore, Penguin Books.

Filson FV (1971): The literary relations among the gospels.
In Laymon CM (1971b).

Findlay JA (1929): *Luke.* In Eiselen FC, Lewis E, Downey DG (1929).

Finegan J (1952): *The Archaeology of World Religions: Volume III.*
Princeton, Princeton U. Press.

Fiqh Al-Sunnah. In *Alim* Multimedia CD Rom. ---,
ISL Software Corporation.

Flaherty RL (1998): Biblical literature and its critical interpretation:
Old Testament literature: The Ketuvim.
In *Encyclopaedia Britannica CD 98.*

Fredericksen LF et al. (1998):
Saint Clement of Alexandria. In *Encyclopaedia Britannica CD 98.*

Frost SB (1971): *The book of Jeremiah.* In Laymon CM (1971b).

Fuller RH (1965): *The foundations of New Testament Christology.*
New York, Charles Scribner's Sons.

Garvie AE (1929): *John.* In Eiselen FC, Lewis E, Downey DG (1929).

Gibbons JA (1990): Introduction to *The Second Treatise of the
Great Seth.* In Robinson JM (1990).

Gottwald NK (1971): The book of *Deuteronomy.*
In Laymon CM (1971b).

Gray J. (1971): The book of *Exodus.* In Laymon CM (1971b).

Grobel K (1971): The languages of the *Bible.* In Laymon CM (1971b).

Guillaumont A, Puech HC, Quispel G, Till W, 'Abd Al-Masih Y (1959):
The Gospel According to Thomas. New York, Harper & Row.

Guthrie HH (1971): *The book of Numbers.* In Laymon CM (1971b).

Hahn F (1969): *The Titles of Jesus in Christology: Their History in
Early Christianity.* New York, The World Publishing Co.

Hamilton W (1959): *The Modern Reader's Guide to Matthew and Luke.*
New York, Association Press.

Harvey DW (1971): The literary forms of the *Old Testament.*
In Laymon CM (1971b).

Hennecke E, Schneemelcher W, Wilson RM (1963):

New Testament Apocrypha: Volume I. Gospels and Related Writings. Philadelphia, The Westminster Press.

Herbert G (1962): The Old Testament from Within.

London, Oxford U. Press.

Hyatt JP (1971):

The compiling of Israel's story. In Laymon CM (1971b).

Josephus F (1988): Jewish Antiquities. In Maier PL (trans.): Josephus: The Essential Writings: A Condensation of Jewish Antiquities and The Jewish War. Grand Rapids, Kregel Publications.

Kee HC (1971):

The gospel according to Matthew. In Laymon CM (1971b).

Koester H (1971a): Gnomai Diaphoroi:

The origin and nature of diversification in the history of early Christianity. In Robinson JM, Koester H (1971).

Koester H (1971b): One Jesus and four primitive gospels.

In Robinson JM, Koester H (1971).

Koester H (1982): Introduction to the New Testament: Volume II. History and Literature of Early Christianity. New York, Walter DeGruyter.

Kohlenberger III JR (1991): The NRSV Condordance: Unabridged: Including the Apocryphal/Deuterocanonical Books. Grand Rapids, Zondervan Publishing House.

Laymon CM (1971a): The New Testament interpretation of Jesus. In Laymon CM (1971b).

Laymon CM (1971b):

The Interpreter's One-Volume Commentary on the Bible. Nashville, Abingdon Press, 1971.

Leiman SZ (1998): Judaism: The Cycle of the Religious Year: Jewish Holidays: Pilgrim Festivals. In Encyclopaedia Britannica CD 98.

Leon-Dufour X (1983): Dictionary of the New Testament.

San Francisco, Harper & Row.

Lernet-Holenia AM (1998): Eugene of Savoy.

   In *Encyclopaedia Britannica CD 98.*

Leslie EA (1929a):

   The chronology of the Old Testament.

   In Eiselen FC, Lewis E, Downey DG (1929).

Leslie EA (1929b): *Psalms* I-LXXII.

   In Eiselen FC, Lewis E, Downey DG (1929).

Lofthouse WF (1929): *Job.* In Eiselen FC, Lewis E, Downey DG (1929).

Mack BL (1996): *Who Wrote the New Testament?: The Making of the Christian Myth.* San Francisco, Harper.

Marks JH (1971): The book of *Genesis.* In Laymon CM (1971b).

Marsh J (1972). *Saint John.* Baltimore, Penguin Books.

Matthews AD (1979): *A Guide for Hajj and 'Umra.*

   Lahore, Kazi Publications.

Milgrom J (1971): *The book of Leviticus.* In Laymon CM (1971b).

Moffatt J (1929): The formation of the *New Testament.*

   In Eiselen FC, Lewis E, Downey DG (1929).

Nineham DE (1973): *Saint Mark.* Baltimore, Penguin Books.

Noth M (1960): *The History of Israel.* New York, Harper & Row.

Norwood FA (1971):

   The early history of the church. In Laymon CM (1971b).

Pagels E (1979): *The Gnostic Gospels.* New York, Random House.

Peritz IJ (1929): *The chronology of the New Testmanent.*

   In Eiselen FC, Lewis E, Downey DG (1929).

Pherigo LP (1971):

   The gospel according to *Mark.* In Laymon CM (1971b).

Pickthall MM: *The Meaning of the Glorious Koran.*

   New York, New American Library.

Platt RH, Brett JA (eds.):

   The Lost Books of the Bible and The Forgotton Books of Eden.

   New York, The World Publishing Co.

Quanbeck WA (1971): The *Letter to the Hebrews.*

   In Laymon CM (1971b)

Ragg L, Ragg L (1974): The *Gospel of Barnabas*. Karachi (?),
The Quran Council of Pakistan (?).

Rahim MA (1974):
How the Gospel of Barnabas survived. In Ragg L, Ragg L (1994).

Reumann J (1971):
The transmission of the Biblical text. In Laymon CM (1971b).

Robertson AT (1929): The transmission of the *New Testament*.
In Eiselen FC, Lewis E, Downey DG (1929).

Robinson JM (1971a): Kerygma and history in the *New Testament*.
In Robinson JM, Koester H (1971).

Robinson JM (1971b): Logoi Sophon:
On the Gattung of *Q*. In Robinson JM, Koester H (1971).

Robinson JM (1990):
The *Nag Hammadi Library in English*. San Francisco, Harper.

Robinson JM, Koester H (1971):
Trajectories though Early Christianity. Philadelphia, Fortress Press.

Robinson TH (1929): *Genesis*. In Eiselen FC, Lewis E,
Downey DG (1929).

Rohl DM (1995): *Pharaohs and Kings: A Biblical Quest*.
New York, Crown Publishers.

Sandison GH:
Jewish sects and their beliefs. In *The Holy Bible: Authorized King
James Version*. Cleveland, The World Publishing Company.

Sarna NM (1998):Biblical literature and its critical interpretation. *Old
Testament* canon, texts, and versions. In *The Encyclopaedia
Britannica CD 98*.

Schonfield JH (1967): *Readers' A to Z Bible Companion*.
New York, New American Library.

Schneemelcher W (1963):
General introduction. In Hennecke E,
Schneemelcher W, Wilson RM (1963).

Scott EF (1929): *The New Testament and criticism*.
In Eiselen FC, Lewis E, Downey DG (1929).

Shelton WA (1929): *Psalms* LSSIII-CL.

In Eislen FC, Lewis E, Downey DG (1929).

Shepherd MH (1971):

The gospel according to *John*. In Laymon CM (1971b).

Silberman LH (1971): The making of the *Old Testament* canon.

In Laymon CM (1971b).

Simpson DC (1929): *First and Second Kings*.

In Eiselen FC, Lewis E, Downey DG (1929).

Smith WC (1943): *Modern Islam in India*. Lahore, ---.

Smith WC (1957):

Islam in Modern History. New York, Mentor.

Smith WC (1964):

The Meaning and End of Religion. New York, Mentor.

Smith WC (1965): *The Faith of Other Men*. New York, Mentor.

Stegemann H (1998):

The Library of Qumran: On the Essenes, Qumran, John the Baptist, and Jesus. Grand Rapids, William B. Eerdmans Publishing Company.

Strugnell J (1998): Saint John the Baptist.

In *Encyclopaedia Britannica CD 98*.

Sundberg AC (1971):

The making of the *New Testament* canon. In Laymon CM (1971b).

Terrien S (1964):

The Golden Bible Atlas. New York, Golden Press.

Toombs LE (1971): The *Psalms*. In Laymon CM (1971b).

Welch AC (1929): *Jeremiah*. In Eiselen FC, Lewis E, Downey DG (1929).

Wilkin RL (1998): Tertullian. In *Encyclopaedia Britannica CD 98*.

Wilson I (1985): *Jesus: The Evidence*. London, Pan Books.

Wilson RM (1971): The literary forms of the *New Testament*.

In Laymon CM (1971b).

Wingren G (1998): Saint Irenaeus. In *Encyclopaedia Britannica CD 98*.

Wright GE (1960): *Biblical Archaeology*. Philadelphia, Westminster Press.